HER KIND

HER KIND

Stories of Women from Greek Mythology

JANE CAHILL

broadview press

Canadian Cataloguing in Publication Data

Cahill, Jane. 1950-
     Her Kind: stories of women from Greek mythology

ISBN 1-55111-042-3

1. Mythology, Greek - - Fiction. 2. Women -- Mythology -- Fiction. I. title

PS8555.A55H47 1995 C813' .54 C95-932829-7 PR9199.3C3SH47 1995

Broadview Press Ltd., is an independent, international publishing house, incorporated in 1985.

North America:
Post Office Box 1243, Peterborough, Ontario, Canada K9J 7H5 3576 California Road, Orchard Park, NY 14127
Tel: (705) 743-8990 Fax: (705) 743-8353
e-mail: customerservice@broadviewpress.com

United Kingdom:
Turpin distribution Services Ltd., Blackhorse Rd., Letchworth, Hertfordshire SG6 1HN
Tel: (1462) 672555 Fax: (1462) 480947 e-mail: turpin@rsc.org

Australia:
St. Clair Press, P.O. Box 287, Rozelle, NSW 2039
Tel: (02) 818-1942 Fax: (02) 418-1923

www.broadviewpress.com

Broadview Press gratefully acknowledges the financial support of the Book Publishing Industry Development Program, Ministry of Canadian Heritage, Government of Canada.

PRINTED IN CANADA

For my mother,
Christine Anne (Farrant) Cahill,
and my daughters,
Leah Elizabeth Cahill and Anna Siobhan Cahill

I have gone out, a possessed witch,
haunting the black air, braver at night;
dreaming evil, I have done my hitch
over the plain houses, light by light:
lonely thing, twelve fingered, out of mind.
A woman like that is not a woman, quite.
I have been her kind.

I have found the warm caves in the woods,
filled them with skillets, carvings, shelves,
closets, silks, innumerable goods;
fixed the suppers for the worms and the elves:
whining, rearranging the disaligned.
A woman like that is misunderstood.
I have been her kind.

I have ridden in your cart, driver,
waved my nude arms at villages going by,
learning the last bright routes, survivor
where your flames still bite my thigh
and my ribs crack where your wheels wind.
A woman like that is not ashamed to die.
I have been her kind.

—Anne Sexton

Contents

Preface

There is a certain tension, I have found, in being both a classicist and a storyteller. This book was written as a response to that tension. As a classicist with a particular interest in mythology, I have felt it my responsibility to try to keep the Greek myths alive in our times, but as a storyteller I found that my audiences felt little affinity with some of them. Many listeners, and these not only women, are not much interested in a story where a hero kills a woman and chops off her head just because she is there. Nor do they wish to hear how Zeus turns himself into a swan or a shower of gold to rape a woman and produce a splendid son. It became apparent that if the old stories were to stay vital then they had to be brought closer to the perceptions and experiences of audiences of our times. But this had to be done without resorting to distortion.

The decision to concentrate on women's stories was not consciously made. Looking back, it is clear that a series of incidents contributed to it: one of my professors, when I was an undergraduate, blithely intoning that Greek women were not much traumatised when their husbands and children were murdered in war and they themselves were taken prisoner—they readily, he claimed, developed loyalties to their new husbands, namely their captors; my daughters, aged seven and five, coming across the story of Pandora in a book of fables and asking unanswerable questions; a student showing me a copy of Charlene Spretnak's *Lost Goddesses of Early Greece,* a reclamation of women's stories from a time before writing; Kay Stone, the folklorist, whom I knew, but not well, saying that she had heard me telling Greek myths on CBC radio—she liked, she said, to hear them told in a woman's voice (until she explained, I thought she meant a high-pitched one; I hadn't realised until then that, as I had brought the literary myths back into oral form, I had also given them a woman's focus); Jennifer Levitt, a student in my classical mythology course at the University of Winnipeg, pointing out that the story of Myrrha was a story that incest survivors would tell rather differently; an old woman, I never knew her name, confiding after a lecture on "Marriage in Mythology" that she would have murdered Agamemnon long before Clytemnestra did.

For years in mythology classes, I told stories about women's lives as they appear in the works of the ancient (male) authors and then explained why they were told that way. I felt some damage control was needed—that harm had been done to women by the very fact that stories such as the rape of Leda existed in our literary tradition; that stories like Hypermnestra's, in which forty-nine of the daughters of Danaüs murder their husbands on their wedding night, had contributed to the misogyny systemic in our society. But this wasn't enough—I was still disturbed that it was possible to read handbooks of mythology that were to be found in any library and discover, without comment from the authors, that all was well with the world until the first woman came along, or that Eriphyle was "a giddy and treacherous mother."

I worked on my own as a storyteller for several years, and many of the stories in this book developed during that time. I began in my children's bedrooms, graduated to their classrooms, and went on from there. I once found myself telling the story of Jocasta and her husband\son Oedipus to a Brownie pack. In the summer of 1990 Kay Stone suggested that she and I join with Mary Louise Chown to form a trio of oral storytellers. "Earthstory" was formed that fall. We have since performed at art galleries, museums, storytelling festivals, conferences, and more. Our rehearsals are the chaos from which whole worlds are born. I have learned more from these two women, and not just about stories and storytelling, than they can imagine.

However lost in the mists of time its beginnings are, this book owes its appearance on paper to many people. We are fortunate when colleagues are also friends. Mark Golden nagged me for years to get these stories into print and helped me in many ways. Bob Gold's door was always open. Both of them have read and remarked upon sections of what follows, as have Kay and Mary Louise. The secretarial skills and calm encouragement of Terry Cooke and Lou Lépine I could not have done without. Terry Teskey has proved a creative and diligent editor. Over the years I have incurred debts to my father, John Cahill, who knows all the fairies of Ireland personally and told me of them when I was young; Veronica Lemon, who first taught me Greek; the late Edward Rushworth, who understood myth to an extent that I have only just begun to appreciate; the many teachers, especially Lois Goertzen, who let me into their classrooms to tell stories when I was just learning the art; Eunice Lavell, who encouraged me to think about the lives of women in new ways; Jean Travis, who has been unfailingly generous with her time, tea, and sympathy; and a whole generation of mythology students. To all of these people I am profoundly grateful.

Last but most I thank my husband, David Koulack, who convinced me that the time for this book had come and who has read every word of it at least three times. His comments and suggestions have helped me to remove the incomprehensible, the recondite, and the strident from its pages, and his support has been immeasurable.

Introduction

As soon as there was language there were stories. These stories were transmitted orally for thousands of years. Communities of people needed to retain information about who their ancestors were, where they had come from, and how they had survived times of trial. Along with knowledge of the past, they needed to provide for themselves explanations of how the world worked. They may also have been aware that they were playing a part in passing on the wisdom of the old times so that the generations of the future would have guidance in moments of crisis.

The stories travelled wherever the people who told them and listened to them went. Some were brought to the place that was to become Greece, a place that already had stories of its own. Still more were created. Eventually, some of the stories from this assortment were written down, and some of those survive. We call them Greek myths.

One can hardly blame classicists, the scholars who study the civilisations of Greece and Rome, for paying more attention to these written versions of Greek myths that have survived than to the oral ones that have all but perished. But what we have in the works of Homer, Aeschylus, and the rest is the *end* of a long tradition. If we look only at their works, and not at what went before them, it is as if we unearth a pyramid and stop digging when we have excavated just the tip. If we are to concern ourselves with Greek myths as *stories,* the relationship between the oral and written versions of the myths needs to be understood and the vastness and diversity of what is missing appreciated.

This is not to say that the place of the Greek myths in the larger scheme of things has not long been recognised. Early in the seventeenth century of our era, Francis Bacon wrote:

> The consideration which has most weight with me is this, that few of these fables were invented, as I take it, by those who recited and made them famous—Homer, Hesiod, and the rest. For had they been certainly the production of that age and of those authors by whose report they have come down to us, I should not have thought of looking for anything great or lofty from such a source. But it will appear upon an attentive examination that they are delivered not as new inventions then first published, but as stories already received and believed. And since they are told in different ways by writers nearly contemporaneous, it is easy to see that what all the versions have in common came from ancient tradition, while the parts in which they vary are the additions introduced by the several writers for embellishment—a circumstance which gives them in my eyes a much higher value: for so they must be regarded as neither being the inventions nor belonging to the age of the poets themselves, but as sacred relics and light airs breathing out of better times, that were caught from the traditions of more ancient nations and so received into the flutes and trumpets of the Greeks.[1]

The search for the "light airs breathing out of better times" manifests itself in numerous ways, particularly in the theories of interpretation of myth, mutually contradictory though they are, and in the comparisons of Greek myth with myths from other places (such as Mesopotamia), but rarely in attempts to reclaim the missing stories. And yet those missing stories may have numbered in the millions.

II

Let us examine for a moment the process by which oral stories are transmitted. One teller tells a story to a group of people of whom several choose to tell that "same" story to new audiences. Some of them may tell essentially the same story; others may make mistakes or alterations. In each of those new audiences there are other potential tellers who will further change the story ... and so on.

But this obvious way is not the only way that variations occur. An oral story changes every time it is told even when it is told by the same person. It changes with the whim and the mood and the purpose of the teller. It changes with the needs or perceived needs of an audience. For instance, a teller may wish to flatter a particular group of listeners by attributing to their ancestors feats usually assigned to other people (the flattery may be necessary if the storyteller wants supper). A teller who feels responsible for the moral welfare of the listeners (suppose, perhaps, they are children) may feel it desirable to omit some details or add an adage to be absorbed. (Interestingly enough, though our tendency is to omit violent and frightening episodes when telling stories to children, this was not, apparently, the Greek style. Greek children were disciplined with tales of monstrous women who, deprived of their own children, came and ate other people's.)

In addition, subtle changes take place over time—changes that a storyteller may not even be aware of—that enable the story to remain current. An audience needs to hear a story that has a familiar ring to it, not one that sounds old-fashioned. So, as customs, beliefs, and values change, stories shift with them.

A story also changes because there is no reason for it *not* to change. A story is not a play wherein the lines have to be the same every time it is performed so that the actors don't lose their places. A story is not bound by ownership of texts and rules about accurate quotation. The spoken word is free—winged, as Homer said.

What all this means is that there are many versions of a single story. Each one is the truth because it contains the essence of the truth. There are then many truths. It depends who is speaking and who is listening.

III

The oral tradition of Greek myth may have died hard, but it did die. None of the stories that we now know came to us by being told and retold over the centuries. This is not to say that the literary tradition alone killed the oral. Oral traditions can more readily be obliterated by war, illness, catastrophe, changing fashions, or simple neglect. (Manuscripts have proved less destructible, with papyri turning up in the sands of Egypt thousands of years after being buried there or codices lurking for centuries in forgotten vaults.) In the case of Greek myth, not only did the oral tradition die, but the literary tradition disappeared also. The growth of Christianity in the Mediterranean area played a large part in the demise of both traditions; the stories, despite their innate ability to change in their oral form, could not change enough and remain "true"—so different was the Christian perspective from the classical Greek. The disintegration of the Roman Empire and the political turmoil that followed it took their toll also, and changes in "scientific" knowledge must have made many of the myths seem eccentric and bizarre. At the end of the Middle Ages, when there was a revival of interest in all things Greek and Roman, the old stories were resurrected, but only in their literary forms. As the true significance of the ability to read and write began to be felt by ordinary people, the written word acquired some of the mystique that the spoken word had once possessed.

IV

If the ability to change is inherent in oral stories, then sameness seems to live in written ones. When literary works were recopied, both in the ancient world and later, during the late Middle Ages and the Renaissance, they were, as far as possible, copied to the letter by scribes who were neither inspired creators nor adaptors of myths. The result is that more than two thousand years on, the versions of myths that the Greeks told in writing have not altered. They are exactly as they were, give or take a few errors from copyists, when Euripides, Pindar, and all the others first wrote them down. There is real magic in that—the very age and durability of the stories make us venerate them as we would a sculpture in Parian marble. We can no more alter them than we could build a new facade onto the Parthenon at Athens.

The quality of the extant texts also makes us reluctant to "update" Greek myth. One reason for the survival of many of the written versions of the stories is that as pieces of literature they are outstanding, unsurpassable. Sophocles has told the definitive version of the Oedipus story in a perfect play. What need have we of any other? And who do we think we are to tamper with the works of masters? Some have dared, of course, Jean Racine, Eugene O'Neill, and Jean Anouilh among them, and we have only to read their works, or watch performances of them, to realise that our misgivings are unfounded, and that two versions of one story can exist without any damage being done to the earlier one. Stories, it turns out, are not the same as statues and temples. We can alter them all we like, and the originals are still there. Ancient literary versions and retellings can co-exist in much the same way as oral stories once co-existed with each other and then later survived alongside written versions of the same stories.

If truth be told, in the ancient world appropriations and adaptations of myths abounded. Aeschylus wrote a version of the story of Electra, and then Sophocles and Euripides wrote their versions. We know them to be different, though the bare bones of the story remain the same, because all three versions survive. Several hundred years later Ovid wrote his *Metamorphoses,* a poem in fifteen books, and probably the single most used text dealing with myth, but an appropriation on a massive scale. Ovid took whatever stories he wanted from Greek myth and slotted them into his framework (his theme was "change"), leaving out the details that didn't fit and enhancing those that did. He updated the stories to include new ideas on how the world worked and the place of gods in it, stressed chosen elements (heterosexual love, for instance, since he had also written love poetry and had an audience for it), and made them suitable for a Roman to tell and for Romans to read. It is this process that returns myth to its truest form—the telling to a community of its own story.

In the effort to appreciate the erstwhile and potential fluidity of the Greek mythological tradition, it is worth looking at the works of those who told stories in pictures. Vase painters and architectural sculptors used myth as subjects for their work. In the absence of captions or explanatory notes (though vase painters sometimes labelled characters by name), they depicted well-known stories that could be instantly recognised. Most of the stories they tell we know from the literary tradition, but not all. On a fifth-century Athenian cup, Jason is regurgitated from the mouth of the dragon that guards the Golden Fleece in Colchis. On an older, black-figure Corinthian amphora, Ismene is killed by Tydeus when the Seven attack Thebes;[2] according to the literary tradition, she is still alive and travels to Attica much later than this.

The story of Philoctetes is an example of the flexibility of the early mythological tradition. Here are two ancient ways of telling it:

In the first story, Heracles is in terrible agony and desperate to die. He builds himself a funeral pyre and climbs up onto it. No one is willing to light the pyre except Philoctetes, to whom Heracles gives his famous bow and poisoned arrows in gratitude. In the ninth year of the Trojan war, the Greeks are told that they need the bow and arrows before they can take Troy. Philoctetes still has them, but he is not there. He is on the island of Lemnos, where the Greeks abandoned him nine years previously on their way to Troy because he had a wound in his foot (from the bite of a snake sent by Hera to punish him for helping Heracles) that gave off so foul a smell that they could not bear to be on the same ship as him. He used the bow and arrows to stay alive.

In the second story, Philoctetes is present when Heracles dies. He alone knows where Heracles is buried. The bow and poisoned arrows are buried with him. Philoctetes promises Heracles that he will tell no one the whereabouts of the grave. Years later, the Greeks who are laying siege to Troy discover that they need the bow and arrows before they can take the city. They try to force Philoctetes to tell them where the grave is. To escape from this difficult situation, Philoctetes decides that he is not breaking his promise if he shows rather than tells where the grave is. He leads the other Greeks to it and then stamps on it with his foot. The dead but enraged Heracles sends a poisoned arrow up through the earth that wounds Philoctetes in his treacherous foot. The bare bones of the stories are the same: Philoctetes in a privileged position at Heracles' death; Philoctetes estranged from his associates; the bow and arrows needed for the taking of Troy; Philoctetes wounded in the foot as a punishment. But the bones are not arranged in the same way, and the whole tenor of the stories is different. There was, and is, more than one truth.[3]

V

The stories that we call Greek myths are men's stories. There is no doubt about this. Their substance is the stuff of men's lives and fantasies—victory in war, glorious death on the battlefield, heroic enterprise, the slaying of monsters, the fathering of sons. None of this has much to do with women. Only rarely do the stories touch on the keeping of families together, the performing of tedious tasks, and the mothering of daughters. Female characters in myth are mothers or wives or virgins, defined always in terms of men. Most of them are bad or unusual women: there is Medea who kills her children; there is Clytemnestra who, though married to the richest king in Greece, commits both adultery and murder; there is Thetis who puts her babies on the fire; there is Jocasta who marries her own son. Side by side with the vicious killers are the mad women and the hapless suicides.

The Greek myths, as we have seen, have come down to us in works of literature. All this literature was produced by men. For the most part, girls were not taught to read or write, nor was it a possibility in their prearranged lives that they might grow up to be poets or playwrights. Of the very few women who were exceptions to this and whose works survive, none wrote myths. So the versions of the stories that are familiar now are not only concerned with men's affairs, they are also reported from a male point of view.

That the Greek myths were not the original work of the men
who wrote them down is not disputed. We have only to look at
the pages of Homer's *Iliad* to see relics of the oral storyteller:
repeated passages, recurring epithets, genealogies, for example.
But what do we know of the people who first told myths?
Almost nothing, because by definition they came from a time
before writing and so no accounts of them exist. It would be
impossible to prove that any of these mythtellers were women,
but it is equally impossible to prove that all of them were men.

Myths probably began to be written down soon after 800
B.C.E. But for some time (hundreds of years, in fact) the oral
tradition coexisted with the literary versions of the stories. We
know regrettably little about informal storytelling situations that
took place during this time (because no one wrote about them),
rather more about formal ones.[4] Most formal ones, though not
all, consisted of men telling or performing stories in some way
for other men: the plays from the fifth century B.C.E. that we
call collectively "Greek tragedy" were performed as well as
written, but all those involved—authors, sponsors, directors,
actors, dancers, and possibly even the audiences—were men
only. There were competitions at Delphi and elsewhere for men
who played the lyre and sang verses from the works of Homer.
There were competitions at Epidaurus and Athens for rhap-
sodes, men who recited epic poetry. There were choral competitions for adolescent males in many places, and the songs
composed for them had mythological themes. Adult males sang
at symposia (dinner and drinking parties at which the only
females present were servers and entertainers). Stories not set
to music were also told at symposia if Plato's account of one
held in 416 B.C.E. is to be considered typical: in his *Symposium*
we are treated to a description of an occasion on which the host
and guests told stories on the theme "Love," and Plato recounts
the stories. One of the participants, Socrates, relates a story
told to him, he says, by a woman! So women did tell stories.

It is tiny snippets of information like this on which we must
rely in order to demonstrate that women told stories. In fact, it

is possible to show that nurses, mothers, and old women told stories, and their subjects were mythological. Choruses of young women sang tales of gods and people of old. Did women tell stories to other women in the women's quarters of the houses in which they lived? Surely they did, though we cannot prove it. Men rarely wrote about what women did when no men were present, for obvious reasons, and so we would not expect to be able to prove it. But it doesn't seem unlikely that storytelling accompanied spinning, weaving,[5] cooking, nursing babies, and hundreds of other women's tasks. Whether some women would have been acknowledged as particularly gifted tellers and would have performed for other women we cannot know.

VII

Classicists know a good deal about the daily lives of ancient Greek men, rather less about the lives of ancient Greek women. Women and men, at least among the wealthier people who lived in cities, about whom we have most information, had separate daily tasks related to their sex rather than to their aptitude. The men, who as we have seen did the writing, left us little information about women's tasks. But someone had to weave the fabric for clothing; someone had to tend to small children; someone had to worry about sick slaves; someone had to make sure that the storeroom supplies were in good condition and would last the winter. These were the women's tasks. It is clear that men did not know much about women's tasks and clear that they did not value them particularly highly. Therefore it is not surprising that lengthy accounts of what women did do not appear in literature of any sort. But it is especially true in Greek myth that what women regularly did is not much mentioned, for the specific reason that it is not the stuff of exciting stories. Women's tasks were dull, repetitive, and did not deliver lasting fame. They were the same for every woman. They did not offer much opportunity for adventure or for rising above the crowd. So, when women were the central characters of myths that men told, they had to be deviant women—women who performed the tasks differently or for some outlandish purpose. One woman (Philomela) makes clothing that bears a message of destruction to a man; another woman (Ino) convinces the peasantry that parched seed is good seed; several women (Ino, Medea, Thetis) kill or are perceived to be trying to kill the children in their charge. Even those who go through the motions of following the expected life-plan of a woman somehow get it "wrong." Myrrha surrenders her virginity to the wrong person, namely her father; Hypermnestra's sisters kill their husbands on their wedding night; Eriphyle sends her lord and master off to his certain death. The men who told the stories, and later wrote versions of them down, were making a statement about their own society without necessarily knowing it. Only by renouncing the conditions imposed on them by men could women achieve fame. Within the existing rules of their society they could not. It is no coincidence that we don't even know the names of the wives of most famous Greek men. If they behaved according to plan, their stories were of no interest. But how different this was for men! In mythology, Agamemnon achieves his fame by conquering Troy, Pelops by winning a chariot race, Perseus by killing a terrible monster. These acts are simply the normal actions of men one step removed into the world of fantasy. In the real world they were to go bravely to war, to compete in sports competitions, to promote the civilised world.

VIII

Is there any reason to suppose that women's versions of the surviving men's stories would have been significantly different, or different in some consistent way? In terms of plot, as we have seen, the bare bones of a story could have been variously arranged, and it seems impossible to determine whether women arranged them differently from men. But in terms of approach and spirit, the sex of the teller may have mattered very much.

When we talk about how the Greeks felt and thought and how they understood the world, we really mean how Greek *men* felt, thought, and understood the world. If Greek women had had a chance to leave their words for posterity, we would now perhaps recognise two separate value systems. Some questions arise over and over:

In ancient Greece unwanted babies were sometimes exposed, placed outside of city limits to die. But were they unwanted by their mothers? How does it feel to be told that you may not rear your child?

After marriage a woman belonged to her husband's family, not to her family of origin. Did she accept that? Where were her loyalties?

Women who were married were subject to extreme sanctions if they committed adultery. Did the women think that reasonable?

In some versions of some myths, particularly in the plays of Euripides, we see signs of values held by women conflicting with those held by. men. Medea talks of the pain that being a mother brings. She finds motherhood tougher than fighting in a war could ever be. Creusa, who exposed her child, doesn't think exposure is a good idea. Hecuba has not a good word for the wars and sieges that so engaged her menfolk. Helen does not feel that her unbridled ardour is to blame for her time spent in Troy with Paris. And though men consistently see women as victims of their own inborn passions, Pasiphaë blames her husband, not herself, for the yearning that grew in her and led to the birth of a monstrous child.[6] It is tempting to imagine the young Euripides snuggled in the arms of a nurse with a formidable repertoire of stories, a nurse who took the trouble to ensure that he saw the world from her point of view. Of all the women who lived in ancient times, she, nameless and faceless though she is, is the one I would most like to meet.

IX

This book is a collection of Greek myths told from a woman's perspective. From dozens of possible stories I have chosen just thirteen, some because they feature a female character who is generally misunderstood or underdeveloped, others simply because they are favourites. The central figure in each story is a woman and the events of the story are described in terms of her life. Thus, in Eriphyle's story the defeat of the Seven Against Thebes is not much connected with a quarrel over the throne of a distant city, but may mean the deaths of Eriphyle's husband and her lover, the one long prayed for, the other greatly dreaded. Another story tells of a famous mythical event, the Calydonian Boar Hunt. But told in the voice of Althaea, queen of Calydon, it is a story not of valour and adventure but of divided loyalties, hard choices, and the death of her son. The plots of the stories have not been changed. With a handful of exceptions, all noted, everything that happens to the characters can be found in the literary tradition. The changes come in perception and interpretation.

Early in the book's history, it became clear that there were many ways of presenting women's stories from myth. Choices had to be made that may require some explanation.

First, the stories told here appear (with the exception of Medusa's story in the appendix) as literary tales. A transcript of a told story is not always satisfactory as reading material, because it requires the teller's presence, voice, and gestures to complete its sense. A literary version gives us the padding we require for our comfort, the descriptions and explanations that we must be given because the writer is not there to provide them directly. It is also my experience that told versions of these stories adapt themselves to suit their audiences and the occasions on which they are being told, and no single told version would appeal to everyone. Sometimes, an orally told story is so distilled, so stripped, for a particular audience, of its ancient context that it requires the presence of that audience to give it life. I hope that by putting these stories in literary form I can see to it that they retain some of the fluidity of ancient myth and can be more things to more people. Thus the tales in this book may be read as short stories by a lone person sitting quietly by a fireside; they are complete enough in themselves that it is possible to understand them without reading their individual forewords or their notes. They can be studied in classrooms alongside ancient texts in any course where myths have a place—in which case the sources and explanations given in the notes may prove useful and enlightening. I am also hopeful that these versions of the Greek myths will be used by oral storytellers as bases for their own tellings. I have tried to give, in each chapter, far more information than any one teller could possibly use in any one telling. The notes contain references to alternate ancient versions and to connected stories, and the forewords explain the circumstances of the major characters and offer suggestions of possible motives for their behaviour, as well as putting the stories in their Greek contexts. I hope that storytellers will feel free to continue the process of reclamation and adaptation of which this book is just one phase. The essential truth of a myth can remain even if revisions are made. Eriphyle will always send her husband to his death, but in one teller's version she will do so because she has reason to hate him, in another's because she is in love with a different man, in another's because she is mad. Please take what you need, and alter what you don't like.[7]

Second, it needs to be made clear that none of these stories is an attempt to answer the question "What really happened that resulted in the existence of this story?" If myth is based on fact, on actual occurrences, as we frequently read that it is, then "What really happened?" is a perfectly reasonable question. Unfortunately, it is also an unanswerable question, and it will remain so until such time as some amazing new technology enables us to hear and understand those winged words spoken thousands of years ago. This book is an attempt to answer a question fraught with fewer difficulties. It is this: Is it possible to produce a version of this story that would have made sense to Greek women? The most obvious difficulty is that there would have been as many different versions of each story as there were women who told them—women from different eras, places, and backgrounds. How much would a woman from Crete in the fifteenth century B.C.E., who perhaps was ruled by a queen and probably knew the power of a Great Goddess, have had in common with the wife of an Athenian citizen from the fifth century who lived a controlled, preordained existence and was without legal and political rights? The answer is, little. But we know far more of the life of the latter, if not of her thoughts. The stories told here would, I think, have been comprehensible to a woman from the fifth century, though some of them would involve a subconscious, atavistic awareness on her part that the position of women had once been different—that birth and motherhood were once magic, not mundane, and that women had once been as mighty as men. (I have resisted the temptation to modernise any of the stories. Deliberate anachronism—bored wives of company directors encountering gods while wandering in sacred groves—is not an easy thing for a writer to sustain, and in a told story, since no believable character is created, pleases nobody.) There is a distance still between the stories as they are written and the experiences of the reader. I hope that the notes will go some way to fill that space.

Third, the vexed question of Goddess worship is not dealt with at length either in the stories or in the notes that accompany them. It may well be that these stories had their origin in a time when the major deity worshipped in Greece was a single all-powerful Great Goddess or Earth Goddess, and I have occasionally referred to such a being, giving her a variety of names, but I have not used the stories as an attempt to prove that Goddess worship existed in Greece, nor have I set them in the context of the overthrow of Goddess worship in favour of the male-dominated Greek pantheon. The stories told here are stories of mortal women and minor goddesses, and though cameo appearances are made by Aphrodite, Athena, and the rest, I have not struggled to connect them to a Great Goddess figure.

Fourth, I have stressed one aspect of the stories that I found particularly appealing, and this is the Greek writers' fascination with placing their characters in situations so refined that every choice of action is catastrophic. For instance:

If two people are defined as enemies, that one should kill the other is normal, to be expected, and certainly not to be punished. This is the premise on which war is based. But suppose the two people are also mother and child.

Suppose a woman is given the power to make decisions. This is a special privilege. She should be able to use the privilege to bring harmony to her family. But suppose one of the decisions means that she must choose her husband over her brother or vice versa.

Suppose a woman has the power to kill her son whenever she chooses. Surely she will never do so? But suppose her son commits an unforgivable crime.

Many of the women, and some of the men, whose stories are told here find themselves in situations like these. The gods, or their own actions, or mere coincidences, place them in positions of no escape, and the Greek storytellers seem to have savoured the ironies in their characters' dilemmas, pinned them neatly down, and watched them squirm.

X

Ancient Texts. There is no better way to become acquainted with Greek mythology than to look at the versions of the stories told by the Greek and Roman writers themselves. Read the plays of Aeschylus, Sophocles, and Euripides—all are available in translation—or watch movie or stage versions of them. Read Homer's *Iliad* and *Odyssey* and Ovid's *Metamorphoses.* Even the work of Apollodorus, who was writing a handbook, not attempting a literary masterpiece, is enjoyable because the material he collected is in itself so compelling.

The first note to each chapter of this book gives the ancient sources for the story contained in it—the works of writers who wrote the story down in its first few centuries of literary life. These works include plays, poems, handbooks of mythology, and much else. I have given each author equal value—nowhere is it suggested, for instance, that Homer's version of a story is better than Apollodorus', even though the quality of writing certainly is. I have included Roman sources with the Greek, even though most Roman writers wrote several hundred years after most Greek writers. I have not referred readers to scholiasts (ancient commentators on texts), to fragments of lost works, or to texts not readily available in English unless necessary information can be found only in these places.

I have used ancient annotations throughout to refer to the Greek and Roman texts. At first glance, this practice appears daunting. But a reference to a page number of a translation is only useful if everyone who uses the reference has a copy of the same translation. Most translators give ancient references—it's a question of looking in the margins and at the top of the pages. Remember that an ancient "book" was much smaller than a book produced today. Thus all twenty-four of the books of Homer's *Iliad* fit into one modern paperback volume. "See Homer, *Iliad* 5.470-92" means "find the fifth book of Homer's *Iliad* and look for the passage beginning at line 470 and ending at line 492." "See Pausanias 3.4.1-2" means "find the third book of Pausanias' only extant work and look up its fourth chapter; the first and second paragraphs of that chapter are the required passage."

XI

Modern Texts. Nowhere does the tension between the discipline of classics and the art of storytelling show itself more clearly than in the modern sources I have examined in writing this book. Few classicists who are serious students of mythology, for instance, have much that is good to say about Robert Graves and his interpretations of myth in terms of ritual. And yet as a storyteller I can safely say that more ideas for angles on how to tell a story, and more interesting and fitting details that might otherwise never have been unearthed, have come from his books than from any other single source.[8]

In *Lost Goddesses of Ancient Greece,* Charlene Spretnak attempted to reclaim the stories that existed in Greece before invaders introduced their male gods. These were the stories of the goddesses Hera, Athena, Pandora, and the rest before they were assigned their secondary roles as wife, daughter, temptress, and so on in the literary tradition. Though Spretnak was restrained in her reconstructions, she did not endear herself to classicists when she wrote "My methodology, once the research was completed, was to study all the index cards of information on a particular Goddess, meditate on the material and then *become* that Goddess as much as possible before reconstructing her myth."[9] As a classicist, upon reading this I should have laid the book aside without a second glance, but as a storyteller

I am delighted to have the stories, however unorthodox the means by which they were recovered.

Many of the modern works that are mentioned in notes for a specific purpose will prove useful general reading for those who wish to read about myths. I have not limited these references to the works of structuralists or feminists or anthropologists or any one group of interpreters, preferring to offer a variety of approaches to the study of myth. I have tried always to refer readers to accessible and readable books rather than to journal articles or foreign-language publications, however recent or apparently definitive. If more questions are thus raised than are answered, this is not necessarily a bad thing. But be warned that as a general rule, these books do not deal with Greek myths as oral stories or acknowledge the existence of a separate women's tradition. There are exceptions, one of which is Richard Buxton's *Imaginary Greece*.[10] Of the general books on mythology currently available, Barry Powell's *Classical Myth*[11] seems to me the most flexible and insightful. It also contains excellent book lists for further reading. But remember that no book about myth will speak to you as the myths themselves will.

Those readers who are also storytellers do not need me to tell them which books to read. But for those who are toying with the idea of using storytelling, in the classroom or elsewhere, for the first time, and wish to read a book on the subject, let it be Betty Rosen's *And None of It Was Nonsense*.[12]

XII

The women whose lives are examined in these stories are not ordinary women. Some are queens, some are princesses, one or two are minor goddesses. In this they are not like most of us. And yet, I venture to suggest that you will recognise these women or else find yourself in them; in fact, I am certain of it. The women whose stories are told in this book are mothers, stepmothers, adoptive mothers. They are first wives, second wives, devoted wives, discarded wives. They are daughters and sisters. Their situations are timeless, and though their actions—the murders they commit, for instance—are extreme, those actions grow from emotions we are all familiar with. Perhaps you will find yourself, or someone you know, only in fleeting moments: a woman's expression of the dangerous intensity of her love for her firstborn child, another's irritation with the cloying and constant presence of her sisters, another's disorientation when her secret lover stands close by. Perhaps you have been Clytemnestra, driven by the need for revenge. Or you have been Myrrha, victimised by those who should have protected you. Or you have been Philomela, silenced ... but unbowed. Over and over, when I tell these stories, I see flickers of recognition on the faces of listeners of both sexes. In workshops, participants sometimes claim ownership of a certain woman's story. They place themselves in it. They say, essentially, "I have been her kind."

As this book goes to press, it is clear that there is much still to do. Dozens of other women's stories wait to be reclaimed: Alcestis chose to die so that her husband might live. What kind of nonsense is that? Sibyl refused to yield her virginity to the god Apollo, accepting instead his punishment of hundreds of years of life as an old, withered woman. Why? Pasiphaë, her daughter Phaedra, Deianeira, even Helen, are women who have perhaps been misjudged. Callisto, Dryope, Antiope, and countless others were abducted or raped. Then there is Circe. According to men's stories, just one year of her life had significance, the year Odysseus was her lover. What of all the other years? And Andromache. I am haunted by Andromache. How does it feel to have been the wife of the greatest warrior of Troy, to have seen your only child, a tiny boy, hurled to his death from the walls of your city, to be taken as a slave by the son of the man who killed your beloved husband, and to bear him a child, also a son?

These stories demand our attention. The process of reclaiming, retelling, appropriating, has only just begun.

Notes

[1] "The Wisdom of the Ancients" (1609) in *Francis Bacon: A Selection of his Works* (New York, 1965), 276–77.

[2] In the Museo Gregoriano Etrusco, the Vatican, and the Louvre, Paris, respectively.

[3] The first story is partly from Diodorus Siculus 4.38, 3–4 and partly from Sophocles' *Philoctetes*. The second is from Servius on Virgil's *Aeneid* 3.402.

[4] See Richard Buxton, *Imaginary Greece* (Cambridge, 1994), Introduction and chaps. 1, 2.

[5] Euripides' *Ion* 196–97 makes it clear that storytelling accompanied weaving, for instance.

[6] In Euripides' *Medea, Ion, Hecuba, Trojan Woman,* and a fragment of *Cretans,* respectively.

[7] If pronouncing Greek names seems difficult, remember this simple rule: every letter is sounded. Thus, "Eriphyle" has four syllables, since the final 'e' is pronounced.

[8] Robert Graves, *The Greek Myths,* vols. 1, 2 (Harmondsworth, UK, 1960).

[9] Charlene Spretnak, *Lost Goddesses of Ancient Greece* (Boston, 1981), 25.

[10] Buxton, *Imaginary Greece.*

[11] Barry Powell, *Classical Myth* (Englewood Cliffs, NJ, 1995).

[12] Betty Rosen, *And None of It Was Nonsense* (Richmond Hill, ON, 1988).

ONE
_____

Philomela's Story

The story of Philomela and her sister Procne[1] is, in most accounts, the story of how the nightingale and the swallow, and sometimes also the hoopoe, came to be. There is some confusion about which sister became which bird, with the Greek writers tending to make Philomela the swallow and the Roman writers making her the nightingale. English poets have tended to follow the Romans. But the story makes more sense if Procne becomes the nightingale, forever mourning her son Itys or Itylos (hence "itu, itu," the nightingale's plaintive song) and Philomela, who is without her tongue but who has a message to convey, becomes the inanely chattering swallow. Tereus, the hoopoe, who was Itys' father, seems to call "pou? pou?" (where? where?) while searching for the dead boy.

The pretty metamorphoses aside, this is the story of near-unspeakable violence and horror. Because the nightingale's song is so lovely, we have been lulled into thinking that anything associated with it is sorrowful yet romantic, even charming. But the nightingale is sad because she chopped up her own son and fed him to his father. The charm is hard to find.

The tale is told here in the voices of the women. (Philomela's is miraculously restored.) They are not birds, though the birds appear in the story. Perhaps the sisters are in the Underworld[2] after death, perhaps not. (Because in the Greek story they are changed into life forms that continue to exist on Earth, there is no story of their punishment in Hades' realm.) They derive comfort, and even some gratification, from going over and over details of the story they know so well, though they have no new audience, just each other. Were they mad? Are they still? Perhaps. There is, in most ancient versions of the tale, at least the suggestion that the murder of the child Itys by the women was committed while they were in the frenzied state achieved by worshippers of Dionysus during celebrations in his honour,[3] though it is agreeable to think of Philomela's rescue, by her sister and the other women of Thrace, as a kind of uprising against male tyranny, merely cloaked in the trappings of a festival of Dionysus.

The most interesting, and surprising, element of this tale is the refusal of Philomela to commit suicide when she reaches a crisis in her life that for most mythical women would be impassable. In the late twentieth century, in the industrialised West, society's position tends to be that life, under almost any conditions, is preferable to death. Physicians strive to keep us alive beyond the point where we can fend for ourselves. We are uncomfortable with suicide and consider it a victory when a suicide attempt fails. It is easy to assume that it was always so. Yet the number of women who die by their own hand in the optionless world of Greek myth is legion. Usually they hang themselves since, though there may be no weapon at hand, there is always the belt that all women wore. Death is chosen when a situation appears unresolvable. Jocasta chooses it when she discovers that she has married her own son, or when her two other sons kill each other,[4] Phaedra when she has falsely accused her stepson (whom she loves) of raping her,[5] Deianira when she has accidentally murdered her husband.[6] But not Philomela.[7]

Also of note is the manner in which Philomela lets her plight be known, by weaving her story into a tapestry and having it sent to her sister. Weaving must have been, in the lives of real Greek women, one of the ways in which stories were told. It is not necessary to assume, as has been done, that all Philomela could do was weave her name into her work. She wove pictures.[8] What the story shows is that a man cannot necessarily silence a woman by cutting out her tongue. Voice is but one medium for telling a story. There are others.

PHILOMELA: Do you remember, sister, how as children we watched the swallow in the springtime? How she soared above us, dancing like a butterfly in the crisp air, and then dipped down to skim the water, chattering madly all the while? She was trying, we thought, to tell us of some great sorrow, a sorrow too monstrous to suffer alone.[9]

PROCNE: Yes, I remember.

PHILOMELA: And do you remember the nightingale, whom we rarely saw, but often heard, her song sweetening the dark with its sadness?[10]

PROCNE: I remember.

PHILOMELA: And the proud hoopoe, his fanned crest like a crown, always searching in the barns and in the stables for some lost treasure. We thought he looked as a king would look if ever he became a bird. And then one day we found the hoopoe's nest in a hole in the wall of the palace, and it smelled for all the world like rotting flesh and death.[11]

PROCNE: I remember. We were young, and knew so little. Our father was the great King Pandion of Athens. He gave me away, as kings do their daughters. I was just sixteen when I was taken from Athens. You were a child, still, your breasts not yet sprouting, your lips not yet full. You never stopped talking. You would sit beside me, walk beside me, whenever you could, and tell me of your dreams. You were the dearest thing in my life. And you needed me there, in Athens, to be a mother to you.[12]

Our father gave me to Tereus, son of the war god, Ares. He was from Thrace,[13] a king himself, though not a wise one. But he was wealthy and powerful, and he had come to our father's aid in war. I was his prize, the reward he received for his effort. It was no surprise. We had known all our lives that this was how it would be. But it was a grievous thing, nonetheless. I remember piling my possessions into a chest, clothing for the queen I was to become, small souvenirs of home, a wooden likeness of Athena, guardian of our city. I remember Tereus' painted ship anchored in the harbour. I remember standing on its deck as it pulled out to sea, looking back at my home for the last time. I remember you, on the shore. A tiny girl waving her arms.

As I lay for the first time with my new husband, on the marriage bed in my new home in Thrace, I heard the screech owl overhead, its shriek piercing the night. It sat on the roof of the bridal chamber, no good omen for my marriage.[14] Where were the gods to bless my marriage? There were only Furies there that night, I think; creatures of foulness, waiting for blood. My son was born in Thrace, my only child. Itys. You hardly knew him, did you? He was small and dark, with solemn eyes, a quiet child, nervous, strange. I had thought all children would be like you.

Five years I had been in Thrace with Tereus when I asked if I could see you again. "Yes," he said, "she shall visit us. I will sail to Athens and fetch her." And he did. In his painted ship he sailed to Athens, and convinced our father to let you leave with him.

PHILOMELA: He watched our father weep to see me go. "Time will hang heavy on your hands," he said, "while she is gone. But you need have no fear. I will look after her as if she were my own daughter. And she will not be long away."

PROCNE: He brought you to Thrace, on the painted ship, but not to our home, not to the palace in the hills where I waited for you.

PHILOMELA: He took me instead to a high-walled house in the woodlands. He raped me there; he raped me many times. I thought that I would be there just a little while, that I should escape and run to you. I wondered how I could ever face you. What if you loved your husband? What if you did not know his nature? What if you thought him true?[15] But though I cried aloud there was no one who heard me, least of all the gods above. He left me there, alone, save for a guard. I dreamed of dying. Of a shield of painless sleep. I thought of other women who had died by their own hand. But there was work to do. A story to make known. Tereus went away a while, and when he came again to the house in the woods I was ready for him. "When I escape from here," I said, "I shall tell my story to your people. They will hear what you have done. For too long we women have kept silent; for too long, through our shame and our fear, men have gone unpunished for their crimes. No more. I am not afraid, nor am I ashamed. If I escape from here, the world will know what you have done to me. If I am kept here, I will sing my story to the trees, and fill the forest with my voice. You shall not silence me."

PROCNE: And then he silenced you.

PHILOMELA: He held me by the hair and tied my arms. He drew his sword, I thought to kill me. But no. He cut my tongue out of my mouth. And left.

PROCNE: He told me you were dead. Did you know that? That you had died of sickness on the painted ship, and he seemed to grieve for you. "She was so pretty," he said. "Her chatter so sweet." I believed him. I cut my hair, short like a slave-girl's, and made a tomb for you, filled only with my sorrow. I wore no embroidered clothes, I wore no jewels. The world became a joyless place, haunted by a memory—a tiny girl waving her arms.

PHILOMELA: He came often to the dark silent world of the forest. I was still pleasing to him, perhaps more so than before. When he was not there, the house was guarded. Its high walls were of stone. I thought I would grow old there. I scratched my name, Philomela, in the stone over and over, so that you might one day know I had been kept there. I chose not to die. I thought of our father, alone in Athens, with cheerless years ahead of him. What would he do without me? I thought of you my sister. Imagined seeing you again. Dreamed of running to your arms as I had done when still a child.

A whole year passed. Women were brought to live with me, to prepare my food and make my clothing. They were frightened of Tereus, and knew that they would pay with their lives if they revealed to anyone outside the forest that I was alive. But their looms were my voice. I wove my torment: figures of Tereus and of myself, first in the painted ship, then in my prison. I wove his rape of me, his cutting of my tongue. I wove my own blood. The cloth grew heavy with it. One of the women knew what to do. She took the cloth to the palace and to you.[16]

PROCNE: A gift unparalleled—my sister's life when I thought her dead.[17] I read your suffering—your clothing torn, your body resisting the man attacking you, your hands flailing, and then aiming for his eyes.[18] The man, and there was no doubt about this, was my husband. I did not weep, I did not tear my hair, this was not death. I kept my silence. No one in the palace knew what news had come to me. Oh, it was hard not to shout my anger to the skies. I waited till the festival day of Dionysus, a time when women are together in their minds. Dionysus, God of sweet terror, you were our saviour, you who know about the ripping, limb from limb, of a mother's young, you who are born over and over, you who know rage and reprisal.[19] On the night of your festival, Dionysus, I dressed in the robes I kept for you, wound ivy in my hair in your honour, draped the skin of a newly slaughtered deer on my shoulders. In my hand I held a spear, sharp for the killing. As the moon drove high in the sky in her carriage, the trance came upon me and the madness. I danced into the hills; I danced death to men, I danced terror to my husband. My heart was full. The women of Thrace were with me, out of mind.

PHILOMELA: I heard shouting in the woodlands, music rising in the night air. The forest filled at last with women's voices!

PROCNE: I followed the guide of your weaving and led my women to the high-walled house in the woods. We broke down the doors. And we found you and we took you.

PHILOMELA: How did you know me? The trance was on you.

PROCNE: In the madness women know each other. We dressed you in fawn skins. We decked your hair with ivy. You were one of us. We killed your guards with our spears. A taste of killing for what was to come. Some of your women came with us.

PHILOMELA: In the palace we wept and embraced. I had longed for this moment. What need had I of a tongue to talk to my own sister?[20]

PROCNE: But we were not safe, my sister. If Tereus had found you there he would have killed us both to save himself.[21] And then Itys came.

PHILOMELA: Itys, your son. I remember Itys. I watched him come to you, skip with little feet across the chamber, and link his arms around your neck. Did you know him?

PROCNE: In the madness women sometimes know their children ...[22] I took him to the grove of Athena, where stood the statue I had brought with me from my home. A corner of Athens in alien Thrace.[23] Itys called me, "Mother, Mother." I was his mother, once. But that was long before.[24] Not a spear for the killing this time, but a sword. I drove his father's sword right through his heart. "Mother," he cried, "this is Itys, your son. Don't you know me, Mother?" And then I cut his throat.[25]

PHILOMELA: Flesh still warm ... blood still fresh ... blood and more blood to pay for the blood of penetration and the blood of my tongue, blood not our own, your child's blood ... flesh ripped from bone ... more blood.

PROCNE: You were there, weren't you? We did it together. Tore him apart, bare-handed; cooked his flesh; some boiled, some roasted.[26]

PHILOMELA: Yes, I was there. Blood on my hands. Look, sister, look.

PROCNE: I served Tereus his supper that night. He sat alone in the dining hall and I brought him his food myself. He did not know what he ate. He found the flesh good ... well flavoured and tender. He asked for more.

PHILOMELA: He was surprised, wasn't he, when I came into the dining hall? He didn't expect to see me there. I brought him his son's head, all wet with death-slime. I held it up to his face. "Look," I said, "look. This is your son. You have eaten his flesh."

PROCNE: I watched his face change. I felt the moment of his understanding.[27]

PHILOMELA: He picked up his sword and ran at us, but we were quicker, you and I. We ran from him and though he followed, raging, sword in hand, he could not catch us. When he knew that we had escaped him, he turned his sword upon himself, and died.[28]

PROCNE: I remember. The world shall end when I forget.[29]

PHILOMELA: Do you hear the swallow, sister, the soft, light swallow? Perhaps she has a tale to tell.

PROCNE: And do you hear the nightingale, singing the grief of the old time? They say she has an ache to bear that passes understanding.

Notes

[1] The major ancient source for the story is Ovid's *Metamorphoses*, 6, 424–674. It also appears in Apollodorus, at 3.14.8. See also Achilles Tatius, 5.3 (where there is a detailed description of Philomela's tapestry) and 5.5. Sophocles wrote a play, *Tereus*, which does not survive, but which must have been the source of some later accounts. Hyginus, at *Fabulae*, 45, tells the story also. In his version, Tereus returns to Athens a while after his marriage to Procne claiming that she is dead, and asking for the hand of her younger sister, Philomela. Their father, Pandion, imprudently one would think, agrees to the request. When they arrive back in Thrace, Tereus hands Philomela, whom he has raped, over to the wife of a fellow king, who sends her to Procne. The sisters recognise one another. Tereus, through divination, learns that his son Itys is soon to be killed by a relative. He suspects his brother Dryas and kills him. This is an exciting story, but since it is without two elements crucial to the demonstration of Philomela's resourcefulness, namely the cutting out of her tongue and the tapestry-letter, I have not followed it here. A strange version of the myth, in which the characters, save for Itys, have different names, is preserved by Antoninus Liberalis, at *Transformationes*, 11: Aedon, a weaver, and her husband Polytechnus, a carpenter, have a contest, the loser of which is to give the winner a slave girl. Polytechnus loses and, in anger, rapes Aedon's sister, Chelidon. He cuts her hair and dresses her strangely and hands her over to Aedon, who does not immediately recognise her. Once she does, she kills and cooks her son and feeds him to her husband. Eventually, she becomes a nightingale, her sister a swallow, and her husband a woodpecker, because he was once a carpenter.

[2] According to Greek tradition, life continued after death in the Underworld, a place of darkness under the Earth. It was ruled over by Hades, a grim character. The Underworld figures regularly in

myth: heroes visit it, dangerous creatures are confined in it, and offenders are punished in it.

3 In such circumstances, in Euripides' play *Bacchae,* Pentheus is killed by his mother. Women under the influence of Dionysus in myth have a tendency to go on murderous rampages and tear into pieces those who stand in their way. See below, n. 19. Dionysiac madness is dealt with more fully in chap. 6, Ino's story.

4 See Jocasta's story, chap. 3.

5 This story is told in Euripides' *Hippolytus.*

6 This story is told by Sophocles in *Women of Trachis.*

7 As an imprisoned, disfigured victim of rape, Philomela can no longer hope for a conventional passage through life. For women in Greek myth, whose role is to be that of "wife," suicide is a permissible escape from situations that threaten to disrupt a marriage or the possibility of marriage. It is also clear that suicide is preferable to slavery. Hyginus, *Fabulae* 243, lists the mythical women who die by their own hand.

8 No such tapestries are extant from ancient Greece (woven fabric does not endure across the centuries under most conditions), but this does not mean they did not exist. The odds were further stacked against the survival of woven stories in that a tapestry cannot be transmitted as a text can. Once a story has been written down, any person with the ability to copy writing can pass it on; this is not the case with a story told in weaving, which can only be passed on by a weaver with skills equal to those of the first teller. One need only glance at the Bayeux tapestry, one of the major sources of information about the Battle of Hastings, to see what detail can be worked onto fabric (though this is an embroidered piece), or the Franco-Flemish tapestries of the late fifteenth century or, for that matter, the weaving currently being produced by women in some South American countries. There is plenty of evidence for the ability of women in ancient Greece to tell stories through weaving. The myths themselves, Philomela's story aside, are a source of it. In the *Iliad,* for instance, which tells the story of the Greek siege of Troy, Homer writes that the Greek queen, Helen, who has been kidnapped by a Trojan (thus the war), oversees and participates in the weaving of a tapestry by her Trojan handmaidens. The subject of the tapestry is the battles between the Greek and the Trojans in the war (*Iliad* 3.125–28 and 6.323–24). A well-known story amongst the Romans was that of Arachne,

who engages in a weaving contest with Athena and is turned into a spider for her pains. Athena weaves stories of gods punishing arrogant mortals, and Arachne weaves stories of gods deceiving mortals for their own ends. See Ovid, *Metamorphoses* 6.1–145, where the tapestries are described at length.

[9] Swallows tend to nest in the eaves of houses, and are not daunted by the presence of humans. John Pollard, in *Birds in Greek Life and Myth* (London, 1977), discusses the habits of the birds in this story. Pausanias notes that swallows make no nests and lay no eggs in Daulis, where according to him the horrible events of this story took place. Even as a bird, Philomela avoids Tereus' domain (Pausanias 10.4.5).

[10] The nightingale, her breast red supposedly with the blood of the child she has killed, prefers to nest in the dark forest, away from built-up areas.

[11] The hoopoe's nest is malodorous—the parent birds do not remove their own excrement and vomit, nor that of their young. Ovid, at *Metamorphoses* 6.673, writes that the long beak of the hoopoe represents the sword that Tereus brandishes at the women at the end of the story. On another level the beak, which probes crevices and cracks for insects, signifies his penis.

[12] The mother of Procne and Philomela, Pandion's wife, was Zeuxippe, his mother's sister, an unparalleled arrangement, as far as I know. No ancient source states that she has died by the time of Procne's marriage, but neither is her participation mentioned.

[13] Though the sources are agreed that Tereus was a Thracian, some have him ruling in Thrace and others in Daulis, in Phocis on the Greek mainland, at the head of a group who had settled there from Thrace. Ovid, who wants to introduce the Dionysian connection, chooses Thrace, where Dionysiac worship possibly originated. Thucydides, at 2.29.3, takes pains to establish Daulis as the site of the events related here.

[14] This detail is Ovid's and reflects the Roman interest in good and bad (mainly bad) omens, in life as well as in literature. The flight patterns of birds, as well as their song, were considered sources of such omens, concealing information sent by the gods that could be decoded in various ways. Some messages were readily interpreted. An ugly sound from an ugly bird would mean that whatever undertaking was currently being initiated would be unsuccessful.

[15] In Ovid's story Philomela is distressed, both during her period of captivity and later, after her sister has rescued her, because she feels responsible for the fact that Tereus raped her and is concerned that her sister will view her as the cause of the collapse of her marriage. Therefore she views a potential reunion between the two with trepidation. Ovid is influenced by the emotions expressed by lovers in personal love poetry (a popular Roman genre not entirely unknown to the Greeks, but not fully developed by them.) Ovid was himself a love poet, having published several volumes of verses and a "how to" guide to relationships with the opposite sex, *The Art of Love,* before writing the *Metamorphoses.* Thus he writes of Philomela being Procne's "rival" (*paelax,* 6.537) and Procne being Philomela's "enemy" (*hostis,* 6.538). The reunion is marred, in Ovid's story, by Philomela's inability to meet her sister's eyes, so ashamed is she. Procne seems to have no such qualms, taking her sister readily into her arms. But in Achilles Tatius' version of this story the emotion that spurs Procne into the action she takes is "jealousy" (*zelotupia,* 5.5.6 and 7) over her husband's sexual activity with her sister. The author comments that women are prepared to suffer pain in order to inflict it on a man who is unfaithful. So, Procne is willing to endure the death of her son in order to punish her husband. This, of course, resembles Medea's story, chap. 13.

[16] This brave woman is unidentified, as slaves tend to be, in Ovid. No other author accounts at all for the transfer of the tapestry from Philomela to Procne. Ovid states that the woman did not know what she was taking to Procne.

[17] This is a recognition scene, a staple of myth. The tapestry is an elaborate token by which Procne recognises that her young sister, whom she thought dead, is in fact alive. In a prototypical recognition scene, a mother recognises the child who is removed from her at birth and supposedly dies soon after, by the woven baby blanket in which the child was wrapped. Such a scene is the climax of Euripides' play *Ion.* Most recognition scenes are distorted. See Jocasta's story, chap. 3, and Ino's story (on the death of Pentheus), chap. 6, for example.

[18] This detail of Philomela's physical resistance is from Achilles Tatius. The struggle of Ovid's Philomela is not described.

[19] Many myths in which Dionysus appears show him taking revenge on mortals for perceived crimes, usually against himself. Thrace, where Tereus rules, is traditionally the place of origin of

Dionysus worship, which existed in life as well as in myth. It seems to have spread through Greece during the seventh century B.C.E. This worship was not orderly and predictable like worship of most gods, at least not to start with. The worshippers were women, by and large, who left their husbands, children, and chores to dance by night on the mountain side in hopes of reaching a state of religious ecstacy. All this was less disruptive to normal family life if it could be staged on a predetermined day, as here. In their state of ecstacy, the women posed all the dangers that a vast crowd of people, too large or too unruly to be adequately controlled by authorities, can pose today. The climax of the ritual was the ripping apart and eating of a young animal.

[20] An Attic red-figure vase in the Louvre Museum (c. 490 B.C.E.) shows Philomela wildly gesticulating with her hands. That she intends the death of Itys is suggested by the sword at her side and the presence of Procne holding her naked son by the armpits in a most unmotherly way. But it is the unnaturally large, long-fingered hands of Philomela that engage the eye and that inspired the recurring references to Philomela's hands in the version of the story told here.

[21] In Ovid's account, the motive for the murder that follows is pure revenge, not fear. Procne lists potential punishments for Tereus with apparent relish—among them burning him alive, cutting out his tongue and eyes, and severing his extremities.

[22] Agauë, whilst under the influence of Dionysus, does not recognise her son, Pentheus. She kills him, despite his protestations and attempts to help her recognise him. (See Ino's story, chap. 6.) Does Procne know what she is doing when she kills the boy? In Ovid there is no doubt that she does. He has her think her plan through and waver, sometimes resolved, sometimes not. She contrasts the boy, who can call her mother, with her sister who, deprived of her tongue, can call her nothing at all. This story is alluded to briefly by Homer (*Odyssey* 19.518–23), and here we find that she "killed her own beloved child when the madness was upon her."

[23] Such a statue is mentioned by Pausanias at 10.4.6, though he is at this point describing Daulis in Phocis, where he prefers to set this story. In his day, the second century C.E., the Daulians boasted a sanctuary of Athena with a stone statue, but claimed that it was a mere replacement for an older, wooden figure that Procne

had first brought with her from Athens on the occasion of her marriage to Tereus.

[24] This is suggested by a line from Achilles Tatius, "[Itys'] mother was Procne, before her anger" (5.5.7). He seems to be suggesting, quite perceptively, that at the moment of the murder Procne is not herself, and therefore does not know who she is killing. This would be consistent with Dionysiac frenzy.

[25] In Ovid's account, Philomela cuts Itys' throat after Procne has driven her sword through him.

[26] This is a gruesome inversion of a common motif in which a mother boils her child with the intention of rendering that child immortal. See Thetis' story, chap. 12. The detail of the way the meat is cooked comes from Ovid. It seems to place the murder in the context of a sacrifice in honour of Dionysus (since Dionysus himself was torn into pieces, some of which were boiled and some roasted, by the Titans, shortly after his first birth). The connection of this story with Dionysiac ritual is discussed by Walter Burkert in *Homo Necans* (Berkeley, 1983), 179–85.

[27] This is another recognition scene, not as close to the standard as the first (see n. 17 above), but effective for that very reason. Here a father recognises his missing child, whom he assumes is alive until this point, as the substance of his dinner. The token of recognition is the head, brought into the dining hall by Philomela.

[28] Pausanias, at 1.41.8, records a version of the story told by the Megarians. They claimed that Tereus had ruled in Megara, not in Daulis or Thrace, and that he died by his own hand there when he could not catch Procne and Philomela. Pausanias also records that Procne and Philomela returned to Athens and died there of their tears.

[29] There are deliberate echoes here of *Itylus,* the poem by Algernon Swinburne (1837–1909), written in the voice of Philomela. Swinburne wrote in the tradition that made Procne the chattering, apparently carefree swallow ("I know not how thou hast heart to sing") and Philomela the ever-grieving nightingale ("the world shall end when I forget").

Clytemnestra's Story

Clytemnestra is one of the most maligned women in Greek myth.[1] *Her story is as follows: while her husband Agamemnon, whom she has reason to hate, since he killed Iphigenia, their daughter, is away at war, she teams up with an old enemy of his, Aegisthus. They kill Agamemnon when he returns. Clytemnestra's son, Orestes, kills her in retaliation.*

When I first encountered Clytemnestra as a student in the 1960s she was presented (in a mythology lecture) as an adulteress, one who had the poor taste, in addition, to take as her lover a man who was too cowardly to go to war. She was also a murderess. Agamemnon was a victim not of his own horrible deeds, but of a curse put on his family two generations previously, by Myrtilus.[2] *Orestes, though it doubtless pained him, was only doing his duty when he killed his mother, and was a greater hero for having the courage to do so. This position, though I did not realise it at the time, represents the view of Homer and presumably most of those who read him, at least until Aeschylus came along. As a class, we students accepted it, merely expressing mild indignation that women were not "allowed" to take lovers but that men, Clytemnestra's husband included, were expected to have mistresses in every port. It hardly seemed fair, but our world at that time rather endorsed this position, and we didn't see anything much we could do about it.*

A year or so later I read Aeschylus' Agamemnon for the first time. Aeschylus' picture of Clytemnestra is of a strong, clever woman. She is man-like (a compliment), audacious, and righteously outraged by her daughter's death and Agamemnon's infidelity. Why was it, she asks, that no one was angered when Agamemnon killed Iphigenia? Why are people so eager to condemn her? I learned that according to Aeschylus' Eumenides, *Orestes, though eventually absolved of Clytemnestra's murder, is first punished for it by the unspeakable Furies. Clearly not all Greeks had as low an opinion of Clytemnestra's character as I had been led to believe. Even so, I was unable to accept this new knowledge. First impressions die hard: I still felt Clytemnestra guilty of terrible crimes. It was years before I began to see that Agamemnon was a murderer by trade, not a mere opportunist, and that he had killed his own daughter to save face with his army. At last Clytemnestra's actions began to seem justifiable—not perhaps in a society such as ours with benefit of a legal system that punishes offenders, but certainly in a society that operated on the principle of revenge.*

The main elements of Clytemnestra's story have come down to us in the plays of the three great dramatists Aeschylus, Sophocles, and Euripides. But details of the background to the story have not been transmitted in such high-quality or widely read literature. Students of drama rarely come across them, and even students of mythology can miss them. The truth is that Aegisthus' father had been much wronged by Agamemnon's, that Agamemnon had killed Clytemnestra's first husband and her child and then married her, that Orestes was not reared by his mother. And more. All sorts of events, from Clytemnestra's childhood and before, affect her story.

Mythology students of the 1990s seem better able to understand Clytemnestra's position than I was thirty years ago. For them, her voice rings out loud and clear from the moment we begin the story. They are accustomed to examining a text, even a male-based ancient one, and finding a place for themselves in it, women and men alike. It is time.

I

The trouble with twins is that they are not the same. Even with identical twins, especially with identical twins, people search for differences, seize upon them when they find them, and exaggerate them beyond reason.

I am Clytemnestra. Helen was my twin sister. You know about her: she was the most beautiful woman in the world; she was a daughter of Zeus the Thunderer; her husband loved her so much that he took all the Greeks to war to get her back when she was kidnapped. And what do you know about me? I was not so beautiful; I was unfaithful to my husband; I murdered him in treachery; my son killed me, and then, poor soul, was driven mad with his blood-guilt. This account of my life will not be quite like the one you've heard before, but never mind. The truth is just as good a story.

In most cities in the Greek world, the birth of twins was not a welcome event. Twins were often exposed, one or both of them, seen as an omen of evil.[3] It was not quite human, it was more the mark of an animal, to produce children in litters, and women paid their midwives well to keep their silence. In Sparta, where I was born, it was different,[4] and my father Tyndareus, who was king of Sparta, was delighted with his own prowess when my mother gave birth to two sets of twins on one day, my brothers Castor and Polydeuces, and my sister Helen and me.[5] Amazingly, we all lived. For my mother, Leda, who was not Spartan born, this was shame and shame again. She felt that all Sparta was eyeing her with disgust, and would not be told otherwise. She exploited an old ruse that women had used to save their twin babies from certain death. She claimed that a god had visited her, Zeus, she said, in the form of a swan. (How did she know, I wonder, that it was Zeus? No one ever asked her that.) Of each set of twins, one would be the child of Tyndareus, the other of Zeus. My brothers never allowed themselves to be divided by the father-difference; this in part was due to Polydeuces' generous nature and profound love for Castor.[6] But Helen wasn't like him. She was "chosen" as the daughter of Zeus and she never let me forget the difference between us. Why was she chosen? Our facial features and bodies looked the same, but hers somehow served her differently. An action that was censored in me was considered charming in her. She drew people to her for no reason

I could see and when she rejected them they fawned on her all the more. They offered to help her do small tasks that she could easily do for herself and she looked at them with disdain and gave then no thanks as they demeaned themselves. I tied my own sandals and combed my own hair and was ignored.

I scarcely saw my father. He could have met me in the halls of our house and not known me. But Helen he loved. For a man to have a daughter was nothing big; for a man to act as foster-father to the daughter of Zeus—now that was something. When Helen was abducted by Theseus of Athens when she was only twelve years old, the royal household went into mourning. My father aged ten years before my eyes and openly wept when Helen was returned to him, a virgin still.[7]

My mother was kind enough in her vague sort of way. They say no woman likes to have a daughter more beautiful than she is herself. (It isn't true to say *no* woman. Oh Iphigenia, my beautiful child!) My mother seemed immune to Helen, but she was equally distant to me. She was, I think, lost in Sparta; we searched our souls too much for comfort there in that bleak place. She was homesick for the gaiety of the north. Her trick backfired on her. When the war came and so many thousands of Greek soldiers died, she was blamed. If she hadn't attracted Zeus the Thunderer, if she hadn't tangled with the gods, Helen would never have been born and no ships would have sailed for windy Troy. She also lived with the hatred of one daughter, me, and the indifference of the other. I know what that's like, too. Perhaps hatred is too strong a word. I was angry with her for the careless way that she allowed my life to be so different from Helen's, and anger at my mother, and then at others, has become a habit that I cannot break.[8]

If you had known Helen as a child, you might have sensed the danger. She could contrive fights between my brothers and me. She could make us crazy. One occasion in particular I remember still. I can even now picture in my mind our nurse comforting Helen after I had attacked her, apparently unprovoked. She confined me to my rooms and joked that with my face like thunder, I would have been far better cast as the daughter of Zeus[9] than Helen. And I remember Helen, smiling.

II

I married before Helen. It didn't much matter, I suppose, who married me. It was Helen's husband, you see, who through her would rule Sparta after my father's death. Helen had it both ways—though acknowledged as the daughter of Zeus, not of Tyndareus, she, not I, would be the one to continue Tyndareus' line. My father married me to Tantalus, the son of an outcast from Mycenae whose own father had been a king. He was neither handsome nor rich, but he was a gentle man and I liked him well enough. I was relieved to be away from Sparta and my family, and I liked to listen to him talk about the places he had visited and the sights he had seen. His family, I soon learned, made mine look almost normal. His father, Thyestes, and his father's brother, Atreus, had quarrelled, over the kingdom of Mycenae and over a woman. She was Aërope, wife of one, lover of the other.[10] Atreus had won Mycenae, banished Thyestes, and many years later had welcomed him back. But the welcome was no true welcome. Atreus killed the children of Thyestes and served them as meat to their own father at the banquet that marked his return. Cut up their limbs and boiled them. Arranged them on a platter. Tantalus, who was to become my husband, and one other child, the eldest daughter Pelopia, whom Atreus wanted to keep around to brighten his nights, escaped. But Atreus, that perjured, impious murderer, had two sons by Aërope. You've heard of them. Their names were Agamemnon and Menelaus. My husband Tantalus feared them, for he knew that he had escaped by chance, not by design, and that these two felt it their duty to finish the vile work their father had begun. He thought it inevitable that he would die at their hands. We lived in this shadow, not settling anywhere lest the brothers find us.[11]

I cannot say I came to love Tantalus. That wasn't a feeling I knew until my first child was born; but he looked after me, and because we stayed nowhere for long we had few friends but each other. We travelled together, ate together, slept together, and I was happy enough. When my son was born, I realized my vulnerability and understood what makes a woman danger-ous: that my husband might die I could bear, indeed I almost expected it; but that my son might be hurt I could not. I knew as I held him newborn in my arms that I could commit murder if my beloved son were harmed. I do not believe those be-reaved mothers who claim they feel no anger towards their children's killers. I do not believe them. And he was harmed, my son, my brown-eyed laughing son. His head was broken on the hard ground by Agamemnon and I saw him die.[12] Tantalus, my husband, lay dead already, beheaded near the road. Agamemnon did not kill me. He was afraid of my ghost per-haps or of my Furies, with good reason. It seemed fitting to him that he should marry me. The family feud had begun, he said, when Thyestes had stolen Aërope, wife of Atreus, so now he would restore the balance by marrying me. It was a sort of elaborate prank to him. He had me taken back to Mycenae, where he was now king, and went himself to Sparta to speak to my father, who probably enjoyed the joke, and gave him per-mission to marry me.

Helen's marriage was a much more serious affair, and my father was occupied for many months in finding a husband for her who would replace him as king of Sparta. Suitors came from all over Greece to admire her beauty and to seek her hand—Diomedes, Ajax, Patroclus, Odysseus, great warriors all.[13] Agamemnon stayed in Sparta to represent his brother Menelaus, who had need of both a wife and a kingdom. They all brought gifts to show their serious intentions, and their wealth, and Agamemnon's gifts were the grandest of all. As Tyndareus hesitated, the suitors began to quarrel amongst them-selves, and he feared that when the winner was chosen there would be much bitterness or even violence, for the suitors were an impetuous group, always ready to draw their swords at the least provocation. He had them swear a solemn oath that those who were not chosen would defend the man who became Helen's husband should he ever be wronged. That way, if one of their number harmed the successful suitor, all of the others would be bound to intervene. The oath had another result, of course, that Tyndareus never dreamed of: when the Trojan, Paris, persuaded Helen that she loved him and took her to his homeland, all those who took the oath, Agamemnon included, sailed to Troy to get her back because her husband had been wronged. But for now, well satisfied with his solution, Tyndareus accepted Agamemnon's gifts and Menelaus' suit, and, married to my sister, Menelaus ruled in Sparta.

III

There were advantages to being Agamemnon's wife. He was wealthy beyond belief. There was enough gold in Mycenae that my children were to grow up playing five-stones with it. I had servants at last, to tie my sandals and comb my hair, and I felt as Helen must always have done.

I did not like Agamemnon. Even if he had not murdered my baby I would not have liked him, but since it made no difference to him whether I was pleased or displeased, it suited me better not to rant. He thought, when he thought about it at all, that I was becoming reconciled to him; he imagined himself the head of an ordered household with a loyal wife. How could he? How could he? He had murdered my son. How could he imagine that I would not rage against him? When he lay with me I turned my mind off—how else could a woman sleep with the murderer of her child—but my body worked despite me and soon a new child filled my womb, a daughter this time, Iphigenia, the exquisite one. A child can be so little its father's, so much its mother's, that I never thought of her as a murderer's child, only as mine. I wasn't a murderer then, you see, and she was enough to turn me, for a while, from my resolve. I knew I would not kill Agamemnon as long as she needed me to care for her.

But he killed her too. Oh my Iphigenia! She was fourteen years old, and so beautiful she would have taken your breath away, her dark hair tumbling to her waist and her smile sweet. She had a peculiar gesture that I loved to watch. She would stroke her own chin with her long fingers and pull at her skin like a worried old man. I remember her standing like that, at Aulis, listening to her father as he announced that he planned to kill her, to sacrifice her to the goddess Artemis like some dumb heifer so that the goddess would let his ships sail to Troy and he could rescue Helen and enjoy his war. Helen. Always Helen. Agamemnon killed my daughter, in cold blood, as the phrase goes now, though her blood was warm. It sprayed on my face as she died. And the foolish man sent me back to Mycenae as though nothing of importance had happened and sailed for Troy with his soldiers. Could he really think that I would not care? That I would sit in the palace and wait and then welcome him home?

By this time, I had other children at home, two daughters: Chrysothemis, who was feeble-minded,[14] and Electra, who looked so much like Agamemnon that I could not set eyes on her for a moment without thinking of him. We had always been wary of each other, Electra and I; I had tried, I think, to love her, but to me she seemed deficient in every way that she did not resemble Iphigenia, and I had never succeeded in loving her well. She stirred in me so many memories of the unhappy child that I had been that her presence gave me no pleasure, and even when she was a baby I sent her away more often than not to a wet nurse. When she grew up I was to bear first her indifference and then her hatred.[15]

I had borne twin sons, too, the one they call Orestes and the other who was never named. Twins are often born to women who are themselves twins and I was not surprised, though I was exhausted and fevered after their birth. In Mycenae twins were never reared, and whenever a complete thought came to me in my delirium it was always that Agamemnon would have them exposed. When I recovered they were gone. He cheated, though. One child he let die; the other he sent to be fostered at the court of Strophius of Phocis, who was married to Agamemnon's own sister, Queen Anaxibia. Only Strophius knew who the child was.[16] Agamemnon needed a son, you see, and feared that the imminent war with Troy would interfere with his begetting another, especially as I was already at the end of my childbearing years. He needed a legitimate son to take over the throne of Mycenae; he had learnt the new ways well. Mycenae would not be ruled by a daughter of mine and her consort, but by his son. Orestes was never my son. You must understand that I did not know he was alive until, long after I had killed his father, he arrived in Mycenae prepared to murder me.

IV

After Agamemnon killed Iphigenia at Aulis, I did not set eyes on him again for ten years. I liked to think of him afraid. I liked to think that in the long nights encamped outside the walls of Troy he lay awake wondering how great my power was in Mycenae and whether he could come safely home. I liked to think that he woke sometimes, cold in his own sweat, from a dream that I would kill him. I wonder now if he worried ever that his precious son would die before he returned from Troy. Tell me, Agamemnon: this son of yours in whom you took such an interest, asking for news of him from Phocis to be sent to you at Troy and crowing over his achievements, would you have sacrificed him if the Goddess of the Wild had demanded it? Would you have slit his throat too?

I thought about Agamemnon's homecoming, swore to myself that he would not sleep a single night in his bed before I killed him. I don't think I ever faltered in this. There was never a moment that I was not aware my beloved daughter was dead. As I woke each morning the first thought that came to me was of her; the second of him, with a knife in his chest.

You have heard of Aegisthus, I'm sure. He was the lily-livered adulterer who dressed up in Agamemnon's robes and sat on Agamemnon's throne while Agamemnon fought so heroically at Troy. Let me say now that there aren't many men for whom I have respect. I find them foolish with their killing-lust and their pride. But Aegisthus I both respected and loved, and believe me, he was no coward. Let me tell you who he was and you might better understand: Atreus, you remember, had murdered Thyestes' children and served their flesh to their father. But two had escaped the massacre. One was my first husband,

Tantalus, and the other was Pelopia, his elder sister. When she was grown, Pelopia was raped by her own father, Thyestes. (Did you expect that he would have acted sanely knowing he had eaten his own children? Think again. He never for one moment recovered his senses.) Aegisthus was born to Pelopia. He spent his life in hiding until Agamemnon and Menelaus left for Troy, for as a boy, as soon as he learnt who he was and understood why his father Thyestes slavered and ranted, he had killed the aging Atreus. He knew that the sons of Atreus, if they were able, would find and destroy him.[17]

Aegisthus had not killed Atreus lightly, for he had no taste for murder. Nonetheless, he approached me. We both had cause, he said, to wish Agamemnon dead. He thought it sensible that we work together. He had not gone to war, he said, not because he was a coward, but because he had no desire to help Menelaus, and because Agamemnon would have had him killed if ever his identity had become known. Aegisthus became my friend, my comfort, my fortress. I loved him well.

Together we plotted Agamemnon's death. I sent a message to Troy asking Agamemnon to light a beacon on Mount Ida there when his ships were embarking on their journey home. When that beacon was sighted on the island of Lemnos another was to be lit and so on, all the way to Mycenae. This way, Agamemnon could not surprise us with his return. We waited for him, and we ruled Mycenae well enough in his absence.

The night came when the closest beacon was sighted from Mycenae, and not many days later Agamemnon, conqueror of Troy, murderer of children, landed in Nauplia. Aegisthus saw him kneel and kiss the soil, so happy was he to be home. Without identifying himself, Aegisthus escorted him to Mycenae and closed the palace gates behind him. Agamemnon was alone among enemies. What happened next you know already. The poets did not lie. I welcomed Agamemnon home. I laid a carpet down for him to walk on, the colour of his blood. Strutting proudly, full of his own importance, he entered the palace. I bathed him, like a dutiful wife. I had made a bathrobe for him, to double as a death shroud. It had no holes for arms and neck. I pulled it down over his head, and as he struggled like a small child with a stiff new tunic I stabbed him three times. The moment of murder was mine. Aegisthus joined me only when Agamemnon lay dead. Once more I felt the spray of warm blood on my face. It was a pleasure. Few murderers have been as jubilant as I.

V

It seems to me it should have ended there. An eye for an eye, or rather one eye for several—the murders of Tantalus, my infant son, Iphigenia, Thyestes' children, all avenged but with just one new death. I did not kill Cassandra.[18] I do not slaughter children. I would not kill an innocent. But it did not end there.

For eight more years I ruled in Mycenae, with Aegisthus as my consort. I kept order at home and there was little trouble in the rest of Greece, but rulers are known for the wars they wage, not the peace they keep. Then, one morning in the summertime, Orestes arrived in Mycenae. The previous night I had dreamed of giving birth to a snake, of swaddling it and suckling it, but it drew blood and not milk from my breast. I felt this to be a portent and gave orders that my daughter Electra be confined to the palace, for I knew that she despised me, and feared she might be plotting with her town friends to end my rule. I did not know there lurked another viper. And then I went about my usual business, the tedious business of state.

But Orestes came to the palace gate, acting the part of a foreigner and begging hospitality. My servants admitted him and I received him myself. I cannot say I recognised him, for I did not know I had a son that lived. When Aegisthus approached, unarmed of course, relaxed, to kiss me and to greet the newcomer, Orestes drew his sword and within moments, so quickly that I could not grasp what was happening, Aegisthus lay dying and I was looking into the face of his murderer. I recognised the look of triumph in his eyes, the triumph of revenge, for I had felt it once myself. "I am Orestes," said the murderer, "your son and Agamemnon's. I am here to kill you because you killed my father."

The poets have told you that I bared my breast and pleaded for my life.[19] It is a favourite scene of theirs. I did not. I looked around me, saw Electra watching from the corner, saw my dear Aegisthus on the ground, and knelt to him. He died as I held his head in my lap and I spoke three words only: "my love, Aegisthus." I did not speak, at all, to Orestes. "He's your love, is he?" sneered this blustering youth. He seemed to me so foolish, so pathetic. "That's good. For you will lie together in one grave." For one mad moment I thought of snatching the sword from his hand, of brawling with him there in the great hall, but I do not slaughter children. I turned instead to Electra, and watched her watching me. Then I knew only darkness.

We are not powerless when we are dead. The Greeks knew that.[20] My anger bore yet more fruit. My Furies came to Orestes in the night, like bats and hoot owls in the mind.[21] He did not rest, he did not eat, he did not speak. He lay for six days screaming, his only wish for death. I remembered Thyestes' madness after he discovered what he had eaten. I remembered my own sorrow in the dark early days after the death of Iphigenia, and I felt it fitting that Orestes, son of Agamemnon, son of Atreus, should suffer this.

And Helen, always Helen. She came to my tomb, to mourn for me, or to be seen to mourn for me. It was the custom for women to crop their long hair short when a close relative died, to scratch their own faces with their fingernails and rub dirt into their wounds. But Helen did not wish to mar her beauty. She came, my sister, and very carefully trimmed a finger's width from her pretty hair, and laid it, smiling, on my grave.[22]

Notes

[1] No one source covers all the details of Clytemnestra's story, but see Aeschylus, Agamemnon, for the homecoming of Agamemnon, and Choephori, for the deaths of Clytemnestra and Aegisthus. In Eumenides, Clytemnestra appears as a ghost, urging the Furies to torment Orestes. Sophocles' Electra also covers the deaths of Clytemnestra and Aegisthus, as does Euripides' play of the same name. Iphigenia in Aulis, also by Euripides, deals with the sacrifice of Iphigenia and contains details (1148–52) of the death of Clytemnestra's first husband, Tantalus, also found in Pausanias 2.18.2.

Apollodorus tells the story of the feud between Thyestes and Atreus at *Epitome* 2.10. Hyginus, at *Fabulae* 87, 88, continues Thyestes' story, in much greater detail than appears here. Other details are taken from Euripides, *Orestes;* Apollodorus, *Epitome* 6.23–25; Hyginus, *Fabulae* 117; and Pindar, *Pythian Odes* 11.1–37. Many other authors tackled this story, which is at least as old as Homer. See *Odyssey* 1.28–43, 1.298–300, and 3.301–310.

² Pelops, who was Agamemnon's paternal grandfather, wanted to win the hand of Hippodamia, daughter of the king and queen, Oenomaus and Sterope, of Pisa. To do this, he had to win a chariot race against her father. He was able to convince Oenomaus' charioteer, Myrtilus, to sabotage the king's chariot by offering him a night with Hippodamia should he, Pelops, win her. Myrtilus kept his part of the bargain, but Pelops reneged and killed Myrtilus when he tried to take what he considered his due. As he died, Myrtilus cursed Pelops and his descendants. See Apollodorus, *Epitome* 2.4–8.

³ It seems that twins were exposed (put outside city limits to die; see Jocasta's story, chap. 3) in real life, since far fewer pairs of twins are recorded as children or adults than we would expect. Perhaps twins, likely to be born prematurely and with more difficulty than most single babies, did not survive birth as often, but it is just as probable that those who did survive were considered too weak, too small, or too full of ill omen to be allowed to live.

⁴ One particular set of twins in Sparta was of great significance. According to tradition, twin boys had founded separate ruling dynasties, and even in historical times two kings, supposedly their direct descendants, ruled the city-state at the same time.

⁵ This is Clytemnestra's family tree:

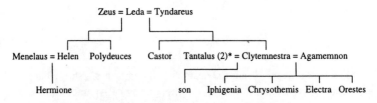

*There was an earlier Tantalus in the family. See n. 17.

⁶ In fact, one should have been mortal and one immortal, but out of love for Castor, Polydeuces relinquishes half of his immortality and gives it to his twin, so that they are each alive for one day, dead for one day, and so on.

[7] Theseus, king of Athens, and his friend Peirithous decide that they both wish to marry daughters of Zeus. Theseus chooses Helen, though because of her youth he does not immediately marry her. Rather he keeps her imprisoned at Aphidnae, in his own territory of Attica. Peirithous chooses Persephone, a daughter of Zeus who is already married—to Hades, god of the Underworld. When Theseus and Peirithous descend to capture her, Hades detains them. Theseus eventually escapes, though Peirithous does not, but while Theseus is in the Underworld Helen's brothers rescue her. See Apollodorus 3.10.7 and *Epitome* 1.23-24.

[8] In myth, being dead doesn't make you any less angry. One of the more poignant scenes in extant Greek literature is Odysseus' attempt to draw Ajax into conversation when he, Odysseus, visits the Underworld and encounters the dead Ajax there. Ajax, still furious because Odysseus won the armour of Achilles in what was, in Ajax's view, an unfair contest, will not speak with him. See Homer, *Odyssey* 11.541-64. The dead Clytemnestra, in Aeschylus' *Eumenides,* has lost none of her rancour.

[9] Zeus, frequently called simply "The Thunderer," is the god who sends storms. He is often depicted in art holding a thunderbolt that he is about to throw.

[10] Aërope had quite a history: she was the daughter of Catreus, son of Minos and king of Crete. Either he threw her into the sea because she fell in love with a foreign-born slave (Sophocles, *Ajax* 1295-97) or he had her and her sister Clymene sold abroad because an oracle had told him that one of his children would kill him. (His son, Althaemenes, and another sister, Apemosune, went into voluntary exile, but years later Althaemenes did indeed kill his father with a javelin, thinking him to be a pirate.) Apollodorus details the little-known adventures of this remarkable family at 3.2.1-2. Eventually, Aërope married Atreus and then became the lover of Thyestes.

[11] For there to be a vendetta between two families was not unusual for the Greeks. But in myth, this becomes a vendetta between two branches of the same family. Only then can the double binds and ironies that the mythtellers so much enjoyed be fully exploited. In this case, the family was cursed in a previous generation (see n. 2, above) and the vendetta fulfills the curse. However, it makes for a story so complicated that it is hard to keep track of who takes revenge on whom for what. Somewhat simplified, the actions of the vendetta are:

    (a) Thyestes seduces Atreus' wife, Aërope.
    (b) Atreus murders Thyestes' children.

(c) Thyestes' son (Aegisthus) kills Atreus.

(d) Atreus' son (Agamemnon) kills Thyestes' son (Tantalus) and Tantalus' son.

(e) Aegisthus kills Atreus' son, Agamemnon.

(f) Agamemnon's son, Orestes, kills Aegisthus.

[12] This part of the story was known to the Greeks, though apparently was not popular. See Euripides, *Iphigenia in Aulis* 1150–52, where Clytemnestra publicly accuses Agamemnon of dashing the baby on the ground; Pausanias 2.18.2 and 2.22.2–4; and Apollodorus, *Epitome* 2.16.

[13] Apollodorus, 3.10.8, lists thirty-one suitors.

[14] This is not stated in any ancient source, but only in Sophocles' *Electra* is Chrysothemis given a role to play in the unfolding of events.

[15] In the ancient sources, Electra invariably dislikes her mother (with good reason, since she is either imprisoned by her or forced by her to live in poverty after Agamemnon's death). She helps Orestes kill Clytemnestra and Aegisthus, according to Euripides actually holding the sword with him as he drives its blade into Clytemnestra's throat.

[16] I have no evidence that Orestes was a twin, but it seems not an unreasonable change to make. As Clytemnestra herself says here, women who are twins may give birth to twins themselves. Orestes is accompanied in his adventures in literature by Pylades, his cousin (the son of Anaxibia and Strophius) and good friend. The two are inseparable, though not equal in prowess. Pylades may well be a remnant of a less powerful twin who appeared in an early version of the myth. See Robert Graves, *The Greek Myths,* vol. 1 (Harmondsworth, UK, 1960), 326, on Theseus and Peirithous.

Most ancient sources have Orestes sent away not at birth, but at the time of his father's murder, lest Aegisthus try to kill him. Either Electra is responsible for removing him from Mycenae, or his tutor or his nurse. See, for example, Apollodorus, *Epitome* 6.24. I have kept this concept of exposure, or removing the child from its family (which does not only involve newborns) but changed the motive for it. Euripides, at *Orestes* 462, seems to suggest that Orestes was brought up in Sparta by his maternal grandparents. In *Agamemnon* Aeschylus has Clytemnestra send Orestes away herself, before Agamemnon arrives home.

¹⁷ This is Aegisthus' family tree:

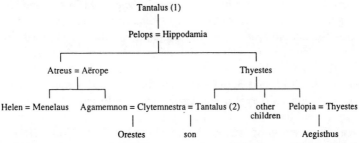

It is Aegisthus' responsibility to kill Atreus, because Atreus killed Aegisthus' brothers and sisters, even though this all happened before he was born. Not all ancient authors know about Tantalus. If he does not exist, Thyestes needs to conceive a son who will avenge the murdered children. A son born of his own daughter will have a double relationship to those children, and thus an enhanced commitment to take revenge. Aegisthus is this son.

Hyginus tells a complex story of the birth and childhood of Aegisthus: Thyestes rapes his daughter Pelopia not knowing who she is. She doesn't know who he is either, but during the attack she takes his sword from its sheath. Atreus marries Pelopia, not knowing that she is Thyestes' daughter or that she is pregnant by Thyestes. When she gives birth to Aegisthus she exposes him but he is suckled by goats and lives. (His name seems to mean "goat-boy.") Atreus finds him and raises him as his own son. At some point Pelopia gives him the stolen sword, telling him that it belongs to his real father. When Aegisthus is grown Atreus sends him to kill Thyestes. As he draws his sword to do so, Thyestes recognises it as the one he lost years before. Pelopia arrives and realises for the first time that her son's father is her own father. She takes the sword as if to look at it more closely, and kills herself with it. Thyestes and Aegisthus acknowledge that they are father and son. Aegisthus takes the bloody sword to Atreus who rejoices temporarily, believing his brother to be dead at last. Then Aegisthus kills him with it.

¹⁸ When the city of Troy was taken, the Trojan men were killed and the women and children enslaved. Cassandra, daughter of Queen Hecuba and King Priam of Troy, became Agamemnon's concubine. The ancient authors, including Homer (*Odyssey* 11.404–454) and Aeschylus in his *Agamemnon,* consider Clytemnestra to be the murderer of Cassandra as well as of Agamemnon. According to most of them she hacks her to death with an axe. A well-known red-figure vase-painting in the National Museum, Ferrara, Italy, shows her doing exactly that. I have chosen to differ. It is interesting to note that

Pausanias (2.16.5) records at Mycenae the graves of Agamemnon, his charioteer, his twin sons by Cassandra (see below, this note), and his daughter Electra as well as those of Clytemnestra and Aegisthus, but states that the authenticity of Cassandra's tomb there is disputed. It was the Spartans at Amyklai who claimed the tomb of Cassandra, though they also claimed those of Clytemnestra and Agamemnon. See Pausanias 2.16.5 and 3.19.6. Perhaps there existed a tradition that Cassandra did not die alongside Agamemnon at Mycenae. If so, no literary source that I have found refers to it. Marion Zimmer Bradley bases the premise of her novel *The Firebrand* (New York, 1987), which tells Cassandra's story, on an inscription on a tablet in the Archaeological Museum in Athens, which suggests to her that Cassandra or at least one of her children lived on past this point in the story. Zimmer Bradley gives Cassandra just one son, but twins ran in Cassandra's family as well as Clytemnestra's. She was a twin herself, to Helenus. According to Pausanias, at 2.16.5, Cassandra bore twin sons to Agamemnon (the return journey from Troy clearly took many months). They were named Teledamus and Pelops, and they were killed along with her and Agamemnon by Aegisthus. Pausanias saw their joint grave at Mycenae.

[19] The point of this act would be to remind Orestes that he had once been suckled at this breast, to impress upon him that it was his *mother* he was about to kill. See Aeschylus, *Choephori* 895–97. An argument follows and then Clytemnestra is killed.

[20] There were, in Greece, hero cults, which involved making offerings at the designated "tombs" of powerful men of the mythical past in return for protection and favours. Heroes had only local power, within a certain radius of their supposed place of burial. Even ordinary people, when dead, were thought to have the potential to affect the living. This is partly why burial rituals were so rigorous, and so much care was taken to ensure that the dead reached the Underworld, from which they could not escape.

[21] The Furies, or Erinyes—female, monstrous, and unspeakably vile— punished perpetrators of crimes against kin by driving them mad.

[22] Euripides, in his *Orestes,* depicts a Helen who is reluctant to visit her sister's grave, so frightened is she that she will be attacked by the families of young men who died at Troy. She asks Electra to take her meagre offering (a libation of honey, milk, and wine and a lock or two of hair) to the grave instead. Electra refuses, more it seems from disapproval of Helen than because she disliked her mother. She suggests that Helen should send her young daughter, Hermione, instead, which she does. See *Orestes* 92–119.

THREE

Jocasta's Story

Most people already know the story that follows.[1] *Laius, king of Thebes, is told by the Delphic oracle of Apollo that his child will kill him. Therefore, plans are made for the child to be exposed on the mountainside with a pin through its ankles, to die, as soon as it is born.*[2] *But the child, Oedipus, does not die. A servant from Laius' household gives him to a Corinthian shepherd, who passes him on to the king and queen of Corinth to rear as their own. When grown, Oedipus himself is warned by Apollo that he will murder his father and marry his mother. The prophecies come true. Oedipus kills Laius when the two meet and argue on a narrow road, and he becomes king of Thebes and the husband of his mother Jocasta when he saves Thebes from disaster by answering the riddle of the Sphinx. It is many years, however, before Oedipus finds out, all in one day, that it was Laius whom he killed, that Laius was his father, and that Jocasta was his mother. His knowledge destroys the family.*

The story as told by Sophocles in his play Oedipus Rex *is rich in situations and angles for the storyteller to capitalise on: the "crime" and predicament of Laius; the brutal relentlessness of Oedipus' fate, which, in struggling to avoid, he meets head on; the fact that he is guilty of kin-murder; the horrifying power of coincidence in his life (after all, he kills only one man as far as we know, and marries only one woman). Part of the story is a murder mystery with a series of clues and with Oedipus as both detective and criminal. Double identities abound—not just mother-wife and son-husband, but servant-survivor and shepherd-messenger.*[3] *The recognition scene, a necessary sequel to the exposure of a child, is here so distorted that it is extraordinary—Oedipus, by identifying a "birth mark" (his scarred feet) and by hearing the testimony of witnesses to his exposure, recognises himself as a murderer and his mother's husband.*[4] *Several characters stand out as worthy of examination. How badly does Creon, Jocasta's brother and periodic regent of Thebes, want to be king in his own right? What about the servant who chooses to let the doomed baby Oedipus live? How does he feel when years later he sees the baby he saved commit unspeakable crimes? Most intriguing of all, though, is Jocasta. At some point she must recognise her son. The question is, when? In Sophocles' play she realises who Oedipus is only a little while before he realises it himself.*[5] *Nowhere is it stated in the ancient sources that she has known all along who Oedipus is. But if, just for a moment, we treat Jocasta as if she were a real person, it must be acknowledged that she did know Laius was destined to be killed by his son, and there was at least a possibility that the son still lived. Laius was killed, yet she had apparently never given much thought to determining who killed him. The nature of the relationship between Sophocles' Jocasta and the servant from Laius' household, called here Phorbas, is unclear. She handed the child over to him personally (according to him but not to her).*[6] *He certainly received compassionate treatment from her when he came to ask if he could be relieved of his palace duties.*[7] *At that point he must have known that Laius' oracle had come true and that the child, whom he had been responsible for saving, had now killed his father and married his mother. At the very least he knew that the murderer of Laius was now sitting on the throne of Thebes and occupying Jocasta's bed. Is it not possible that he told Jocasta his real reason for wishing to leave the palace—that his knowledge made it impossible for him to be in close proximity to the king? Sophocles' Jocasta, and his Oedipus, too, for that matter, should certainly have realised earlier on the day of discovery who Oedipus was. Before there is any real proof of Oedipus' identity and crimes, Oedipus tells Jocasta that he is fated to murder his father and marry his mother. She should see that this oracle matches the one given to Laius, about which she knows,*[8] *and since by this point in the play it is at least possible that Oedipus killed Laius, she should draw the obvious inference. But she doesn't. Why not? Because she too can recognise scarred ankles? Because she has known, all along, who Oedipus is?*

In the version of this story told below, Jocasta realised that Oedipus was her son on the very day he arrived in Thebes, and she discovered that he was Laius' murderer soon after that.

I

It may be that I made some mistakes, that I could have tried harder to see to it that none of this happened. But at what price? At the cost of killing my baby boy? Of refusing the young man, the saviour of our city, who came to my bed? I knew who he was. How could I not have known? What woman could lie with her own son and not know it? Do you think me a fool?

Let me take you back, to the beginning, before the troubles. I was born here, in Thebes, of one of the old families, the Sparti, or Sown Ones. Legend has it that when Cadmus founded this city, it was peopled at first by men who sprang from the ground when he scattered the teeth of a serpent he killed. Perhaps I have not gone back far enough after all. It may be that it all began with that serpent, which was sacred to the god Ares, implacable hater of humankind.[9]

There I go, in the way of women. Forever we search our minds for a cause for what goes wrong in our lives.

I grew up like a creature of the forest, free to do whatever I wished. No one planned my days for me, or decided what I should learn. As children my brother and I explored every corner of our city and beyond, into the hills. The northern slopes of Cithaeron, the arbutus bushes dripping with fruit, were as familiar to us as the walls of our own house. My brother was wild then, fierce as a lion. We took what we wanted from our days and nothing frightened us.

I grew up proud of my city. I remember my father crouching down beside me once as I made my castles in the roadside dirt. He helped me to fashion splendid buildings, and smaller ones, a Thebes in miniature. That day he explained to me our family's obligations to the other citizens of Thebes. He could not have known that I would one day be her queen, but he must have thought it possible. I was five years younger than Laius, son of Labdacus. Labdacus was the handsome young king who was dead before my birth, killed in battle with Athenians. Laius, still too young to rule, lived in Pisa, for his safety. Our fair city was ruled by Lycus, but not justly, and the people were glad when Laius, as handsome as his father, came home to reclaim the throne of Thebes.

I remember the first time I saw him. It was my sixteenth summer. He was presented to his people in the palace courtyard. We came, all of us, to greet him and to love him. Did he know, then, what horrors he would bring on our city?

A year later, I was his bride. He chose me himself. The daughters of those who were descendants of the Sown Men were paraded before him, and he chose me. I was dark where he was fair, as tall as he, and nearly as strong. This was my chance, my father said, to do my duty for my beloved city, to be the foremost of her queens. My mother was pleased when I was chosen, though my brother Creon, and I don't think I imagined this, was quiet, and slow with his congratulations.

Laius seemed to me a distant man. They say he loved elsewhere, that the beautiful boy Chrysippus who had come from Pisa to Thebes with him was his true love, that after the boy was killed by his own half brothers, in Laius' bed, Laius was never the same.[10] The people of Thebes knew nothing of this, but the palace servants knew. I hear it said that this was why it all happened, not because Laius loved the boy—men can love where they like and no one cares—but because he stole him from his parents while he, Laius, was their guest. And this, this could be crime enough? To account for all that happened later? If so, the gods are fools, or depraved, or both.

Laius rarely approached me. I knew I was not plain, was beautiful in fact, and I wondered what it was that kept him from my arms. Grief for that boy, I think now, though I knew nothing of it then. The people of Thebes began to wonder at our childlessness. Years later, I knew, though not from his own lips, that Laius had asked Apollo—I warn you now, I have no good words for Apollo—whether children would be born to us. We were childless because he did not sleep with me. Did he need a god to tell him that? Apollo revealed that any child born to us would murder Laius. When I heard this later, though before the prophecy had come true, it made me smile. I liked the economy of it. Perhaps all sons should kill their fathers, if those fathers do them wrong.

One night, Laius, muddled with wine, came to my bedroom uninvited, the first time for many months. He was too drunk to remember Apollo's words, or else drunk enough to challenge them. A child was conceived that night, my first son.

I was overjoyed to be carrying the child. But Laius' horror grew with my belly. I could not imagine why. Most kings want sons, and the people were happy enough. He told me, plainly, without artifice, that when the child was born, it would be exposed on Mount Cithaeron, left for the wolves to mangle. A manservant, he said, had been ordered to see to it. I knew, immediately, which servant he meant: a young man who had been born and raised in the palace, spent the winters there and the summers with the flocks in the hills. He had taken Laius' fancy. I visited the young man in his quarters. His name was Phorbas.[11]

"If you will see to it that my child lives," I said to him, "I will give you privileges beyond the dreams of slaves."

II

I remember my child's first cry. He was born with the dawn on a bleak day at summer's end. I did not hold him in my arms. His father snatched him from the midwife's hands, drove a pin through his ankles and then left, without a word, without a glance behind him. The midwife screamed and went on screaming. She moved towards the child on the floor. The servant Phorbas was already there.

"Take him." I do not know how I managed the words. "Take him now."[12]

He came back later that same day, and sent word to me that he had removed the pin, lain sweet herbs on the child's ankles and bound them. And then he had given him to a shepherd on the hillside, a man he had known for years.

Many summers went by. After each, when Phorbas returned to the palace, he gave me a report on my son—first that he had been taken to Corinth and was being reared there by a childless woman of high birth and her husband. I sent gifts, supposedly of congratulation, when I heard this—a blanket for the child, that I had embroidered myself, and a chest of palace-woven clothing. And so it was that my son grew up wearing clothes his mother made, just as it should be. In his second year I learned that he was dark, like me, and later that he was taller than most boys, and stronger, scarcely troubled by his scarred ankles. I heard too that he was not the best runner in Corinth, though after twelve summers he walked without a limp, but that he was fast becoming the best swordsman.

Laius grew no warmer towards me. We scarcely spoke, yet in the sixteenth year of my son's life he seemed to grow more silent still, sterner, angrier. I learned from Phorbas that Apollo's seer, Teiresias, had warned him that his fate would soon be upon him, and I knew, also from Phorbas, what that fate was supposed to be. Apollo had predicted that Laius' own son would kill him. He wanted to go to Delphi to ask the god how this could be, when his only child did not live.[13] He left, all in a hurry, seated in his carriage with four attendants, one of them Phorbas. He was never to return, and though I did not know this as the carriage sped away, my heart felt light as down to see him go.

III

Phorbas alone came home, with news that our king was dead. The story he told, to us all at first, was that robbers had killed Laius, a whole gang of them, rough men who lay hidden in the undergrowth and surprised the party where the Daulis road and the Delphi road meet the road from Thebes. Whoever they were, I blessed them many times in the shadows of my mind and did not allow myself to dwell on that prophecy from Apollo heard by Laius long ago.

But I took no chances. Phorbas was ill, delirious, for a long time. And he was looked after, at the palace, by me.

My once-carefree brother, Creon, had been managing Thebes in Laius' absence, because he was my brother and because he was descended from one of the oldest families here. His position made him officious; I hardly knew him. He issued proclamations as though they were invitations to dinner.

When Thebes learned that her king was dead, the citizens were eager that Creon be named regent. With great solemnity he took up his duties, not least of which was finding a new king. He needed a crisis to give him ideas, and it came, the crisis, almost before we had taken a breath. You have heard of the Sphinx, the Strangler. She was a lion, but also a serpent; an eagle, but also a woman. She perched on Mount Phicium, and looked down on Thebes. She would wait until our streets were filled with people, then fly down and settle on the walls of the citadel. She would pick young men out of the crowd, one, then another, then another. She would ask them each a question, always the same question,[14] and throttle them when they could not answer. Our citizens were terrified. They pleaded with Creon to rid them of this scourge. We like economy in our family. He sought to solve two problems with one bold manoeuvre. A proclamation, his best yet: "Whoever solves the riddle of the Sphinx shall become king of Thebes and husband of the queen."

I knew my son lived. I knew he was grown. But I did not know he would arrive at Thebes and answer the riddle. I had nothing to do with that.

I remember the day he came. It was raining and cold. The people were going about their business. From amongst the crowd of tortured citizens a traveller emerged. They directed him to the palace. His bearing was dignified; it was as if his shoulders were ready to be draped with robes of office.

"My lady," he said as he kneeled before me, "I am Oedipus, son of Polybus and Merope, king and queen of Corinth. I bring you greetings on their behalf." He reminded me of someone—his leanness, his spareness, his ease of movement. His kind, bright eyes never left my face. He confronted the Sphinx, answered her riddle in a moment. Before we knew it she was gone, had flung herself from the citadel walls. The people saw her die. Oedipus returned to the palace. He smiled, confident beyond his years. Suddenly I realised that he reminded me of myself. And then I knew. The scars were there, on his legs. I saw them. I held out my hand for him to kiss. Ours was the swiftest marriage ever staged, that very night our wedding night. I held my son in my arms at last.

IV

Four pretty babies in as many years. Can you believe me that I was so much their mother that I all but forgot I was their grandmother too? And Oedipus. He was so powerful, as king and husband and lover, that I could not connect him with the child I had carried in my womb years before. I knew, yes, but I did not believe. And we were happy, and Thebes was happy. Our children grew up fine and strong: My daughter Ismene fair and winsome, like pear blossom. My daughter Antigone dark and wiry, tiny, monkey-faced. Polynices, a solemn child inclined to pretension, like his uncle, inclined to puff out his chest and strut, proclaiming that he would be king one day, with his brother. And Eteocles: my youngest child.[15] A replica of his father—his eyes kind and intense, his smile almost wicked. Four babies. If what I was doing was so wrong, why did the gods bless me so?

We had been together sixteen years when the changes came—slowly at first—the palace women miscarrying, waves of sickness in the villages. But the sickness did not go away. And then ... blight on the crops, animals starving in the fields, our people dying in the streets. Oh my gods, why punish them for my wrongdoing? Through it all, we, the royal family, remained unscathed. The children grew; we were not ill. Our food seemed always enough to nourish us.

The people of Thebes were not angry. Rather, they looked to us for help, coming daily to the palace, advancing on us like insects, dark and thin. Oedipus and Creon discussed the trouble and nothing else. Creon seemed almost to enjoy it, his eyes gleaming with concentration. They decided that Creon should travel to Delphi to ask Apollo what was wrong, and how we could save our city. I prayed that Apollo would not ask me to give up another child. But what he did was worse. It didn't seem so at first; when Creon came back what he said seemed like a joke. In his blustering, self-important way he told us that we needed to find out who had murdered Laius, my husband of years ago, and cast this wretch from the city, whoever it was who had felled the king at the place where three roads met.

"May the curses of the gods fall on the killer of Laius," proclaimed Oedipus, Creon at his side, "and on anyone who harbours this man, or who knows who he is, yet does not tell." He cursed himself and did not know it. And cursed me too.

I had known, for many years, that Oedipus killed Laius. Apollo had said he would, and Phorbas told me he had. When he, Phorbas, finally recovered from his injuries, he revealed the true story of Laius' death. A young man, taller than Laius, dark, sun-beaten, was walking alone on the road towards Thebes. Laius' carriage approached the spot where the Daulis road and the Delphi road meet the road from Thebes. The way is narrow there. Laius called out to the stranger, ordering him to step aside. Before the man could even move, Laius' horses had trampled his feet. An argument followed. The young man killed Laius and three attendants, ran them through with his sword. Only Phorbas escaped. He left the bodies where they lay, unburied, and returned to Thebes on foot to tell us that our king was dead. He had recognised the murderer from the scars on his ankles. He told his lie about a robber gang.

Months passed before Phorbas was well enough to speak again. By then, all had changed at Thebes. Oedipus, Laius' son, my son, he of the scarred ankles, a murderer, now shared my bed and ruled our city. Phorbas wanted no trouble for himself or anyone. He asked to be sent away from the palace, to live in the hills all the year far from the sight of Thebes. He knew too much. I let him go.

V

With his usual fervour, Oedipus set about finding the murderer of Laius. First, he sent for Apollo's blind seer, Teiresias, thinking he would pluck the murderer's name out of the air like some magician. He could have done so. It is clear to me now that he knew, all along, who Oedipus was and what he had done. But Apollo would not let us escape so easily. Teiresias refused straight answers, talking only in riddles that Oedipus could not understand, of fathers who were also brothers, of husbands who were also sons. And then, suddenly, shouting in anger, for all to hear, "This I will tell you. *You* are the murderer of the man whose murderer you seek. You are the cursed polluter of this land."[16] Apollo must have dulled Oedipus' wits. He didn't understand how this could be. He sent Teiresias away, mocking him for his blindness. Then he grew quarrelsome, squabbled with Creon like a boy whose toys are stolen.

He told me of the accusation and I saw the danger hanging over us, felt its power like the hot breath of a rapist on my neck. Too much said, and Oedipus would know he was my son. That he be denounced as a murderer, I could bear. I would go with him into exile. I would follow him anywhere. But that he, and our people, find out he was my son ... this was unendurable. I took a risk: "Take no notice of Apollo's fool," I said. "This is dangerous nonsense." And then, because I needed him to hear this from me, and no one else: "I lost a child, once, because of Apollo and his prophecies." He stopped his ranting, and listened to me.

I told him of the prophecy Laius was given, of his determination that our child be put out to die. "That child did not kill Laius," I insisted. "That child died before he saw his second sunrise." If I could convince him that Laius' son, and mine, was dead, the danger would be less. It would never occur to him that he could be that child.[17]

Oedipus seemed comforted to think that Apollo could be wrong, but he returned to his search. He questioned me about the attack on Laius. As I told him what I knew about the place where Laius died, he recognised my description, realising that he had killed a man at a place where three roads met. Perhaps, he thought, he had killed Laius after all. But I told him the old lie that Phorbas told to everyone, save me, that robbers had killed the king. He clung to this like a child to its mother's neck. "This Phorbas," he asked, "is he here?"

"No," I answered, glad that this was true.

But I had underestimated Oedipus' tenacity. "I must speak with him," he said. "He alone can clear my name."

I was truly frightened. "But I assure you," I insisted, "that this is what he told us—told us all—all our citizens heard him. He cannot change his story now."[18]

"Send for him anyway," said Oedipus. And I had no choice.

VI

And then the Corinthian came. A messenger. A slow old man, too stupid for his own good. He told Oedipus that Polybus, king of Corinth, his supposed father, was dead, and told him more besides. That Oedipus was not the son of this dead man and Merope, his queen, but that he, this old Corinthian fool himself, had once been a shepherd on Cithaeron and had taken a baby from another man. This baby he had given to the queen, who had reared the child as her own. "You are no more Polybus' son than you are mine," he said, rocking with merry laughter.[19]

"Who gave me to you?" Oedipus asked carefully, sensing the closeness of the truth.

"A manservant from the house of Laius."

And to me: "Jocasta, who is this man of whom he speaks?"

I begged him to press no further, tried to push the old Corinthian to leave. If he would only go, Phorbas could come and tell his old lie about robbers, deny all knowledge of a baby. Phorbas, old himself now, came, more frightened than I had ever seen him. He did not let his eyes meet mine. He had kept his secret well, this slave-born man who knew more of a queen's mysteries than should ever have been known. He came to talk about the killing he had witnessed, prepared, perhaps, to name Oedipus murderer of Laius at last. But it was worse, far worse, than this. The murder of Laius, the robbers, the place where three roads met were all forgotten. Oedipus wanted to know one thing only. He wanted to know who he was. Phorbas pretended not to recognise the Corinthian, who was chortling with pleasure at meeting his old friend again, then tried to warn him to be quiet. But the Corinthian rolled on, inexorable, like a river roaring home. He spoke of a summer in the mountains, of a baby, of a pin through its ankles. Oedipus listened and turned, at last, to Phorbas.

"This child he speaks of. Did you give him a child?"

"Yes."

"Your own child?"

"No."

"Whose child?"

"For love of the gods, my king, do not ask me this."

"Whose child?"

"Ask your wife."

"She gave you the child?"

"Yes."[20]

VII

I have had years to think about this moment. Now, it seems impossible. Impossible that it took him so long to understand. How could he not have realised until then? Think of what he knew: he had just come from Apollo's oracle at Delphi when he killed Laius. Apollo had told him what he would do. He was to murder his father and bed his mother. But when he killed a man, he didn't pause to wonder whether this man was his father. And when he became my husband, he didn't pause to wonder whether I could be his mother. Apollo's oracle, you may say. Apollo told him that Polybus and Merope were his parents. But Apollo couldn't have told him that, could he? Because it wasn't true.

Even supposing that when he killed Laius he didn't imagine that he had killed his father, why did it not occur to him that he had killed the king of Thebes? He arrived here and learned that the king was newly slain. And yet he married the dead king's wife. He should have fathomed it, shouldn't he, should have seen that he was doing what the god had told him he would do?

I am grateful for his blindness. Blindness comes in many forms. Teiresias had one. But Oedipus, oh, Oedipus—he had another. His blindness gave us all those years of joy.

VIII

Oedipus left the Corinthian standing there astounded, Phorbas a shattered man. Rushed inside the palace, screaming my name, howling that I was a whore, and worse. He tore my dress from my breast. Took the pins that had held it at my shoulders and drove them straight into his eyes. Afterwards he stood, bemused, bewildered. Creon asked him why he had put out his eyes. What kind of question is that? This is how he answered it: "What need have I of eyes when all is ugly?"[21]

IX

What next? I can scarcely remember. My dear Oedipus, blind, creeping like an old man, gone from the city with our daughters. The plague abating now the murderer was found. Word that he had died near Athens, my name never passing his lips. And trouble here. It never ends. My son Eteocles defending Thebes from attack. Polynices, my other son, the attacker.

My sons met at the highest gate of Thebes. Brother fighting brother to the death. Killing each other with their swords, cursing their father with their dying breaths. I closed their dead eyelids with my own hands.

Can a woman curse a god? If so, Apollo, then I curse you. I curse your priests and your prophecies. May your temples crumble and may future generations be indifferent to your name.

And I ... What's for me now? What need have I of life when all is loathsome? Let Creon, my dear brother, blunder on; let him enjoy his proclamations. There are few left to hear them. Oh my city ... that you should come to this. The noose is too slow for me. I need a quicker death. The sword is good. I will take the sword.[22] And who will mourn me, knowing what I have done?

Notes

[1] The most obvious source for this story is Sophocles' *Oedipus Rex,* the story of Oedipus' discovery of what he has done and who he is. The events that precede this discovery need to be gleaned from conversations in the play. Nowhere does Sophocles state precisely what happened. This play begins with distraught citizens asking for Oedipus' help to combat troubles that have befallen the city of Thebes. It so happens that Oedipus has already taken action and consulted the Delphic oracle. The oracle seems to tell him to find out who murdered Laius, the last king of Thebes, many years before. Towards the end of the play, Jocasta hangs herself, realising that Oedipus is about to find out that she is his mother. From Sophocles' *Oedipus at Colonus* we learn that after this Oedipus is sent into exile and Creon becomes regent of Thebes. Oedipus dies far from home, in Athens. In Euripides' *Phoenician Women,* which deals with the fate of the sons of Oedipus and Jocasta, Jocasta is still alive, until she dies by her own hand over the dead bodies of those sons, and even Oedipus is still there, lingering on in the palace, though useful to no one. Sophocles' *Antigone* and Euripides' *Suppliant Women* also deal with the fortunes of the royal family of Thebes, though their action takes place after the deaths of Jocasta and Oedipus. Fragments of other plays survive also, as do fragments of an epic poem, the *Thebaid.* Homer knew of Oedipus, though he calls his mother-wife Epicaste and mentions no children of the pair (*Odyssey* 11.271–80). Seneca wrote an *Oedipus* in Latin, based on Sophocles' *Oedipus Rex.* See also Apollodorus 3.5.7–9 and Hyginus, *Fabulae* 67. A different story, in which Oedipus has another wife, Euryganeia, who is the mother of his children, is alluded to by Pausanias at 9.5.5.

[2] Laius cannot have the child killed, precisely, since this would be kin-murder, exactly what he is trying to avoid. Exposure solves the problem nicely. The gods can decide if the child is to live. In stories that employ this device, the child does live, and in adult-

hood confronts his or her parents in some significant way, in this case by killing one and committing incest with the other. Oedipus' ankles are pierced not to prevent him from crawling away, but so that when he dies his ghost will not walk.

3 The servant who is given the task of getting rid of the new-born Oedipus turns out also to be one of the men who accompanies Laius on his last trip, the only one to survive it. Sophocles does not name him, but Seneca calls him Phorbas. The Corinthian shepherd who takes the baby Oedipus from Phorbas and gives him to Merope and Polybus of Corinth to rear also has another role in the story: years later it is his task to run from Corinth to Thebes with the news for Oedipus that Polybus is dead. Sophocles doesn't name this man either, but on an Attic vase, c. 450 B.C.E., in the Bibliothèque Nationale, Paris, he is clearly labelled "Euphorbus." Generations of students laughingly point out how absurd it is that a man who was a shepherd thirty years before would now be a long-distance runner, and then realise that they have fallen into the very trap that the story sets for them over and over, namely to think complacently that something can't happen because it is too unlikely or too outrageous.

4 Aristotle thought this play the greatest of Greek tragedies because the recognition, of Oedipus by himself, and the reversal of fortune that is a common element of plays like this, happen at the same instant (*Poetics* 11.1–6). In a play full of coincidences, not at all accidental on Sophocles' part, this is one more.

5 In the *Oedipus Rex* she is in possession of more information than Oedipus is. The Corinthian shepherd announces that he received a child from a member of Laius' household and took it to Corinth. It is already known that this was Oedipus. Jocasta knows, though Oedipus does not (yet), that the child in question was her own. She begs him to stop asking questions, and when he refuses, rushes away. We are told later that she hanged herself immediately.

6 Sophocles, *Oedipus Rex* 1173 and 719.

7 Sophocles, *Oedipus Rex* 758–64.

8 Sophocles, *Oedipus Rex* 791–93 and 711–14.

9 The story is that Cadmus' followers were killed by the serpent when they attempted to fetch water from the spring it guarded. Cadmus killed the serpent and, on Athena's advice, planted its teeth. Men in armour sprung up, who, when Cadmus used the common ruse of tossing a stone amongst them (see Medea's story,

chap. 13), fought each other to the death, except for five. The surviving five became the founding fathers of Thebes, and so Cadmus' followers were replaced. The story does not acknowledge that women, as well as men, are required to ensure that the city survives into the next generation.

[10] Chrysippus was the illegitimate son of Pelops, king of Pisa. Pelops' wife, Hippodamia, was the mother of his better-known sons, Atreus and Thyestes (see Clytemnestra's story, chap. 2). There is an obscure story that Hippodamia committed this murder, at Thebes and in Laius' bed, more to prevent Chrysippus from becoming king of Pisa than to protect his honour. Laius is first accused of the murder, but later exonerated. See Robert Graves, *The Greek Myths,* vol. 2 (Harmondsworth, UK, 1960), 42.

[11] See above, n. 3.

[12] I have tried to reconcile this account of the removal of the baby Oedipus with Sophocles'. This is not entirely possible. 1173, "She gave him to you?" "Yes, sir" (meaning Jocasta to Phorbas) contradicts 717–19, "the child was not yet three days old when [Laius] pinned his ankles together, and had him thrown, by other's hands, onto the pathless mountain."

[13] Diodorus states clearly that Laius went to Delphi to enquire about the child who was exposed many years before. At much the same time, as he points out, Oedipus had been goaded into consulting the oracle also, about his true parentage. This is another of the "coincidences" that pervade this story. It makes sense, then, to assume that Laius did not travel to Delphi to find out from Apollo how to answer the riddle of the Sphinx, and that she began to terrorise the city only after the death of Laius, as Apollodorus suggests.

[14] The question was this: What has four legs in the morning, two at noon, and three at the end of the day? The answer was: a person, crawling as a baby, walking upright in later life, and using a stick in old age.

[15] In the ancient sources, Eteocles is not necessarily the youngest child. Euripides, for instance, clearly states that Eteocles is older than Polynices (*Phoenician Women* 71). But in Sophocles' *Oedipus at Colonus* (at 375) Polynices is the older brother.

[16] These lines are a paraphrase of *Oedipus Rex* 362 and 353.

[17] The quest for the murderer of Laius is in itself harmful to Jocasta's position, since she is knowingly harbouring a kin-murderer. But worse than this, it can clearly lead to Oedipus' discovery of his own identity. Teiresias knows the truth. Phorbas also knows it. At this point in Sophocles' play, Jocasta tells Oedipus about Laius' oracle, which according to traditional inter-pretations she believes not to have come true, in order to prove to him that oracles and seers are worthless and thus Teiresias can be ignored. In the version told here, wherein she knows only too well that the oracle *has* come true, her only reason for giving Oedipus this information and claiming that all oracles are useless is to convince him that whatever anyone may say to him in the next lit-tle while, he cannot be Laius' and Jocasta's child, because that child is dead. Dramatically it is necessary, in Sophocles' version, for Oedipus to learn during the process of discovery that Jocasta had borne a child years before: when Phorbas tells him in their eventual confrontation near the end of the play (at 1173–75) that he, Phorbas, was given a child by Jocasta, and that the child was her own, Oedipus must be able to accept that this could be so with-out further questioning that would detract from the moment of recognition. It is equally necessary, for the same reason, in the version told here.

[18] This conversation is condensed from *Oedipus Rex* 754–854.

[19] This is a paraphrase of *Oedipus Rex* 1018. Of all the secondary characters in Sophocles' play, it seems to me that this one is the most finely drawn. If he had known his place, he would not have presumed to discuss the personal affairs of kings with queens. If he had not been so eager to help, he would never have told Oedipus that Merope was not his mother. If he had not been so delighted to see his old friend again, and could somehow have understood that Phorbas didn't want to tell the truth about their exchange on the mountainside all those years ago, Phorbas could just have repeated his old lie, the lie about robbers, and they could all have gone on as before.

[20] This conversation is condensed from *Oedipus Rex* 1156–73.

[21] This is a paraphrase of *Oedipus Rex* 1334–35, spoken to the chorus, not to Creon.

[22] According to Sophocles, Jocasta rushes away and hangs herself (offstage) when she realises that Oedipus is about to discover she is his mother. Yet this was not the most common version of the story. Suicide by the sword is her usual end, either when Oedipus

is on the verge of making his discovery, or later, over the bodies of her sons, Polynices and Eteocles. In *Phoenician Women,* Euripides describes the scene on the battlefield in some detail, how Jocasta hurries to her dying sons, too late to talk to Eteocles but in time to hear Polynices' dying words. His words are very significant: "He was my dear brother and became my enemy" (1447); this is kin-murder admitted. Eteocles was someone whom Polynices should never have come close to killing, and yet he killed him. The Greek text is more precise than any translation can be: "'Philos,' he became 'echthros.'" Kin-murder was, to the Greeks, a crime most terrible. Jocasta, according to Euripides, lives long enough to recognise that the fortunes of her family have fallen so low that they include it again. In addition, she is forced to suffer the deaths of her children while she herself is still alive, a reversal of the natural order of things. She dies by plunging the sword of one of her sons into her own throat. She falls dead between them, one arm around each dead body, a mother to the end (1455–59). According to Euripides, Oedipus is alive and still in Thebes. For further discussion of kin-murder, see the foreword to Medea's story, chap. 13.

Medusa's Story

Medusa and her sisters, Stheno and Euryale, are the Gorgons,
usually said to be the daughters of Phorcys and Ceto, a sea god
and a sea monster.¹ Literary accounts give them a variety of
ugly features—swine's tusks, bulging eyes, snakes for hair, and
lolling tongues. Their brazen hands and golden wings made them
even more monstrous. Paradoxically, we are told that Medusa was
so beautiful that the god Poseidon fell in love with her. The
ancients made sense of the discrepancy by saying that Medusa
incurred the wrath of Athena when she lay with Poseidon in a
grove sacred to the goddess. Athena's revenge was to make her
so vile to look at that anyone who saw her was turned to stone.

Oddly, two of the Gorgons are immortal, and only one,
Medusa, is subject to death. When she dies, the surviving sisters are so distraught that even the snakes of their hair hiss in
lamentation. The sources contain next to nothing of Medusa's
life. Only in death is she famous, as the object of a hero's
quest. Two creatures, the winged horse Pegasus and the warrior Chrysaor, are born from her decapitated body. Her head
becomes a weapon, first in Perseus' hands and then emblaz-
oned forever on Athena's battle dress.² Those who look on it
are turned, instantly and permanently, to stone.

The version of the story told here relies for its effect on
Medusa's death occurring when she sees her own image for the
first time. In the usual story Perseus journeys to the ends of the
Earth to find her in response to the request of Polydectes, king
of Seriphos. Once there, he looks at her apparently harmless
reflection in his shield and uses it to guide his arm behind his

back as he decapitates her. All the written sources have Perseus
performing this contortionist-style feat, but they may stem from
a desire to give Perseus more credit (what, after all, is heroic
about standing around while a monster kills herself?) or a mis-
understanding of the way the shield could be used.[3]

I have used this story to explore a common theme—that of
knowing one's fate. As Medusa herself states, Prometheus, who
according to the Greeks made the first humans, originally gave
them a share in his own talent—foresight. But they were too
unhappy when they knew their fates, too overwhelmed by the
shadows of future terrors and death.[4] *In the story below,*
Medusa has been told what the future will bring as part of her
punishment from Athena. If the ancient writers are to be heed-
ed, Medusa had no life. She existed only to be killed. For her,
knowing her fate means seeing beyond death.

The appendix of this book contains a transcribed text of an
oral telling of this story.

I

To know your fate. To glimpse behind the veil of death whilst
still alive. To be told how you will die. To understand that you
will be hated and feared long after your death. Imagine this.
They say that mortal men, long before women were thought of,
were given this gift by Prometheus, their creator. Possessing
foreknowledge himself, he saw no reason why his men should
not know their fates. But imagine. Imagine knowing as you arm
yourself before a battle that it will be your last. Imagine knowing that you will kill your own father. However hard you try to
avoid it, somewhere, somehow, it will happen. Prometheus'
men were not strong enough. Their lives were clouded always
by their knowledge, and so Prometheus took his gift away and
gave them hope instead.

To know your fate. A curse. My curse. I know that I will die
soon, though my sisters try to keep me safe; I know that the mere
mention of my name will strike horror into the hearts of mortals

for all time. That I will cause harm where I mean no harm, when I bear no grudge, when I have no vengeance in my heart.

We live, my sisters and I, at the very edge of the Earth. We came here long ago, after Athena laid her curse on me. No mortal, man or woman, will ever look on your face and live. That was her curse. And she told me how I would die, and what would happen after.

Why? Why did she hate me? Because Poseidon loved me; because I was beautiful; because she herself can never know the love of a male, man or god.

Poseidon convinced me that he loved me, that we two creatures of the sea should know one another, that I was more beautiful than the daughters of Nereus, that to look on me was for time to stand still. He took me to where there were soft grasses in the woods, fields of white narcissus, like snow in the lowlands, to a grove of oak trees. We made love there and I loved him. He didn't tell me whose trees they were, whose flowers, whose air. Athena's sanctuary desecrated, Athena's home on Earth defiled. Oh gods, I meant no harm. I loved him, that was all. I would have lain with him anywhere on Earth. Must she still punish me? No mortal, man or woman, will ever look on your face and live. I hear her words still in my mind. See her hard grey eyes. Feel her anger.

My sisters found me lying on the grass, alone now, Poseidon gone. My sisters are not mortal. They are unaffected by my face. They can look on me whenever they wish, and when they do they weep. They do not tell me how I look.

One day, not far away now, I will see myself, see my own face reflected, know how hideous I am. And at that moment I will die. So promised Athena.

My sisters took me away to a place where they hope this cannot happen, on the western edge of the Earth. There is little daylight here. It is like living forever in the darkness of the underground. We sleep by day, so that there is no chance I can see my reflection in a lake or a river. No chance for me to play Narcissus.[5] This land is barren like the sea that borders it. No one lives here, save we three.

This is no life, but it is mine: to sleep; to see no living soul; to fear; to know how death will come. I long to look behind its veil, to see the other side. Death could not be a greater torment than this. I want, if truth be told, to know how I look, what monster I am.[6]

Once, I heard footsteps outside our cave and ran to its entrance while my sisters slept. There was a man there. Who he was I do not know—some adventurer, perhaps. Certainly not the one who will bring me my death. And I knew that the curse was indeed on me. He was still in an instant. His body changed to grey granite, his features an image of horror.

If only I could have talked with him awhile, told him who I once was, and how beautiful. Sent him on his way to tell my story to the world. But he is cold stone ... And I ...? There are worse fates than his.

I am in need of sun, of light, of fields of white narcissus. Of some spark of fire to warm me. I am past loving my sisters. We are too much together. Though I will die alone.

And they have seen my face. They know what I do not. How else is solitude to be defined?

II

Athena gave me knowledge of how I will die. Like Prometheus' men, I can scarcely bear it. This is what will happen. A young man—Perseus is his name—will come for me. He is a pleasant young man, who loves his mother and hopes to save her from a distasteful marriage by foiling her suitor.[7] He has no thought of me save that he will kill me without looking at my face. With Athena's help, he will approach the Grey Ones, also my sisters, they whose white hair, white like snow, frames their hideous aged faces, they whose four eyes are sightless save for one which the gods let them share. He will steal from them their eye as they pass it from one to the other, and to get it back from him they will betray me. They will tell him how to find what he needs: a cap of invisibility, so that he can escape when he has killed me; winged shoes so that his flight may be faster; and, most important, a bag to put my head in, to conceal my face so that he will never see it. Athena will give him a curved sword and a shield, her own shield, polished so that it gleams like a mirror.

He will come when we are sleeping. Since that man came, the one who is stone now, my sisters sleep like mothers alert to the cries of their babies, waking at the slightest sound. But they will sleep through this one's approach. Athena will see to that. He will call me, by name, and I will answer him, tell him I am coming. And when I come to the entrance of the cave into the dim light that is all we have of day here, he will turn his eyes away and hold the polished shield up between his face and mine. In the half-light I will see myself and I will know, at last, what I am. For a moment before I die I will know. When I am dead he will cut off my head with his curved blade and place it in his bag without ever looking at my face. My sisters will wake as he leaves. They will find my body, headless, faceless, their hideous child dead in the night, and they will reproach themselves for sleeping too soundly. They will follow Perseus, but will not catch him. Invisible and fleet of foot, he will be gone. My head is not heavy; it will not hold him back.

III

I will be a murderer after my death. How strange a notion; a curse all on its own. My head will be the finest weapon ever known. Perseus will kill the rightful husband of Andromeda, princess of Joppa, when that man comes to his own wedding banquet to claim his bride. Perseus will himself become Andromeda's husband. Then he will return to his own island and kill the king there, who is his mother's despised suitor. Killing them will be easy. He will just show them my face, and they will die.[8]

IV

And I will be known for all time as a monster—people will say that my great eyes bulge, that my hair is a mass of writhing snakes, that I have a boar's tusks on my cheeks, and that my tongue lolls grotesquely from my mouth.

Oh gods, what fate is this? I meant no harm.

Notes

1 The story of Perseus' quest for the Gorgon's head is told in Apollodorus 2.4.2-3. See also Pindar, *Pythian Odes*, 10.29-48. The Roman poet Lucan (*Pharsalia* 9.619-99), though he places Medusa's home in Libya, not at the western edge of the world, gives an account of Medusa's death that is not unsympathetic to her. See also Hyginus, *Poetica Astronomica* 2.12, and Pausanias 2.21.6-8. For Pausanias she is beautiful, even in death. It is Ovid at *Metamorphoses* 4.772-803 who relates that Medusa was once beautiful but was rendered ugly by Athena after Poseidon violated her in Athena's sanctuary. The ancient literary sources for Medusa's story are collected in Jocelyn Woodward, *Perseus: A Study in Greek Art and Legend* (Cambridge, 1937). The various artistic representations, ranging from gargoyle-like to beautiful, are also shown and discussed.

2 The goddess Athena plays a large role in Medusa's story: cursing her, helping Perseus to kill her (or, according to some authors, killing her herself), and then wearing her head forever on her armour. It may be that Athena and Medusa are two sides of the same mythical character—that Athena is merely displaying her other face. See Tobin Siebers, *The Mirror of Medusa* (Berkeley, 1983), among others.

3 In European legend there is a creature called the Basilisk whose glance also brings death. The Basilisk is killed when, surrounded by mirrors, it cannot avoid seeing its own reflection.

4 Other myths that touch on this theme are Jocasta's story, chap. 3; Eriphyle's story, chap. 5; and Thetis' story, chap. 12. In folktale the most obvious example is *Sleeping Beauty,* wherein all the characters know that the princess will die on her sixteenth birthday. Their lives, and hers, are blighted by the knowledge.

5 Narcissus fell in love with his own reflection in a rock pool. He had never seen himself before. He wasted to nothing, staring enraptured at his image. He was destined to live until old age unless he came to know himself, which he did when he saw his own image. See Ovid, *Metamorphoses* 3.339-510. It should be pointed out that here in the industrialised West, at the end of the twentieth century, most of us know precisely what we look like. We have mirrors in the bathroom, the hallway, and the car. We catch sight of ourselves in shop windows as we walk along the street. But there are plenty of people in the world who have never

seen their reflection in anything that passes for a mirror. The story of Narcissus depends for its effect on the relative absence of mirrors or other reflecting agents. So do stories in which two characters look alike. Other participants in the story can see the resemblance, but the characters in question, who do not know what they look like, cannot see what the fuss is about. See, for instance, the Roman playwright Plautus' plays, *Amphitryon* and *Menaechmi*. The latter was the basis of Shakespeare's *A Comedy of Errors*.

[6] Medusa's curiosity is here akin to the notion, common to several ancient peoples, that to look behind the veil of a veiled goddess is to see one's own death. We want to look, but we are afraid. It may be that Medusa is a relic of a veiled goddess figure, and if so, this would explain why her face was dreaded and deadly in the first place. This is suggested by Barbara G. Walker, *The Women's Dictionary of Symbols and Sacred Objects* (New York, 1988), 161, amongst others. In one respect, Medusa has already looked beyond the veil, for she knows how she is to die. What she does not know is what her own face looks like—is she beautiful still, or does she look as the mythtellers have described her, hideous and deformed? It seems to me not necessary that we imagine her as ugly when we read or listen to this story. Her face can be terrible in its surpassing beauty or in the pain it registers, as well as in monstrous ugliness. When I ask audiences, including mythology students who are familiar with the iconography of Medusa, what they see in their mind's eye when Medusa approaches Perseus in the moment before she dies, fewer than half see the ugly gargoyle of sculpture. Some see a woman with an unreadable expression in her eyes. Some see a striking, inhuman, but nonetheless beautiful face. Some see nothing at all, and for them Medusa's concern over how she looks is never resolved. Since the essence of the story is that no mortal, man or woman, will ever look on her face and live, this is no surprise.

[7] See the story of Danaë, chap. 11.

[8] There is a story that Perseus killed himself using Medusa's head. He quarrelled with his father-in-law, Cepheus, and at the height of the argument held up Medusa's head to quieten his opponent once and for all. Cepheus did not turn to stone. Thinking that the head had lost its power, Perseus turned to examine it, and it killed him. The reason that the head didn't work was that Cepheus was blind. This is a late story; its author, John of Antioch (4.544, fragments 6 and 18), may have lived as late as the sixth century, C.E. See Woodward, *Perseus,* op. cit. (see n. 1 above), 23.

Eriphyle's Story

Eriphyle's story is this: a woman, allowed more power than almost any other in myth—the power to make decisions for kings—succumbs to the lure of gold. She sends her husband to his certain death, and is killed in revenge by her own son.[1] In the ancient sources that survive, Eriphyle is a shadowy figure. We are told that she accepts a bribe, from Polynices, in exchange for sending her husband to war, but not why. Did she fall in love with Polynices? Was her marriage unhappy? If we look back to what happened before her marriage, we find that the families of her father (Talaüs) and her husband (Amphiaraüs) were jointly responsible for ruling Argos. There was trouble between them, and Talaüs' son, Adrastus, was driven out of the country. Since there is no record of Talaüs fleeing, possibly there was once a story in which Amphiaraüs killed him to set himself up as sole king. If Amphiaraüs indeed killed Eriphyle's father, she had motive enough for wishing him dead. I have chosen to downplay this possibility, preferring to attribute Eriphyle's actions to her dissatisfaction with her marriage and her lot.

Central to Eriphyle's story is the necklace that is used to bribe her. It belonged to Harmonia, loyal wife of Cadmus, the founder of Thebes. It became an heirloom of the royal family of Thebes and eventually found its way into the hands of Polynices, Oedipus' son. He needed allies to march against his own city to reclaim the throne from his brother, and used the necklace to get them. The necklace was given to Eriphyle, and as payment for it, her husband Amphiaraüs was to go to war against

Polynices' brother. Had the choice been his he would not have gone, because, being a prophet, he knew that he and all of the other leaders, save one, would die. How was it that Eriphyle could make him go? It had been decreed (the story is sketchy here) that whenever there was a dispute between Amphiaraüs and Adrastus, king of Argos and Eriphyle's brother, Eriphyle was to decide it, and the men were bound by her verdict. Adrastus wanted to go, Amphiaraüs didn't. Eriphyle decided in Adrastus' favour. He would be the one leader who would return.

A present-day storyteller is able to do with this story what Aeschylus did for Clytemnestra, and what Euripides did for Medea—fill in the motives. Suppose that when Amphiaraüs married Eriphyle Apollo had warned him about her, so that he knew, already, that she would cause his death. Suppose this knowledge blighted their married life. Could it be said that his awareness of his fate actually brought it about? That his own actions, based on the information given to him by Apollo, caused the death that Apollo had predicted? Could it be that her long-time husband caused Eriphyle such misery that she sent him deliberately to his death, preferring a necklace to his life?

Eriphyle is a tragic figure, however the story is told. In the version given here, she thinks she is wise enough to know that appearances can be deceiving, and yet she is blind to the possibility of an ulterior motive behind Polynices' approach to her. There may not, in fact, be one. At the end of the story she is faced not only with Amphiaraüs' death, but also with Polynices'. Perhaps her descent into madness begins here; perhaps it has been longer in the making.

How beautiful it is. I feel it heavy on my throat like the hands of a lover before his kiss. Gold. The golden necklace of Harmonia. Made by a god for the daughter of gods. Hephaestus' craft beyond the ken of mortals. When I wear it I am Harmonia herself, decked all in gold on her wedding day, walking before the twelve golden thrones of the sons and daughters of Cronus and the sons and daughters of Zeus. Apollo himself played the lyre at her wedding, and sang a song of love requited. Can you imagine that? The Muses sang at her wedding—golden tiaras in their hair.[2] This is what they sang, these daughters of Zeus, "What is beautiful is good."[3] The necklace, then, is good. Harmonia was marrying a mortal. The gods came to no other wedding of a mortal man save that of Peleus.[4] Did you know that? Twelve thrones of gold were set up in Cadmus' house. Gods and mortals were never so close.

Hermes gave a lyre, harmony for Harmonia. Athena gave a flute. Discord for whom? The robe, too, was a gift of Athena. The necklace, also, was a gift. Made by Hephaestus, given to Harmonia by her new husband, placed around her neck by his own hands, gold on gold, flesh on flesh.[5]

She was a goddess, Harmonia, daughter of the shrill-voiced Aphrodite and her lover, Ares. Her young husband was Cadmus, founder and king of Cadmeia, or Thebes. Harmonia loved him, mortal though he was. He was brave and beautiful. She stayed with him and loved him, though there was much to bear. All their daughters dead or mad. Cadmus punished time and time again for killing Ares' snake.[6]

When I am not Harmonia, who am I? I am Eriphyle, daughter of Talaüs and Lysimache. My brother is Adrastus, king of Argos. My husband is Amphiaraüs, but not for much longer. He will be dead soon, so he claims. Amphiaraüs, the seer, the boar-hunter,[7] an Argonaut,[8] Argive-born, as my brother and I are; in fact he is a cousin of ours. Zeus and Apollo love him, people say.[9] Not that it has done him any good.

We were children still when they gave me to the seer as his wife. Even then I was disappointed. No golden thrones, no gifts from gods at my wedding. And an unwilling husband—this the worst trial. I had known him all my life. When no one else would accept that he had the gift of foreknowledge, I would listen to him and believe it. We had walked together in the groves of cypress trees, dipped our feet together in the mountain steams. He told me of the still shadowy visions sent to him by Apollo, that all but overwhelmed him. He spoke of the god's words ringing in his mind. Sometimes he held his head in his hands and wept in pain and fear. In those days I was his comfort.

I loved them both, my cousin and my brother. Both of them had hereditary rights to land in Argos. Generations earlier, so the story goes, another seer, Melampus, the greatest prophet ever known, won Argive land, one third of it for himself, one third for Bias his brother, by ridding the Argive women of madness.[10] That Bias was my grandfather. Melampus' son was Antiphates, his son was Oïcles, and his, Amphiaraüs. Too many kings, too little land. My father, Talaüs son of Bias, thought that if he married me to my cousin the seer, there would be fewer quarrels. Adrastus, my brother, and Amphiaraüs, my husband, would be bound together by ties of friendship through me.[11]

It was only when he heard we were to be married that Amphiaraüs turned against me. He argued with his father, their shouts resounding through our halls. Marriage, he said would be the death of him, especially marriage to me. He knew, he said. He had seen it. Apollo had shown him. He had seen himself among the dead, a young man still. But to his father, seers were blind old men, not boys who had yet to shave. And he would not hear.

Amphiaraüs pleaded with my father also, and told him that he was afraid to marry me. My father laughed and tousled his hair, thought him only shy.

Amphiaraüs talked to anyone who would listen: "'Beware a wife of your own blood.' Those were Apollo's words to me; he warned me because he loves me."[12] Not so. If Apollo had loved him he would have held his peace.

Can you imagine how it is to marry a man who fears you? A man who knows you will bring him death? In those early days, Amphiaraüs could not bring himself to touch me, lest I kill him with my closeness. His gift was imperfect then. Later he knew, he said, how I would bring about his end. He described a tall, gaunt young man, a golden gift, and a battle outside a city wall.

Can you imagine how it is, when your husband lies with you, to hear these words from him? "I do this only so that sons may be born who will avenge my death. Sons who will kill you."

Can you imagine how it is, when you hold your first-born son in your arms, to know, because you believe the seer, have always believed him, that this son, this helpless child, will grow up to kill you? For this you must nourish him. For this you must shepherd him through the trials of youth. For this you must make him strong. Grow in power, you must say. Do all that you have to do. Do it well, and with conviction. Even killing your mother.

Can you imagine how, after years of pains like these, you come to hate your husband, come to wish him dead? The very fate he has predicted for himself—death through me—has happened over and over in my mind. I have poisoned him. I have burned him. I have cut him with a thousand knives.

Adrastus, my brother, became king when still a young man. Our father was dead by then, so also the seer's. The seer was jealous. He and Adrastus quarrelled constantly. The marriage did not bind them. Young Argives were dying every year in feuds caused by their quarrels. This was no way to lead a nation. Wise men were consulted. "Between King Adrastus and Amphiaraüs, Eriphyle is the bond of love," said the wise men. "Through her they are friends. They must swear that, whenever they have a disagreement, Eriphyle will resolve it. She is not as other women. Like us, she is wise. Passion does not sway her. This is what the gods declare."[13]

So this is how it will come about, said the seer to me. This is how you will kill me. Resigned, he swore, as did my brother, to abide by any decision I made. I did not understand, then, what would happen.

Years and years and my life passed by. The seer spoke not one word of kindness to me in all that time.

Have you ever recognised, precisely and absolutely, a moment when your life changes? In retrospect, we often know such moments, but that's not what I mean. I knew it then, as sharply as I have ever known anything. A young man had requested an audience with the king. He was ushered in. He was indeed tall and gaunt. He looked hungry and wasted. His fair hair curled onto his neck like little moons. I loved him instantly. He said that he was Polynices, son of Oedipus, brother of the self-styled king of Thebes, Eteocles. The throne was rightly his, he said. His brother had refused to acknowledge the agreement they had made—to share the rule, a year apiece. Another young man stood beside him, but this one did not move me. Tydeus, his name was, and he was son of Oeneus, king of Calydon.[14] He had murdered his brother and fled his native land, but considered himself the rightful king there. Both Polynices and Tydeus wanted help from Adrastus, help in regaining what was theirs. Adrastus invited them to sit with us, and rest, and eat. Polynices sat beside me. I remember still the smell of him, the touch of his hand to mine when I passed him wine, the exquisite agony of his closeness. His face visited my dreams that night and every night thereafter.

Adrastus consulted the wise men again. They told him nothing of wars and thrones, but only to marry his daughters to the newcomers.[15] They were two little girls, younger even than I had been on my wedding day. On the very eve of the weddings, I dreamed that Polynices would spend his wedding night with me. I dressed his bride, Argeia, in the morning, and prepared her marriage bed in the evening. She was, and is, a sunny, giggling child, as fair as a golden flower. She laughed prettily all day, but as the sun left the sky she began to tremble. It was my task to comfort her.

When I was a child, I was not like her. Eriphyle is a solemn girl, my mother would say. Her smile is rare. Not for her the girlish dreams of love, the frivolities of youth. It is good to be steady, she said to me. You are wise, you have a good mind, and a strong character. Passionate women are no use to men. But she did not look deep enough. The outside of a woman, like the outside of a fruit, does not necessarily show what is within. It is in knowing this that I am wise.

Amphiaraüs saw more of his death—though not a death exactly. He would be buried alive. He saw his chariot on the river's edge, the city wall and battlefield behind him, felt his own fear, a coward's terror, in his throat, saw the earth opening and the bank along which he fled bare, as if he had never been. Night after night he told me of his visions. Our one intimacy was his death. Both of us lived it, over and over.

Still, I did not see how I would cause it, and yet in this city they call me wise.

Polynices first came to my room not on his wedding night, but soon after. He seemed to shine. So must his father have bewitched his mother.[16] So must Cadmus have appeared to Harmonia. At last I knew the touch of a lover on my neck, a man's fervid breath on my cheek. I loved with all my soul. Love for a brother and children is nothing to this.

When Polynices talked to me, often long into the night, he told of a devoted family torn apart by knowledge that came too late. The knowledge that his mother, Jocasta, and his father, Oedipus, were, in reality, mother and son. Jocasta had killed herself, Oedipus was a beaten man, subject to his own curse,[17] blinded by his own hand. He lived in exile. His sons had not seen him for many years. When they were still young, motherless and frightened, their mother's brother, Creon, had ruled in Thebes. He still lived, but when Polynices and his brother Eteocles grew to manhood, had stood down from the throne that Eteocles had first assumed, promising to step aside for his brother at the end of a year. But power changed his mind and character. He would not step aside, would not even talk with his brother. Polynices wanted the throne. Nothing else would satisfy him. He needed an army thousands strong, with capable leaders and courage in plenty. He wanted Adrastus, my brother, to command this army with him; he wanted his companion in misfortune, Tydeus, now a relative by marriage, to be his comrade in battle also, and he wanted Capaneus and Hippomedon of Argos, and Parthenopaeus of Arcadia, son of Atalanta,[18] to go along. Above all he wanted Amphiaraüs, my husband, a brave man and a clever one, to be his advisor and to fight by his side.

One night he brought the necklace ... I had heard of it, of course. What Greek woman does not know of Cadmus' love for Harmonia? But I could not, in all my dreams, have imagined its beauty. I had presumed it a gold string worked with amber beads like one my mother wore. But it is gold alone, pure, precious gold.[19] He placed it around my throat. "Eriphyle," he said, and when he said my name all reason left me, "as, long ago, Cadmus gave this necklace as a love-sign to Harmonia, so now, I, to you. For all eternity I will love you."

The next day I was summoned to my brother's presence. My husband was there in the throne room before me, grim-faced, hateful. Polynices stood to one side of the king, with Tydeus and other men behind him. Adrastus explained to me that there was a dispute. That Polynices had formally requested an Argive army to aid him in enforcing his claim to the Theban throne. That Adrastus was willing to provide the army, with himself, Tydeus, Capaneus, Hippomedon, Parthenopaeus, and Amphiaraüs as commanders (he motioned to them to step forward as he spoke), but that Amphiaraüs had refused. Adrastus explained that Polynices was his own daughter's husband, so too Tydeus, whose claim to the throne of Calydon would be settled later by the same army. Glory would be brought to our family if it were linked to the royal family of Thebes in so tangible a way. Despite myself, I reeled and clutched my breast, where the necklace of Harmonia had so lately lain. Adrastus insisted that it was the duty of one king to restore another to his rightful throne; that they were all diminished by the misfortune of one. He explained how the rich cities of the Argolid had resources to spare. To what better use could they be put? Then it was my husband's turn.

His statement was brief: "Eriphyle knows why I do not wish to go. I have nothing more to say."

The king's eyes flashed with anger. "You are in danger of being thought a coward, my lord Amphiaraüs," he said. "How will your sons live down such weakness in a father?"

"My sons will do what they must do," the seer replied, not looking at Adrastus, but at me.

"Eriphyle?" I had been watching my husband, and my brother's address took me by surprise. "Eriphyle, the dispute is yours to decide. What is to be done?"

My lover stood an arm's length from me. I was dizzy with his closeness. I tried to think clearly. If Polynices won the throne he coveted, then he would never come back to Argos, but in Thebes he would be king, and I, if the seer's predictions were true, would be husbandless. I would go to him. Become his mistress openly. Love him. Wear Harmonia's necklace in her own halls. On the other hand, if no Argive army stood behind him, he would travel to every Greek city until he found an army, and I would never see him again.

"My brother and my king," I replied, my voice shaking with the joy of pleasing my lover, "the Argive army shall march with Polynices." The cheering in the throne room was loud enough to echo in the Halls of the Dead.

It took them just eight days to raise their army. Young Argive men, eager to fight for their king, greedy for glory on the field, lined the palace courtyards like palisades and were divided amongst the seven commanders. The entire army gathered early on the morning of the ninth day. Priests made sacrifices to the gods, to Zeus and Apollo, and to the lady Athena, mistress of war. Mothers, fathers, wives of soldiers said their farewells. Words of good omen filled the air. With their men in ranks behind them, the Argive leaders prepared to climb onto their chariots. My duty as the seer's wife was to embrace him, in front of all. To bring his children out to say goodbye to their father and to be greeted, as a family, by the crowd. My younger son, Amphilochus, was brought out in the arms of his nurse. I think he did not know his father in the strange armour that makes all men look alike. My daughters, Demonassa and Eurydice, born before their brothers, stayed one on either side of me, and close. My elder son, Alcmaeon, stood solemnly in front of me, stretching out his arms to touch his father. Amphiaraüs paid him scant attention, brushing him aside after a moment. It was to me he spoke. "I go now to my certain death. This child, when grown, will fight the battles I have lost and take revenge for me. All that you know. But this you do not: he too will die, your lover Polynices. So look your last on his yellow hair. He will perish at the hand of his own brother. His body will lie outside the walls of Thebes, a feast for dogs and vultures. The limbs you love will be picked clean of that firm flesh."[20]

He stepped towards me, raised his hand as if to strike me, though he did not, and climbed onto his chariot.[21] Within moments they were gone.

I caught a last glimpse of Polynices, his hair gold-yellow in the morning sun, his head held high and proud, as his charioteer drove him down the path from the palace and out of my sight.

The seer has never, to my knowledge, made an error in prophecy. The god Apollo talks to him as I talk to my own children. The pictures he sees in his dreams are as true as an artist's masterpiece. Polynices will die, as the seer predicts. He will never return.

And I will send my sons to war, to march again against a king of Thebes, this time to take his city. Alcmaeon will return and kill me, the necklace no protection against cold steel driven through my throat.

I place the necklace around my neck. It is a reminder that I am loved, that I am an immortal queen, that the gods came to my wedding and sat on golden thrones, that I am Harmonia. The necklace. How beautiful it is. I feel it heavy on my throat like the hands of a lover before his kiss.

Postscript

Polynices died at the Hypsistan gate of Thebes. He and his brother Eteocles killed each other in single combat. Tydeus, Capaneus, Hippomedon, and Parthenopaeus were all killed. Adrastus escaped through the speed of his divine horse[22] and lived. Amphiaraüs, apparently abandoning his men, ordered his charioteer to drive away from Thebes along the bank of the river Ismenus. They were chased by Periclymenus of Thebes. Amphiaraüs would have died a coward's death, a spear in his back, but the gods who loved him saved him. Zeus sent a thunderbolt to cleave the earth, and the riverbank swallowed him up, chariot, charioteer, and all, as if he had never been. His dream come true.

Alcmaeon and Amphilochus, sons of Eriphyle and Amphiaraüs, grew to manhood. They, along with other sons of the first Seven Against Thebes, planned an expedition to Thebes to avenge their fathers' deaths. The Thebans fled their city and the Epigonoi, as the second Seven were called, looted and destroyed it. Upon his return, Alcmaeon learned that his mother Eriphyle had persuaded him and his brother to join the expedition only after receiving, as a bribe, the robe of Harmonia from Thersander, son of Polynices and Argeia.[23] On the advice of Apollo's oracle, and with help from his brother, he killed her. No mortal avenged her death, but Alcmaeon was persecuted by her Furies[24] and driven insane. He was purified of murder by Phegeus, king of Psophis. He married the king's daughter, Arsinoë, and presented her with the necklace and robe of Harmonia. This purification, though, was not enough. Phegeus' kingdom became barren because of Alcmaeon's presence in it, and he was forced to leave. After some wandering, he was purified a second time—by the river Acheloüs, and given the river's daughter, Callirrhoë, as his wife. Callirrhoë demanded the necklace and the robe, which he obtained from his first wife by trickery. When the deceit was discovered, his first wife's brothers killed him and retrieved the necklace and robe. They intended to dedicate them to Apollo at Delphi, but were themselves killed in the meantime by the sons of Alcmaeon and Callirrhoë, who were suddenly full-grown by Callirrhoë's wish and Zeus' decree. They—their names were Amphoterus and Acarnan—dedicated the necklace and the robe to Apollo at Delphi. So ended Eriphyle's story.

Notes

[1] Sophocles wrote a play entitled *Eriphyle* of which only a few fragments survive. Apollodorus, at 3.6.2, 3.7.2, and 3.7.5, gives a complete account of Eriphyle's treachery and eventual death. So also does

Diodorus Siculus, at 4.65.5–66.3. Hyginus (*Fabulae* 73) knows the story, but the necklace is for him no heirloom of the Theban royal family. Adrastus has it made and bribes Eriphyle with it. See also Pausanias 5.17.7–8, where a carving on a cedar chest depicting the departure of Amphiaraüs for war is described, and 9.41.2, where the appearance and eventual whereabouts of the necklace are discussed. The wedding of Harmonia and Cadmus is described by Diodorus Siculus at 5.49.1, by Apollodorus at 3.4.2, and by Pindar at *Pythian Odes* 3.88–97. Homer, *Odyssey* 15.223–48, gives relevant details of Amphiaraüs' background. Aeschylus' *Seven Against Thebes* and Hyginus' *Fabulae* 68, 69, and 70 tell the story of the first expedition to Thebes to set Polynices on the throne there. So also do Euripides' *Phoenician Women* and Apollodorus at 3.6.3–8. Details of Amphiaraüs' "death" are to be found in Pindar, *Nemean Odes* 9.24–27. The expedition of the second Seven against Thebes, the Epigonoi, is recounted by Apollodorus 3.7.2–3, who also gives an account of later troubles caused by Harmonia's necklace at 3.7.5–7.

[2] The details of the golden thrones and the gold-crowned Muses come from Pindar, *Pythian Odes* 3.88–97.

[3] Theognis, *Elegies* 15–18.

[4] See Thetis' story, chap. 12.

[5] Diodorus Siculus contradicts himself on the provenance of the necklace. At 5.49.1 he writes that it was the gift of Athena, at 4.65.5 of Aphrodite. Apollodorus writes that it was made by Hephaestus, the metalworker of the gods, but given by Cadmus to his bride. Interestingly, Apollodorus mentions the possibility that this was not custom-made, but was a gift of Zeus to Europa. Whether she passed it on to her brother Cadmus somehow before she was abducted by Zeus, or whether she turned up at his wedding, is not clear. See Apollodorus 3.4.2.

[6] Harmonia and Cadmus had four daughters, Ino, Autonoë, Agauë, and Semele. Ino and her husband, Athamas, were mad. He shot their son, Learchus, possibly mistaking him for a deer. She jumped to her death from a cliff into the sea carrying their second son, Melicertes, whom she may have already boiled and killed (Apollodorus 3.4.3). See Ino's story, chap. 6. Autonoë was heartbroken when her son, Actaeon, was set upon and eaten by his own hounds (Apollodorus 3.4.4 and Pausanias 1.44.8). Agauë, maddened by Dionysus, killed her son Pentheus and was banished from Thebes. Semele, by her own account a lover of Zeus, was burned by his brightness and died. She was the mother by Zeus of the god Dionysus. Agauë's story

and Semele's are the subject of Euripides' *Bacchae.* For the snake, or serpert, that Cadmus killed, see chap. 3, Jocasta's story, no. 9.

[7] He joined the Calydonian Boar Hunt. See Althaea's story, chap. 8.

[8] He also went with Jason to Colchis, as a sailor on the first Greek ship, the Argo. Parts of this story are told in chap. 13, Medea's story.

[9] Homer, *Odyssey* 15.244–46.

[10] Apollodorus, 1.9.12.

[11] This is a simplified version of Eriphyle's family tree:

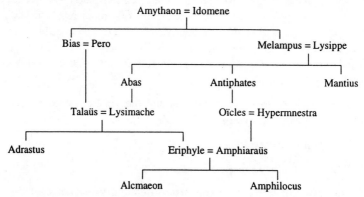

[12] This is my invention. No such warning from Apollo is mentioned in the extant ancient sources.

[13] According to Pindar, *Nemean Odes* 9.13–27, the sequence of events is very clear. Elsewhere it is not. Pindar writes that Adrastus was forced to flee Argos, driven from his father's halls by Amphiaraüs. Amphiaraüs became king for a while. Adrastus fled to Sicyon. (According to Pausanias at 2.6.6, his maternal grandfather, Polybus, was king there. Polybus died, leaving the kingdom to Adrastus. Adrastus ruled in Sicyon for a while before returning to Argos.) After this period of exile, writes Pindar, Eriphyle was given to Amphiaraüs as a pledge of good faith. Presumably it was at this point that the cousins, her brother and her husband, agreed to abide by her decision in any dispute.

[14] After Althaea died, Oeneus remarried. Tydeus was a son of this second marriage. See chap. 8.

[15] The best-known story is that Adrastus has been advised by the god Apollo to join his daughters in marriage to a lion and a boar. He is puzzled by this until he comes across two young men brawl-

ing at his palace gate. The story is told by Euripides, at *Phoenician Women* 408-23. Traditionally, Polynices has a lion-faced sphinx as the device on his shield, Tydeus has on his the boar that terrorised his father's kingdom of Calydon not many years before.

[16] Polynices' parents were Oedipus and Oedipus' own mother, Jocasta. See Jocasta's story, chap. 3.

[17] As king of Thebes, Oedipus had laid a curse on the killer of Laius, the previous king, not knowing that he himself was the killer. The enormity of this crime was magnified a thousandfold because Laius was Oedipus' father, though neither knew it at the time of the murder. The story is told in Sophocles' *Oedipus Rex*.

[18] Most male characters in mythology take their identities at least partially from their fathers, but Parthenopaeus (his name means "child of a virgin") is known as the son of Atalanta, the famous hunter. His father is variously Meleager (see Althaea's story, chap. 8), the god Ares, or Melanion, who was the only one of her many suitors who was able to beat her in a foot race, and then only with trickery and the help of the goddess Aphrodite. Ovid tells the story at *Metamorphoses* 10.560-704, although he calls the victorious suitor Hippomenes.

[19] Pausanias is intrigued with the necklace and its eventual resting place. He states that it was made entirely of gold. See 9.41.2.

[20] All this happens. Euripides' *Phoenician Women* tells the story of the fatal meeting between the brothers at the Hypsistan gate of Thebes. Sophocles' *Antigone* deals with the casting of Polynices' body to the vultures, and the efforts of his sister Antigone to give his body fitting burial.

[21] The moment of parting is preserved on two famous vases: the currently missing but much photographed archaic Corinthian crater (Staatliche Museen zu Berlin, 1655) and a red-figure hydria (Boston Museum of Fine Arts, 03.798). The former shows Amphiaraüs mounting his chariot but looking back banefully at Eriphyle. All four children are present, Amphilochus held by a nurse; the children hold their arms out towards Amphiaraüs, who has his sword drawn—in anticipation of battle, or to kill Eriphyle? The necklace, white and gigantic, is there in Eriphyle's hand. The second vase, now missing Eriphyle and the necklace, shows Amphiaraüs ignoring his younger son, again held by a nurse, but reaching out towards his wife, though not looking at her. For a full discussion of both vases and

the storytelling techniques employed by the painters of them, see Jane Henle, *A Vase Painter's Notebook* (Indiana, 1973), 14–19.

[22] The horse, black-maned, was Arion, offspring of the goddess Demeter and the god Poseidon. The horse ran wild until Heracles tamed and gave him to Adrastus, who used him, in harness with Caerus, to pull his chariot. He moved more swiftly than the wind. See Pausanias 8.25.7–10.

[23] The ancient story is not complete here. No agreement that her sons will abide by her decisions is mentioned, nor would one be logical. The pattern of the story alone requires that she be bribed by Polynices' son with Harmonia's robe. Thersander, perhaps surprisingly, marries Eriphyle's daughter, Demonassa. He and his son by her, Tisamenus, succeed to the throne of Thebes. See Pausanias 9.5.7–8.

[24] See Clytemnestra's story, chap. 2, for the same motif more fully expounded.

SIX

Ino's Story

Ino is the original wicked stepmother.[1] As the second wife of Athamas, king of Orchomenos in Boeotia, she is placed in a difficult position, as women in the real world must have been. How is a second wife's security in old age to be guaranteed if there are sons from the first marriage? She must somehow ensure that she bears sons herself and that they are at least equally favoured by their father. In stories, the second wife goes one step further and attempts to remove the children of the first marriage. Almost invariably our sympathies lie with the children, and not with the wife.[2] Ino is unusual in that she seems to make a career of disposing of her rivals' children.

Ino is invariably connected with Dionysus, the wild god who drives women mad. She is his dead mother's sister, his wet-nurse, and his guardian. She is said to have participated in at least one dismemberment of a human, namely the son of her sister Agauë, while in an altered state of consciousness brought on by Dionysus-worship. Several authors relate that it is a spate of Dionysiac madness that causes her to abandon children, husband, and royal duties in order to wander in the forest for a period of time long enough for her husband to marry again and father two new sons. The deaths of Learchus and Melicertes, her sons, and her own death, are the indirect result of association with Dionysus. And it is Dionysus who resurrects her as a minor goddess.

Amongst the pre-classical Greeks, worship of Dionysus involved the disruption of daily routines. Women would leave their homes, their children, and their looms and go dancing *together on the hillsides. They would experience religious ecstasy, a communion with the god. Myth, as usual, takes the possibilities of reality to extremes. Women don't just refuse to listen to men, they tear them limb from limb; they don't just neglect their children, they eat them.[3] It may be, though, that the myths are exaggerating but not distorting actual practice, and that real women who were caught up in the communal frenzy did sometimes claim a human victim to sacrifice to their god. It is typical of the depictions of Dionysus in myth that his followers do not derive only pleasure or only pain from involvement with him. He is at once gentle and violent, creative and destructive.[4]*

In the ancient sources the goddess Hera figures rather more prominently than she does in the version of the story told here. It is she who sends madness upon Ino and Athamas because they shelter the child of Zeus and Semele, Dionysus. (Many myths tell of her feelings of jealousy towards the children that her husband Zeus fathers on other women.) Hera is also the divine protector of marriage, the sanctity of which is certainly not upheld here, at least not by Athamas. Even if Dionysus were not her rival's son (interestingly, Hera, too, is a stepmother) he would surely incur her wrath on similar grounds, since he encourages married women to leave their husbands and children and run off to the mountains.

That too much happens in Ino's life is this story's major difficulty. Individual episodes are complete in themselves—the elimination of Phrixus and Helle; the concealment of the baby Dionysus; the rivalry with Themisto; the ripping up of Pentheus on Mount Cithaeron; the deaths of Learchus, Melicertes, and Ino herself; the good deed Ino performs for Odysseus—but it is hard to find a time sequence for them, and they do not fit very well together. Of course, it may be that ancient oral tellers were not at all disturbed by problems of chronology and unity. The episodes of this story may have been strung together much as the episodes of a television drama series are strung together, with a recurring cast of characters facing new predicaments every week. Ancient authors, on the other hand, seem to have perceived a problem and tend to select just some episodes to relate, differing in the logic they use to combine their preferred scenes.

I have chosen to have this story narrated by an imaginary woman who is a storyteller, not a participant in the action. She clearly believes in the power of Dionysus to enthral and to madden. She tells variations of the story as she goes along, stating which she finds credible and which not. But she is close enough to the action to believe that the people were real and to try to determine why they might have acted as they did. This approach accommodates, but does not solve, the problem of having many and contradictory versions of the same story, and the problem of there being more than one way of perceiving Ino. Either she is a woman faintly tinged with madness for much of her life; or she is evil, but eventually redeemed; or she is simply protecting her interests in a reasonable manner, by removing her stepchildren so that her own children can flourish. I have no means, either, of alleviating the problem of not really understanding what Dionysiac madness was about except in a removed, academic way. This story and its characters remain inscrutable. You had to be there.

The story I have to tell is not an easy one; the deaths of children are seldom easy. But it's hard for other reasons too, reasons I can scarcely explain—some of the things that are said to have happened couldn't have happened, and I don't always understand it even as I tell it. But it is a story of madness. What else can I expect?

Where to start? Let us try beginning at the end. With Odysseus. You've heard of him. There he is on his way home from Troy after ten years of war. His companions are lost; his ships are lost; and now his little home-made boat is in pieces. There's just Odysseus and the angry wine-dark sea. Since Poseidon hates him, he has little chance to live.

But deliverance arrives. In the form of Leucothea, the goddess of the white foam. She throws him one end of a scarf, a veil if you like, and he holds on to it like—well, like a drowning man. And he does not drown. She tells him to abandon his boat and to swim to shore, the veil tied around his waist. "When you reach dry land," she says, "throw this scarf back into the wine-dark sea and as you do so, turn your eyes away."[5] Odysseus knows when to do as he is told. He reaches dry land safely and tosses the scarf into the sea. And Leucothea, or Ino, as she once was, raises one hand out of the water to recover it and then delivers him to the tutelary care of Athena.

Our story does not concern Odysseus any more. He was soon home and in the arms of his faithful Penelope, and the world was neither a better nor a worse place for it. But the sea goddess, Leucothea—you might wonder who she was and where she had come from, and why she troubled to rescue inconsequential heroes when they ran afoul of the waves. I do believe, though some will laugh at me when I say it, that she was compensating for her crimes, making amends in the only way she was able.

Her name was really Ino. She was the daughter of the king and queen of Thebes.[6] She was the wife, the second wife, of Athamas, king of Orchomenos.[7] For a woman to be a man's second wife is not unusual, but it can be a grievous thing if her husband has children already when he marries her. Athamas had two. Phrixus and Helle their names were. Remember them. The sequence of murder began with them.

Ino had three sisters whose names were Agauë, Autonoë, and Semele. Agauë was the wife of Echion, who was born of the Earth in Thebes; their son was Pentheus.[8] Autonoë was the wife of Aristaeüs, who made his home for a while in Thebes, though he was a wanderer at heart. Their son was Actaeon, whose warm blood now is stilled for ever in cold stone.[9] Semele was the youngest and loveliest of the sisters and was enjoyed by Zeus. She carried his child, the child that was to be Dionysus, the tender, mad god, but she died before he was born, consumed by the flames of Zeus' lightning. Until the moment of Semele's death, Ino had not believed that the father of the child was Zeus. She thought her sister a liar and worse. It was an old trick of princesses to say that Zeus had got to them when their bellies were stretched with child. The other sisters still didn't believe it. They scoffed at Semele even as she died. Zeus' punishment for her lies, they said. But Ino saw the look in Semele's eyes as the flames whipped around her body. It was neither repentance nor indignation. It was surprise. For Semele knew that she had done nothing wrong. She had merely asked to see Zeus in his true form, and Zeus had complied. He was too brilliant for her and she burned. Simple.

The story they tell of the birth of the child Dionysus I cannot believe. It is a man's tale and men know nothing of birth. They say that the young god Hermes snatched the child, no bigger then than a baby hare, from the flames as Semele died. That the child was sewn into Zeus' thigh and stayed there until it was ready to be born. And then Zeus cut the golden stitches and gave birth to the baby god from his own loins.[10] But even Zeus cannot nurse a child. He called for Hermes to come and take the child away. I saw an image once, worked in white marble, of Hermes holding the pig-faced baby in one arm, eyeing it with some distaste, as if he knew the havoc it would wreak.[11]

Hermes took the child to the daughters of Lamos, nymphs of the river, who gave him milk from their breasts and left him lying unswaddled on his back, his legs kicking the air, while they went about their work. But something strange happened to them. They began to dance, to skip with careless feet along the riverbank. Some say their eyes grew wild, and they howled and foamed at the mouth, and Hermes was so frightened for the baby's safety that he snatched him away and found him a different nurse, Ino.

So there was Ino, queen of Orchomenos, already the mother of two small sons, presented with a new child, a child she had last seen torn from her sister's womb at the moment of her death. "Lady," said Hermes, grandly, "take to your breast a new son, your sister Semele's child. Keep him safe here, for already the daughters of Lamos have tried to kill him in their madness." Ino opened her arms and the motherless child found a refuge, and then Hermes was gone.

I have heard it said that it was the closeness of the baby Dionysus that tainted Ino with madness. That as his golden head nestled on her white breast somehow his mania seeped into her—that it was a kind of exchange, milk for madness. But I'm not sure. She may have already killed, you see. This is where the story starts to fall apart, the point beyond which I cannot move with any certainty. Either Ino had already tried to kill two children and had succeeded in killing one, her husband's daughter, Helle, or else that all came later, after the baby Dionysus had come to stay. It makes no sense either way. If she had already killed a child, what was the guarantee that she would not harm this one, this tiny, helpless baby god who could barely lift his head from his chest? I want it to have happened later, after the madness of Dionysus had crept into her bones; only then is it bearable. Otherwise she committed a cold, deliberate act of murder, not with her bare hands, it's true, but in a way that was infinitely worse. But for all I want it to have happened later, I don't see how it could have done. There wasn't time. She was obsessed with her foster child, with the golden baby.[12] She was with him night and day. When could she have laid her plans, when visited the houses of the country folk, when bribed the messengers?[13]

I see that I must tell you the story of the plan to kill Phrixus and the death of Helle. They say that Athamas, king of Orchomenos, husband of Ino, was married, once, to Nephele, and that she bore him these two children and then they parted. This is when he took Ino of the slender ankles as his wife. In due time, Ino bore two sons, Learchus first, and then Melicertes. She fretted over her sons. Not so much about the fevers and frailties of childhood as about what was to come. Who would become king of the glorious city of Orchomenos after Athamas? Not either of her own sons, but Phrixus. And Phrixus might fear her sons as usurpers, might he not, and have them killed before even they were grown? These thoughts went round and round in her head; she was never free of them; when she held her babies in her arms, she felt, as the mothers of sons have often felt, that she was Death's surrogate, nursing them only until he was ready to snatch them away from her.

Now Ino was no witch. She had no magic at her fingertips. But she was a clever woman, and the plan that formed in her mind was worthy of the greatest generals. This is what happened: the women of Orchomenos loved Ino. No affection had been inspired in them by the aloof, impassive Nephele, but this young princess from nearby Thebes, who spoke and laughed with the people and whose bonny sons went everywhere that she went, had easily won their loyalty. They would do any thing she asked. And what she asked them to do was roast the seed grain. Some say the women knew full well that if parched grain were sown it would not grow. Others claim that Ino persuaded them that it would. However she managed it, the women, without the knowledge of their husbands, had parched grain sown in the Boeotian soil, and that year nothing at all grew in the fields. The men were perplexed. They came to their king, and Athamas, as perplexed as any, sent envoys to Delphi, to communicate with Apollo, the god who speaks the truth to mortals, when it suits him. They were to ask what was causing the bare fields and meagre harvest. No one knows, now, what Apollo thought about this, whether he knew what Ino had done and was prepared to reveal it to the questioners, because Ino bribed them, perhaps before ever they left Boeotia, to bring back a certain answer. It was this: the famine will end, and the curse on the land be lifted, if Phrixus the king's son and Helle the king's daughter are sacrificed to the powers of Heaven and Earth.

How gullible can a king be? Athamas swallowed every word the envoys spoke, and reluctantly, and oh so heavy of heart, he took his son Phrixus and little Helle, who held her father's hand tightly as they walked up the mountainside, to the very summit of Mount Laphystion, where the sanctuary of Zeus lay almost hidden in the clouds. He stood at the altar with his son, prepared to believe that the death of a beautiful youth, the first-born son of a king, would atone for whatever offences had been committed, and bring his people bountiful harvests and peace of mind.[14] I see him now, in my mind's eye; he is every foolish priest who ever trusted that spilled blood, as long as it wasn't his own, would lead to renewed life. He waves the sacrificial knife, intones the prayer, and prepares to strike.

I have heard different tales of what happened next. Just how credulous are you? Did Nephele, the children's mother, send a ram with a golden fleece to rescue them? Did it stand patiently by the altar until Phrixus understood that he should climb onto its back and pull little Helle up behind? Did the assembled company just stand there and watch, chins tilted to the skies, as the ram flew up and away into the vast blue ether? The ram, with Phrixus on its back, flew all the way to Colchis, and Athamas, the poor fool, had no idea that Phrixus lived. Helle wasn't so lucky. She fell off the ram into the sea far below and drowned.[15]

It's more likely, isn't it, that one of the men who had been sent to question Apollo had a pang of conscience when he saw the boy Phrixus, with sacrificial garlands around his neck, about to die. He must have stopped the sacrifice in the nick of time. Perhaps he even told Athamas that it was Ino who had bribed him to tell the crucial lie.[16] It may be that Phrixus and Helle decided themselves to leave Orchomenos, assuming that Ino would get them somehow if they stayed. At any rate, they were never seen in Boeotia again.[17]

So, however it was, whether they were dead or not, Phrixus and Helle were gone, and it was all Ino's doing, there's no doubt of that. She was a dangerous woman. And yet she nursed the baby Dionysus at her breast.

This was the richest time of Ino's life, the time when she loved a child who was not her own. The baby was enchanting— golden haired and plump, all smiles. Keep him close to you, Hermes had said, and so at first Ino kept him in the dark halls of the palace, and rocked him, and he played there with rattles and cymbals. And while he played, ivy, heavy with berries, wound itself around the doorposts and the pillars of the palace. And the women sang to him, sweet, sad songs of delight.[18] But Dionysus was not to remain long in the palace. The hills were his place. The hills and the forest, where the ivy creeps over the ground and the cones from the pine trees crunch underfoot. One day, as suddenly as he had arrived, he was gone. From then on the mad, wild god has never rested, a motherless child always searching for his nurse.[19]

It was when the child left that Ino changed. Her own sons had been dear but were now abandoned. She left the palace in

the night's dark cover, without even the knowledge of her servants, and ran, unshod, hair streaming, up into the hills. She
wept for Dionysus, and she danced for him, calling his name to
the skies. When she slept she lay on a bed of pine needles. She
offered her breast to the cubs of a wolf. Poor deranged woman.

Back at the palace, Athamas made some effort to locate
her. The servants were sent out to search in the hills, to follow
any likely trail through the woods. But they did not find her,
and returned in sorrow to the palace.

And here we are in trouble again. Was it then, while she
was missing from the palace—for as long as four years I've
heard it said—that she travelled to Thebes? Was this when she
joined with her sisters in the fatal dance on Mount Cithaeron?
It's a long way, Orchomenos to Cithaeron. Was this when she
severed the arm of her sister Agauë's son, Pentheus lord of
Thebes and prince of fools? They lured him up onto the mountainside, oh he was little more than a boy. The Thebans made
him king too soon, he didn't know what he was saying, they
didn't have to hurt him, did they? I don't even understand why
Ino would have been part of this. If Dionysus wanted to punish
Agauë for her refusal to acknowledge that he was the son of
Zeus, I can see the reason in that—can't condone it, for gods
should be forgiving, not like mortals—but I can see the reason
in it. He compelled Agauë to kill her son. Simple. But why
would he punish Ino? Ino who had loved him, believed in him,
Ino whom he had loved? Why would he have her kill the boy-
king in that hideous way? And yet every story I have heard has
her right there in the middle of it all, blood on her hands, flesh
flying, ripping Pentheus limb for limb as mad as any of them.

The other thing that puzzles me, and it's silly really, but I
can't get my mind around it, is that if Dionysus was grown
enough to punish his aunt Agauë like that, how was it that Ino's
sons, Learchus and Melicertes, who were already born when
Dionysus was brought to Orchomenos, were children still when
Ino returned to her palace after Pentheus' death? They died as
children. They never did grow up. So when did Dionysus? Do
gods mature faster than mortals? Is that it? Did Dionysus grow
like his own ivy, fast and lithe and wild? Is that how it was that

he could be out driving the world mad while Learchus and Melicertes were still babbling in their cradles?

Wherever she was, whatever she did, Ino was gone for a long time. I wonder just how hard Athamas tried to find her, for soon after she vanished a new wife was installed in her place, the beautiful Themisto, soon the mother of two sons.[20] And what was more natural than that Themisto should fear the sons of Ino and want them dead? Athamas never learned, did he?

When Ino was at long last found, and brought home, Athamas was secretly pleased. Of all his wives, he loved her the best. He thought he could have two wives at once if he was careful, and so he brought her to the palace. This was perhaps his worst mistake. She roamed through its hallways, calling still for Dionysus, and at night she came to the nursery and rocked the children in her arms, her own two sons and Themisto's sturdy twins. Themisto was a frightened woman. She heard that Ino had been found, for the palace was all a-whisper, and she knew, though she pretended not to know, that the poor mad dishevelled thing who haunted the nursery and crooned in the dark of the night to the babies must be the once-loved queen.

So here they were, the two remaining wives of Athamas, each stepmother to the other's children. It was Themisto who struck first, by planning the deaths of Ino's sons. She summoned Ino to her. "Dress the children that are mine," she said, "in robes of white for joy. Dress the children that are Ino's in robes of black for sorrow." But Ino dressed the children of the young and lovely queen in robes of black for sorrow and her own dear sons in robes of white for joy. And when Themisto, dagger in hand, crept into the nursery that night, as Ino even in her madness knew she would, she slit the throats of the two children dressed in black, not knowing until the light of morning that she had killed her own young sons. Oh, but this is a man's tale again. Even in the dark a mother knows her own children. She knows them by their whimpers as they sleep, by the softness of their cheeks, by their very smell. No mother could kill her child in mistake for another. If this happened at all, if anything like this happened, then Themisto sent killers who did not know her children into the nursery that night. This is the only way it could have been.

And of course there's another thing: no woman could mistake newborns, as Themisto's twins were, for boy children who had lived for six and seven summers. It isn't possible.

At any rate the twins were dead. "My babies are slain," cried the young and lovely Themisto, who had not hesitated for a moment to order her rival's children killed. And she hanged herself. Ino was queen again, sole surviving wife of Athamas, madwoman extraordinaire.

You would think by now I would be accustomed to describing the deaths of children. But these last deaths are the hardest to tell. There was Athamas, two more children gone and his lovely bride hanging from the rafters, angry or mad or both. It is strange, isn't it, the logic of the man? He has four children dead or missing. He takes revenge by killing the other two. It makes no sense.

What made him do it? Was it that Ino's crimes were just too great? A famine that was no famine, an oracle that was no oracle. The absurd scene on the mountain top and then Phrixus and Helle gone and now the babies with their throats cut in their cradles? All Ino's doing. Or was he mad, with the same creeping madness that afflicted her? There was enough in his house to make a man mad even without the ivy tendrils of Dionysus curling round the doorways.

There's another possibility that some have suggested and I have never really considered until now. There was another player in this whole drama. Remember how Semele died? How she burned in Zeus' lightning? It was Hera, Zeus' wife, who made that happen. She was jealous of Semele's overpowering beauty and of the love Zeus had for her. She went to Semele in disguise and persuaded her to ask Zeus to show himself to her in his full splendour. And so Semele burned. And it was Hera who threatened Dionysus. It was because of her that Hermes brought Dionysus to be hidden in the dark in Ino's halls. And when Dionysus vanished it was Hermes that took him again, because Hera had discovered where he was. Did Hera punish Ino for loving Dionysus? Hera, herself a stepmother, herself worried that her own children would be overshadowed by the sweet and dangerous Dionysus, which of course they were?[21] Did she hate Athamas too, and punish him, for making such a mockery of marriage, of which she was the guardian? It's a thought, isn't it? I don't want it to be so. I would like to think that the gods were above this sort of thing, and that Hera, at least, would not harm the women who revere her. But I'm not sure; Hera has never been much help to me.

Whatever it was, whatever or whoever drove him, Athamas would not stop until Ino and her children were dead. This much was clear.

Ino in the palace heard him call. She recognised his cry. It was the summons to the mountain. So had Agauë cried as she tore her dear son limb from limb on Mount Cithaeron's heights. Ino's place now was the hills. The woods were hers; she knew them well and ran with sure feet through them to the cliffs that tower over the sea, calling out to the man bent on murder to follow. She was ready for more blood. Ready to tear her own sons limb from limb. She called to her sisters, wherever in the world they were, to join her in the slaughter. Another killing. New blood. The blood of children. Her own children. For this they had been carried in the womb. For this nurtured. For this loved. She ran with Melicertes in her arms. He was no longer a small child, but she was stronger than you could imagine a woman could be. Learchus, tall and long-legged by now, ran easily beside her, not understanding why he was there, that the child's part in Dionysus' revels was quite unlike the mother's. On and on he ran, until, stumbling on a root of a tree, he fell and couldn't rise. [22]

Athamas appeared behind them. Eyes rolling. Hair on end. Howling as the dead howl. With his bow he took aim at his son. The arrow flew true, caught Learchus in the heart. But this was not the boy's death. Torn limbs, flesh scattered like the grain at sowing time, calling father father ... Oh, I have not the art to tell you how he died. [23]

Ino stood at the cliff's edge and watched. Where is madness when you need it? She saw her son die and she understood that it was her son and why it was her son. In the end it was absence of madness, not madness, that was her ruin. [24] The sea behind her was inviting and dark. A promise of oblivion.

Some say she listed her crimes as she dropped from the cliff with the boy Melicertes in her arms. "It was I who brought famine to Boeotia. It was I killed children. I lived in the wilds like an animal, danced in the death dance. The Earth is done with me now."

She knew the depths and anger of the sea. Its foam took her and smothered her, and her son. It was perhaps a kinder death than she had dealt. A bloodless death. Bloodless and white.[25] And so the goddess Leucothea, helper of sailors in distress, profferer of veils, was born.[26]

This story will end as it began, with a man. I can't help it. The women are dead, or else removed into the realm of goddesses—Semele, Ino, Nephele, Themisto. So here is Athamas, wifeless, childless, his wits recovered. He has learned something from all of this after all—he never marries again. He adopts his brother's grandsons to rule when he dies. A sensible decision. I commend him.

Years later a youth arrives at Athamas' court claiming to be the son of Phrixus. Presbon, his name is.[27] To a man who believes all his sons dead, and dead before they became fathers, that youth is a sight more welcome than a field of wheat to a starving kingdom. Thus it is that a son of Phrixus becomes king of Orchomenos.

And so it was all for nothing. It was as if Ino had never been. All the murders, all the madness. All for nothing.

Notes

[1] All the elements of Ino's story told here can be found in Hyginus, *Fabulae* 1–5 and *Poetica Astronomica* 2.20. He knows of all three of Athamas' wives and makes Ino the pivotal character in both the removal of Phrixus and Helle and the deaths of Themisto's children. Apollodorus tells the stories of Phrixus and Helle, the birth of Dionysus, Ino and Athamas' guardianship of him, the deaths of Learchus, Melicertes, and Ino, and the resurrection of Ino. He knows of Themisto but has Athamas marry her after Ino's death. See 1.9.1–2 and 3.4.2–3. Ovid, at *Metamorphoses* 4.464–562 tells how Ino and Athamas are driven mad by Hera (he calls her Juno) and kill their children. Both Apollodorus and Ovid, along with numerous other authors, state that Melicertes becomes a sea deity after his death. The story of Ino\Leucothea's rescue of Odysseus

is told by Homer at *Odyssey* 5.333–53. The main source for the episode in which Ino participates in the dismemberment of Pentheus is Euripides' *Bacchae*. Nonnus, in his *Dionysiaca*, tells most of Ino's story; his work is particularly useful for details on the concealment of the baby Dionysus in the palace of Ino and Athamas. Details of Athamas' life after the deaths of Ino and his sons can be found in Herodotus 7.197 and Pausanias 9.34.5.

Many authors tell portions of Ino's story. See, for example, Ovid, *Metamorphoses* 3.259–315 and 3.701–33 and *Fasti* 3.849–76 and 6.485–568; Pausanias 1.44.11; Apollonius Rhodius, *Argonautica* 2.1140–56; Diodorus Siculus 4.47.1–6; and Lucian, *Dialogues of the Sea Gods* 6. Euripides wrote an *Ino* and Sophocles an *Athamas* that are no longer extant. We know that the former told the story of the deaths of Themisto's children.

² Medea's story, chap. 13, in which the children of a first marriage are abandoned by their father when he marries for a second time, is unusual in that the new wife is not depicted as the perpetrator of harm against the children. Instead, it is the cold-heartedness of their father that is stressed. Medea herself becomes a stepmother after she escapes from Corinth to Athens. She marries Aegeus, king of Athens, bears a son by him, and tries to murder his older son, Theseus, by slipping aconite into his wine. The attempt is a failure. See Ovid, *Metamorphoses* 7.404–24.

³ Orpheus, for instance, was torn to pieces, and the daughters of Minyas cast lots to determine which of their children would be eaten. See Apollodorus 1.3.2 and Antoninus Liberalis 10 respectively.

⁴ For information on Dionysiac rituals see Walter F. Otto, *Dionysus: Myth and Cult* (Bloomington, 1973). What the celebrations amounted to was an attempt by an oppressed class, in this case women, to assert itself, to take on, at least for a short period, the role of oppressor. In time, Greek authorities tamed these celebrations, so that they became less threatening to the status quo.

⁵ These words are taken from Homer, *Odyssey* 5.348–50.

⁶ This is Ino's family tree:

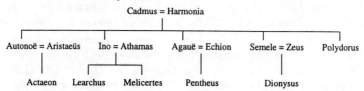

Polydorus escapes the disasters that befall his sisters.

[7] Orchomenos is a Boeotian city north of Thebes.

[8] Echion was one of the Sown Ones who sprang from the ground when Cadmus founded the city of Thebes. It was common for a city to have a story that said that its first inhabitants had not immigrated to the city, but had grown from the land on which it was built. Agauë was exiled from Thebes for her part in her son's death. She travelled to Illyria, married a king there, and then killed him, apparently so that Cadmus, also exiled from Thebes, could rule.

[9] Aristaeüs was hunter, prophet, and healer. He was the mythological expert on bee keeping, olive growing, and cheese making. Actaeon was torn to pieces on Mount Cithaeron near Thebes by his own, maddened, hunting dogs. This poignant story is told by Ovid at *Metamorphoses* 3.138–252. So distraught were the hounds without their master that a statue of Actaeon was made to calm them (Apollodorus, 3.4.4). Autonoë left Thebes after the death of her son.

[10] This is not the only story in Greek myth in which a male character gives birth. The goddess Athena, for instance, is born not from Zeus' thigh but from his head. Such stories may originate from male fantasies of commandeering the magic of birth for themselves, and may owe their details to confusion on a topic about which male storytellers knew little.

[11] This is the Hermes of Praxiteles, sculpted c. 350 B.C.E.

[12] Nonnus (*Dionysiaca* 9.103–10) writes that he glows with his own light.

[13] In Hyginus (*Fabulae* 2) the attempted murders of Phrixus and Helle appear to occur after the concealment of Dionysus (Hyginus calls him Liber).

[14] According to Ovid in *Fasti* 3, both children are to be sacrificed. The myth here describes what may well have been a real-life pattern: crisis (here the famine), consultation of oracle or seer, demand of sacrifice from gods via oracle or seer, sacrifice. The assumption was that the community had transgressed in some way and that the crisis had been caused by the anger of a god. The greater the god's anger, the more valuable the sacrifice had to be. Logically, then, in cases where the god was not easily appeased, the sacrifice was likely to have been a young, beautiful, unsullied human. What is unusual here is that Ino, though not yet divine, takes the role of the god.

[15] The ram here is differently used from the one stuck by its horns in the thicket that turned up in the nick of time to save Isaac when his father Abraham was about to sacrifice him (*Genesis* 22). In that case, Abraham sacrificed the ram instead of the boy. Phrixus' ram is usually said to have been sent by his mother Nephele, whose name means "cloud" and who has taken up residence among the clouds. Its fleece turns up in the story of Medea (chap. 13) and is the object in quest of which Jason undertakes the first known sea voyage. Helle loses her grip on the ram and falls off into the strait between Europe and Asia, thereafter called the Hellespont (Helle's sea) in her honour. According to Hyginus, Phrixus and Helle encounter the ram in a different way. Ino is handed over to Phrixus for punishment after Athamas finds out that she is responsible for the famine (see n. 16, below). But Dionysus saves her. Later he drives Phrixus and Helle mad and sets them wandering. Nephele finds her children lost in a forest and gives them the ram.

[16] This is Hyginus' suggestion (*Fabulae* 2). In Ovid (*Fasti* 6) a serving woman with whom Athamas secretly consorts gives him the information.

[17] This is the story Diodorus Siculus tells.

[18] Several sources state that Dionysus is disguised as a girl so that Hera cannot find him. A relief sculpture in the Lateran Museum, Rome, shows Ino feeding a toddler Dionysus not from the breast but from the Horn of Plenty. A huge vine grows up around him, indicating that he has the power to cause spontaneous growth and perhaps that madness is not far away. In the *Homeric Hymn to Dionysus* (7), vines grow from the mast of a ship, and ivy entwines itself around the oars just before panic, caused by Dionysus, strikes the crew.

The toys with which Dionysus plays here (following Nonnus) are to become his cult implements.

[19] According to most authors, Hermes removes Dionysus from Ino's care because Hera has discovered his whereabouts. He is taken either to Zeus' mother, Rhea (Nonnus), or, in the shape of a kid, to the nymphs of Nysa (an elusive or perhaps even movable mountain, and therefore a fine hiding place). He rewards the nymphs with renewed youth whenever they grow old (Apollodorus 3.4.3 and Hyginus, *Fabulae* 182). From this point on, Dionysus settles nowhere. As an adult god, his pattern is to arrive in a place, cause havoc, and disappear as suddenly as he came.

[20] According to Nonnus, she has four sons, Schoineus, Leucon, and the twins. The twins will be Ino's victims.

[21] Although Hera is Zeus' legitimate wife, her offspring, Hebe, Eileithyia, and Ares, are weaker and less important than many of the children of earlier wives (such as Athena, daughter of Metis) and current mistresses (Apollo and Artemis, children of Leto, and Heracles, son of Alcmena, for instance). To many of these children she is openly hostile.

[22] The chronology of the story is particularly awkward here. For optimum poignancy Learchus and Melicertes need to be babies when they die rather than older children, yet this is impossible if the account of their deaths is combined with other episodes of Ino's story. Nonnus runs into difficulty, describing Melicertes as a newborn at his death, even though after his birth Ino is missing from the palace for four years and four children are born to Themisto.

[23] According to Apollodorus (3.4.3), Athamas kills Learchus thinking he is a deer. In Euripides' *Medea* 1283–92 it seems as though it is Ino who kills Learchus and Melicertes. If the story is told that way, then Athamas' part must be to run after her to try and stop her, or to take revenge on her for killing his last remaining sons, both equally good stories.

Nonnus has Athamas kill Learchus and then return to the palace, where he places Melicertes in a cauldron of boiling water on the fire. Ino removes him before the water has completed its work. But what, precisely, is the water supposed to do? Kill Melicertes or make him immortal? This story is reminiscent of Thetis' attempts to immortalise Achilles (see her story, chap. 12) where the child's father, Peleus, assuming that Thetis is trying to harm the child, removes him too soon from the fire. If the boiling is supposed to bring immortality, it seems to work in Melicertes' case, since he is soon to become a minor god. In various versions of this story it is Ino who boils Melicertes. Again, it is not clear whether she is trying to murder him or to render him immune to Athamas' attempts to murder him; moments later she leaps from a cliff holding the child. Is he dead or alive?

[24] I have borrowed this element of understanding the enormity of one's actions from recognition scenes in myth. Oedipus' tragedy (see Jocasta's story, chap. 3) is not so much that he has killed his father and married his mother as that he understands that he has done these things. In Euripides' *Bacchae* Agauë is under the impression that she is killing a mountain lion when she is tearing her son Pentheus

to pieces. This is Dionysus' punishment for her for denying his godhead, but the punishment is not complete until she recovers her senses and understands what she has done. Ino's understanding is such that through it she moves beyond the realm of normal human experience. This is her preparation for becoming a goddess.

[25] The name "Leucothea" means "white goddess" and may refer to the foam from which the new goddess is created.

[26] According to Lucian, Ino is to be saved on Dionysus' orders. In Ovid's *Metamorphoses*, Aphrodite (Venus), who is actually Ino's grandmother, strange as that may seem, is the one who pleads for Ino to be reborn as a sea goddess. She reminds Poseidon (Neptune) that she became a goddess in a similar way herself: when Uranus was castrated by his son and his genitals were thrown into the sea, the foam that they created became Aphrodite. See Hesiod, *Theogony* 188–206.

Some authors notice a symmetry in the deaths of Helle and Ino. Both fall from a height into the sea. Ino herself, according to Nonnus (*Dionysiaca* 10.96–98), supposes that Nephele has sent the Furies after her, to avenge her daughter Helle's death.

Melicertes becomes Palaemon or "wrestler," another minor sea deity. He is carried off by a dolphin to Corinth, and the Isthmian games, held there in historical times, are instituted in his honour. The point from which Ino leaps is identified as the Molourian rock on the Saronic coast of the Corinthian Isthmus. The rock itself is sacred to Leucothea and Palaemon, but the rocks beyond it are accursed: from these rocks the infamous Sciron hurls passing travellers into the sea, to be dashed to pieces on the rocks below, or eaten by a giant turtle that lurks there. So writes Pausanias (1.44.11).

[27] These details are from Pausanias 9.34.5. According to Apollonius Rhodius, Phrixus reaches Colchis on the back of the golden-fleeced ram and settles there. He marries Chalciope, daughter of the king of Colchis and older sister of Medea. She bears him four sons, none of whom is called Presbon. The four attempt to sail to Greece to claim their grandfather's land in Orchomenos, but are shipwrecked and return to Colchis with the Argonauts. See *Argonautica* 2 and 3 passim. Herodotus relates that one son, Cytissorus, encounters his grandfather Athamas in Alus, where Athamas is about to be sacrificed to Laphystian Zeus (at whose altar near Orchomenos he once tried to sacrifice Phrixus). Cytissorus is able to rescue his grandfather.

SEVEN

Procris' Story

This story[1] *is not well known now. The names of Procris and Cephalus trip off nobody's tongue nowadays. Nonetheless, they were favourites of the ancients,*[2] *and their story still fascinates—perhaps because of the coincidences it contains, and the agonies of mistiming it involves. Here are intense love, overwhelming jealousy, and interfering outsiders. Like Oedipus, the major characters struggle hard on what they believe to be the best course of action, only to be plunged further into their inescapable doom. The story is more like a later romance than a typical Greek myth. The twists in the action, the disguises and mistaken identities, the very personal nature of the trials, all these contribute to a feeling that there is little of a traditional core to this tale. It must owe a good deal to the imaginations of storytellers, or perhaps to their willingness to join unrelated stories together. At times the story verges on the realms of the humorous and the absurd.*

Procris herself is a complex character: loyal yet suspicious (with good cause), she dedicates her life to her marriage to Cephalus. But according to some of the ancient writers who tell her story, she is an accomplished hunter. It is also recorded that she travels in disguise to Crete, heals sickness, and plots and plays an elaborate trick on her husband. All these elements are included in the version of the story that follows.

I

Procris was the daughter of the king and queen of Athens; she was both beautiful and sweet tempered. She was to be married to Cephalus, by her father's order but, and we must remember that this was unusual, she loved him—she loved the curl of his hair on his forehead, the sharp profile, and more than that. She believed him sound, and true. Did he love her? Yes, in his way, he did. But men seldom love as women do.

Procris felt that she belonged to Cephalus, and that he, though he might have laughed at this, belonged to her. It was her misfortune to love too much—forgive her, please. She hardly knew what she was doing ... We cannot imagine, now, such devotion, if that is what it was. She had been a daughter and she was to become a wife. No other destiny presented itself. She could be a wife willingly and with joy, or grudgingly. She chose the joy.

Orithyia was Procris' sister[3]—a gentle soul, slender and small boned. Oh, they joked when she was a child that she was so light she could be lifted up by a puff of wind. The jokes died on their lips the day Boreas took her—Boreas the North Wind. He had tried long and hard to win her love—begged her father Erechtheus, king of Athens, to give the beautiful girl to him as his wife,[4] but the Athenians did not trust him. Who, after all, can trust the spirits of the air? So Boreas swept down one moonless night from the heavens, when the sisters, Procris betrothed at this time but still unmarried, were walking through the courtyard of their father's palace. Orithyia screamed even before he touched her, for she sensed what the great dark thing was that was coming at her, and knew she had no defence against it. Boreas enfolded her tiny body in his great feathered wings and she was gone. Procris was left cowering alone beside the altar of the goddess Artemis. She ran straight to her father and mother. My sister has been taken by the wind, she said. And they believed her, though this was little comfort. She never saw her sister again, though sometimes, on a moonless night, she thought she caught a familiar voice, straining to be heard on the midnight air.[5]

II

When Procris was married to Cephalus she could scarcely believe her good fortune. They lived together in King Erechtheus' palace, each delighting in the other's company. But the gods do not look kindly on mortals who relish life, who have put past sorrows behind them. It is most dangerous of all to love too much. One morning, when they had been married only for two new moons, Cephalus left their shared bed early, before the dawn, to set traps to catch deer on Mount Hymettus, as he often did. On this day, he never reached the mountain.

The sky was beginning to turn from black to yellow. Eos, the moon-banishing dawn, she of the web-fine wings, all but invisible, took Cephalus against his will. Procris saw him struggle, in the same courtyard, by the same altar, as if with the breeze. Then he was gone. This time no one believed her. What sort of a wife must she have been, they wondered, for her husband to desert her after so short a time? On that day began the unravelling of her heart.

III

Cephalus had been kidnapped by Eos simply because she desired him. There was no other reason. Her lover Tithonus had grown old and unsightly.[6] She wanted a new and beautiful love. And the gods take what they want. Never forget that. Despite himself, Cephalus found her captivating, irresistible; she was like no one he had ever known. He was frantic with desire for her. She bore him a son while they were together, Phaethon. He was kidnapped for his beauty also, by Aphrodite, who loves all men, but loves handsome men best.[7]

In time, Cephalus came to loathe his new life. He was a man of the outdoors, he said, a great hunter, not a toy for a goddess. And Eos, if truth be told, began to tire of Cephalus. He talked endlessly of Procris, his young wife in Athens. He imagined her, ensconced in her chamber, dreaming about him, awaiting his return, weaving her anguish, as Penelope would do in years to come, into a tapestry.[8] Eos was enraged. No woman, scoffed the goddess, acts that way. You can be sure she is unfaithful to you at every turn, with any man who comes her way. Any grief she shows is feigned—designed to make her more desirable to men. A widow is an easy mark, even your widow.

Cephalus knew little of women. Eos' vision of Procris seemed as likely to him as his own. It tormented him. How would he ever know whether she had remained faithful to him? That she would take him back when he returned he did not doubt. But to enjoy her as he had once enjoyed her he must know, for certain, that she was his alone. Then test her, said the goddess, taunting him. Test her to see how she behaves. Eos smiled. She changed him just enough that none at first would know him. She gave him gifts with which to tempt his wife—jewels the colours of the dawn, mauve and golden yellow.

IV

Procris saw him arrive at the palace at dusk. In the fading light the guards did not recognise him as Cephalus, but they judged him to be of noble blood, and he was welcomed. For the first time in many months he set eyes on his wife. It was all he could do to refrain from taking her in his arms. If she seemed less delicate than when he had married her, the fingers clasping the wine goblet thick and unlovely, he thought little of it. After all, she had been weaving all those months. Procris did not know him. She seemed detached, distant. Though her parents spoke to her often and kindly, her silences hung heavy in the air. Her father explained to Cephalus: she grieves for her husband who left her many months ago. He vanished one day at dawn without a trace. It is hard for her to accept that he tired of her so quickly. Erechtheus did not tell this stranger that he feared for his daughter's sanity or that she too disappeared in the early hours of many mornings and had been found more than once wandering on the mountainside near deer traps that looked freshly laid but surely could not have been since there was no man close who could have set them.

Procris went wearily to bed that night without a thought for the stranger, though Cephalus could hardly contain himself until the household retired. She had no idea that he was skulking beside the altar of Artemis in the courtyard, waiting until the last of her serving women left her.

When he entered her room, she did not cry out. She seemed to him sad rather than frightened. She listened as he flattered her, assured her she was the most beautiful woman he had ever seen. She said she would wait for her husband to return and wanted no other man. I know he will come back to me, she said. I have no doubt. She sighed when he pressed her, when he told her that her husband could be in his grave, that she would soon be old and withered, her life wasted for a dead man. He will return, she said, and sighed again, eager to be rid of him. He took the jewels from the pouch he carried, tumbled them into her hands in the half-light. They shone like fire. She gasped. They were beautiful beyond words and so she spoke none. For the first time she did not protest. It was enough for him. Into her silence he read the betrayal of his other self, her husband. He came at her, as if to strike her. And then she knew him.

V

Procris remembered little of what happened next. The husband she had longed for hated her. This alone she knew. He warned that he would tell the world he had trapped her in her faithlessness, she who had doubtless sold herself for jewels a hundred times while he was gone. Not once, she said, not once. You would better use your guile to trap your deer, not trick your wife.

VI

Cephalus shouted his wife's perfidy to the rooftops. Though it was night, the palace came alive. Every servant knew him now, and though they had seen, with their own eyes, Procris grieve for her absent husband, and though they recognised that he had deceived her, still they thought her treacherous, the lure of jewels her ruin. That was how it was in those days. But Procris knew none of this. She ran to Mount Hymettus, her husband's old hunting ground, by now her second home. When Cephalus had lain with Eos all those months, she had escaped there many times, had listened to her sister's singing on the wind, and had taught herself, with the guidance of the goddess Artemis, to be as fine a hunter as her husband. And now, in her new misery, she lived as Artemis' devotee, built her own altar to her goddess in a sheltered glade and daily laid on it some animal, freshly killed, for goddess and worshipper to share. She made herself a javelin of knotted cornel, the wood supple, comfortable in her hand as if moulded to it. From the crones of the mountain she learned to cure such illnesses as women sometimes suffer when they consort with men.

VII

Cephalus soon tired of telling the tale of his faithless wife. Those who believed him urged him to take a new one. A few, and these not only women, stared at him incredulous. Where is she now, they asked, this wife who loved you? Find her, before it is too late, and beg her to forgive you.

VIII

Procris lived for many months on Mount Hymettus. I cannot say she was happy; she wandered in the box-groves, remembering the time when she was loved. Cephalus, too, came to Hymettus, though he had no reason to look for Procris there. Procris caught sight of him one morning, standing on a ridge calling his hounds to his side, and she loved him still, the curl of his hair on his forehead, the sharp profile. But she did not wait to be seen by him. His closeness was unbearable. There is a limit, after all, to what even a woman who loves her husband can take.

IX

She left the mountain then, and Athens too. She sailed, alone amongst men, to Crete. Though her stature was small, with her close-cropped hair and her darkened skin she could pass with ease for a youth.

Once in Crete, Procris made her way to the palace of King Minos, who recognised her, through her disguise, from the serpents on her rings.[9] She told him of her trials and of her skills, for she was by now a fine hunter, though no other mortal knew this. A hunter himself, he asked her to join him in the chase. Their days were marked by the yelping of Minos' hounds as the dogs followed their prey through the woods. He whose own daughters would desert him in times still to come[10] offered her keepsakes: a javelin, with a golden tip, finer even than her own; and his best dog, lop-eared and lean, gifts to him from Artemis the goddess, one hunter to another. The javelin never missed its mark, the dog never failed to catch his prey.

But nothing is without its price. Minos had an illness, or was under a spell: a woman who lay in his embrace, whoever she was, and there were many, would suffer. His wife was the witch Pasiphaë. She had seen to it that whenever he took a woman to his bed, he let loose inside her scorpions and worms that gnawed at her body and drove her to death. Procris cured him—mixed him a brew of roots and leaves to drink, and he could lie with any woman then.[11]

X

Procris thought, constantly, of Cephalus. It is plain she loved him still. Minos' bed held no attraction for her. And so she ran away again, back to Athens, still disguised as a youth. If truth be told, she feared the wrath of the witch Pasiphaë. It is not wise to make an enemy of one so powerful. But one more powerful still was watching: Artemis, goddess of the hunt, goddess of young women who are pure, and sometime champion of witches.[12]

Back in Athens, Procris preferred the life of a hunter to that of a shamed princess. On Mount Hymettus, wearing still the leather tunic of a woodsman, her hair cropped short, she joined a troop of hunters. Their leader was Cephalus. She was ready, now, to be close to him, surer of her innocence than she had once been. She could watch him, remember how he had once loved her. Cephalus noticed not her, but her gold-tipped javelin and the dog, Laelaps.[13] He asked where they had come from and she told him they were the gifts of the king of Crete. Who are you, then, he asked, that the king of Crete should so honour you? My name is Pterelas, she replied. My story you will discover for yourself. But Cephalus asked her no more questions. It was the hound and javelin he coveted. Their owner was nothing to him. I must have them, he said to the boy who stood before him. I will give you gifts in return—all the jewels you like. Oh, I have jewels enough, said Procris. Take me to your bed, and I will give you what you ask.

XI

That night they lay together by the fire. And as the youth removed his clothes, and revealed himself to be a woman, Cephalus recognised his wife, and was filled with joy to have found her.[14] Procris was content again. She gave the dog, Laelaps, and the gold-tipped javelin to her husband and grudged them not at all. And he was happier with his wife than he had ever been. They stayed together on the mountainside all through the months of summer, and when the sun began to make a quicker journey through the sky and the evening frost grew harsh, Procris found that she was to give birth to a child. She returned to the palace of her father in Athens, Cephalus came with her, and there their son was born, Arcesius the artful, whose son was Laertes, father of Odysseus.[15]

For years they were happy, all past sorrows forgotten. Procris loved Cephalus with all her old passion. They lived in the palace, an easeful life. But the gods do not forget. Years before, the hound and the javelin that Cephalus valued so much had been given to Minos, king of Crete, by Artemis, goddess of the hunt. They were no true gifts. She had watched him, noted how he used them. Artemis loved chastity, not the wanton couplings of an adulterous king. Procris, too, had surrendered them for love, or what passed for it, Procris, who had once been a finer hunter than her husband, had once lived alone on Mount Hymettus, even in the wintertime, learning the ways of the forest and shunning the comforts of the palace and the beds of men.

The child Arcesius had lived for twenty new moons when Cephalus began again an old habit of his. He would rise, before dawn, leave the palace and travel to Mount Hymettus, to set traps for deer. The javelin that never missed its mark was always in his hand, the dog, Laelaps, at his side. Procris would rise too and watch him cross the courtyard under Artemis' moon. She remembered that dawn, long ago, when he had disappeared into Eos' arms. She remembered too how it felt to be on the mountainside in the morning stillness. At first merely envious of his freedom, at length she began to believe, for Pasiphaë had found a place in Procris' mind, not that he was going to hunt, but that he was going to meet a lover there in a woodland cave, perhaps even Eos herself. She thought of Artemis as her ally. But the gods like to deceive. Remember that. Her prayers were many, and all to Artemis. My lady, may my husband love me and only me. May he hold no other woman in his arms, see no other image in his dreams. Her sister Orithyia's voice came to her on the breeze more and more often. Her parents, old now, pleased in past years that their daughter was with them, heart and mind intact, feared for her sanity. Cephalus knew she was sad, but thought it just some woman's grief. She would be easily pleased—another child, or a lovely jewel—he thought he had learned enough about women now to know what she would want.

XIII

Artemis chose a beautiful morning for Procris' death. Stars still shimmered in a silent sky. It was windless[16] and warm. As the first flush of dawn appeared, Procris crept out after her husband, and followed him to the flower-cloaked mountainside. By the light of the dull moon she could see him as he stood on the ridge, the dog alert at his side. She crouched in the thicket, listening, straining to hear her sister's voice. It was the time of the dawn, the yellow glow of day returning; the time of the goddess, the lustful Eos. Artemis, be with me, whispered Procris.

Suddenly, Laelaps tensed, a low growl signalled something skulking close by. Cephalus heard a noise, of leaves rustling, from the bushes. He held the javelin poised, the javelin that had yet to miss its mark. He let it fly. It did not miss, but struck Procris in the heart. She was not long in dying. Long enough, though, for Cephalus to draw the low branches apart and meet her eyes. Her pain was beyond words, and so she spoke none. She died thinking him faithless and her murderer.[17]

XIV

Some stories seem never to end. Cephalus stood trial in Athens and was found guilty of the murder of his wife. He was banished for all time from Attica. He travelled to Thebes, where, in those days, Creon still ruled. The hound Laelaps travelled with him, always at his heel. There was in Thebes a need for the hound that never failed to catch his prey, for Creon's people were troubled by a fox that killed their cattle and their children. This fox, it was said, could never be caught by any dog. I leave the rest to your imagination.[18]

Notes

[1] The major source for this story is Ovid, *Metamorphoses* 7.668–862. Ovid takes a variety of elements from older stories and blends them into one. The tale is told by Cephalus. Procris is a faithful wife, who is accused of infidelity by her husband when, in disguise, he attempts to seduce her by offering her gifts. Ashamed, and presumably angry that she has been tricked, she leaves Athens and devotes herself to hunting and to the goddess Artemis, whom Ovid calls Diana. Diana gives her the javelin and the hound that play such a big part in the story, and she in turn gives them to her husband when they reconcile. Disaster occurs, however, when Procris spies on her husband as he hunts. He kills her, accidentally, with the javelin she had given him. According to Apollodorus (3.15.1), Procris is seduced not by Cephalus disguised, but by another man, Pteleon. Minos readily seduces her too, and presents her with the javelin and the hound. Apollodorus tells a later part of the story, Cephalus' adventures in Thebes, at 2.4.6–7. Sophocles wrote a tragedy entitled *Procris,* of which only a few words survive. Hyginus tells this story at *Fabulae* 189 and continues it, with

some contradictions, at *Poetica Astronomica* 2.35. He, and he alone, states that Procris' father, Erechtheus, was guilty of incest with her (*Fabulae* 253). Elsewhere (*Fabulae* 189) he states that Pandion, not Erechtheus, was Procris' father. The motif of father-daughter incest is dealt with in the story of Myrrha, chap. 9, and is omitted here. It is Antoninus Liberalis who gives the details of Minos' disease and its cure, at *Transformationes* 41. Procris is greedy in this version. Cephalus sends a friend of his whom she doesn't know to give her gold, telling her that an admirer has sent it and it is hers if she sleeps with him. When he doubles the amount, she consents to do so.

[2] Pausanias seems to suggest at 10.29.6 that the tale was familiar to all, even hackneyed. Shakespeare mentions Cephalus and Procris in *A Midsummer Night's Dream,* act V, scene 1.199–200. He has the characters of Flute and Bottom, playing Thisbe and Pyramus respectively, mispronounce their names as "Shafalus" and "Procrus." The story must in Shakespeare's time, then, have been well enough known for the audience to understand the joke.

[3] The parents of Procris and Orithyia, Erechtheus and Praxithea, had other daughters. Erechtheus on one occasion learned from an oracle that his people would only be victorious in the war with the Eleusinians if he allowed one of his daughters to be sacrificed. He killed the youngest, and other daughters committed suicide in sympathy. (Or perhaps he killed the second youngest, since a daughter called Creusa is said to have been an infant at the time, and yet she grows to adulthood and marries. Her story is interesting in itself. Euripides tells it in his *Ion.* Raped by Apollo, she exposes the resulting child. Years later, when he is grown, she meets him again. Euripides describes with compassion the agonies of a woman forced by society's pressures to abandon her child.) See Apollodorus 3.15.4–5; Euripides, *Ion* 275–82; and Hyginus, *Fabulae* 238. The following family tree does not tally with all accounts of the rulers of Athens. According to Euripides' *Ion*, for instance, Creusa's husband Xuthus becomes king when Erechtheus dies.

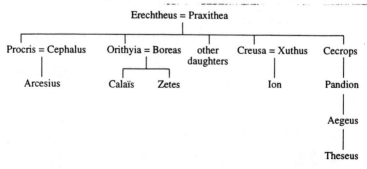

⁴ Several Greek myths have as their central theme an examination of a girl's troubled transition from her role as her father's daughter to her role as her husband's wife. The fathers frequently make trouble, as they do not wish to give up their daughters. Thus, Oenomaus will not relinquish his daughter Hippodamia to anyone who cannot beat him in a chariot race, a near-impossible task since he owns horses that are swifter than the wind. For further discussion on this theme, see Hypermnestra's story, chap. 10.

⁵ Orithyia went on to become the mother of Calaïs and Zetes, human in form except that as young men they grew wings like their father's. Calaïs and Zetes joined Jason on his quest for the Golden Fleece. They made good use of their wings for fighting monsters, but did not use them for the purpose of carrying off women. See Apollonius Rhodius, *Argonautica* 1.211–23 and Ovid, *Metamorphoses* 6.682–721. Ovid tells the story of Orithyia's abduction by Boreas in some detail.

⁶ This in itself is a good story. Eos, an immortal goddess in love with Tithonus, a mortal man, pleads with Zeus that he be allowed to live forever. Zeus grants the request. Eos neglects to ask, however, that he not grow old. She ceases to desire him as he ages, and he becomes a burden and an aggravation but, of course, she is unable to be rid of him. The blessing of eternal life becomes a curse. She shuts Tithonus away behind brazen doors, but his constant mumbling still annoys her (*Homeric Hymn to Aphrodite* 5.218–38). Other sources have him wither away until he becomes a grasshopper. His grating voice still irritates. Thetis' story, chap. 12, deals more fully with the theme of the incompatibility of the mortal and immortal worlds.

⁷ Not the famous Phaethon who drove the chariot of the Sun God across the sky and lost his life; this Phaethon is chosen by Aphrodite to watch over her sanctuaries at night, in the form of a star (Hesiod, *Theogony* 986–91). Being snatched away is apparently a common fate for members of this family.

⁸ Penelope was the wife of Odysseus. She waited for him while he was away fighting at Troy and then trying to get home, approximately twenty years. Her most famous activity during this time was the weaving of a shroud for her father-in-law. She accomplished little else, since every night she unravelled all the weaving she had done during the day. The whole story is told in Homer's *Odyssey*. At the time that Procris' story takes place, the Trojan war has not yet occurred and Penelope is not yet born. Odysseus

is either the grandson or the great-grandson of Procris and Cephalus. See below, n. 15.

⁹ Procris' father was Erechtheus, son of Pandion (an earlier Pandion than Procne's and Philomela's father), son of Erichthonius. Erichthonius was Earth-born, and the serpent appears to be able, like the Earth, to renew itself indefinitely by shedding its skin. Either Erichthonius was a serpent from the waist down like an earlier Athenian king, Cecrops, or he was guarded by a pair of entwined serpents as a child. In Euripides' play *Ion,* the god Hermes tells the audience that the descendants of King Erechtheus adorn their children with a necklace of golden serpents. See *Ion* 20–26. Since serpents do not attack their own, and since Athens, at least in mythology, is replete with serpents, this would seem to be a necessary precaution for keeping children safe.

¹⁰ Ariadne and Phaedra are presumably not yet born, since Theseus, who will be the lover of one and husband of the other, will not be king of Athens for another four generations, after Erechtheus' son (a second Cecrops), his son, Pandion, and his son Aegeus. See the family tree in n. 3, above. (Minos' apparent longevity troubled some ancient writers, who like to think there were two of him, one the grandson of the other. It may be that "Minos" was a word used by Cretans to mean "king" and that not all mythtellers understood this.)

¹¹ Although it doesn't fit well with the version of the story given here, Antoninus Liberalis relates a more interesting method of curing Minos' affliction. Procris inserts the bladder of a goat into a model of a woman and Minos uses this as a repository for his dangerous excretions. The model is reminiscent of the various mechanical wonders that figure in the myths about Crete, such as the wooden cow that Pasiphaë used to satisfy her passion for a beautiful bull, and Talus, the man of bronze who guarded the whole island, and was alive only as long as ichor (gods' blood) flowed in a single vein. Antoninus Liberalis' language is ambiguous enough that some prefer to think Procris inserted a goat's bladder into her own vagina, thus protecting herself from the scorpions. See Barry Powell, *Classical Myth* (Englewood Cliffs, NJ, 1995), 353–54.

¹² Artemis figures in this story, and in most, primarily as goddess of the hunt; as such she is youthful, robust, and wholesome. She leads the chase carrying her torch, followed not just by hounds but by a troop of virgins. But she is also identified with Hecate, crone of the Underworld. Her torch still blazes, but her hounds howl

terrifyingly, and she is skilled in black magic. Artemis is the goddess of the new moon, and Pasiphaë may have been a moon goddess also, at least in Crete. She is said to be the daughter of Helius, the Sun. She appears in Medea's story, chap. 13, where also note the ambiguity of Artemis' position in Medea's spells against Pelias. That Artemis would disapprove of the various sexual intrigues in this story (Cephalus with Eos, Procris with "the stranger," Procris with Minos) is certain. She consistently in myth disapproves of sexual encounters, even punishing innocent female victims of rape for the "crime" of being raped. In this case, the fact that Minos so casually gives away the unavoidable javelin and the inescapable dog, and in return is given a trouble-free sex life, must further annoy her.

[13] Laelaps may have originally belonged to Zeus. He perhaps employed him to watch over Europa after his abduction of her.

[14] Cephalus seems not to realise that he is guilty of the very crime that he so despised Procris for, willingness to surrender "virtue" for riches.

[15] Odysseus' father may have been Sisyphus, a rogue who seduced his mother. Some authors omit Arcesius' generation entirely, and make Laertes the son of Procris and Cephalus.

[16] In Ovid's version of this story the morning is warm and there is no wind. Procris has been told by a nosy stranger that her husband is meeting a lover on the mountainside. The stranger has heard him calling "Aura" and whispering such sentiments as "relieve the heat with which I burn" and "you are a great joy to me," and has mistakenly concluded that he is addressing a woman. In fact, Cephalus is often hot, and he is talking to the breeze, "aura" in Latin, which does sound like a woman's name. The pun can be rendered into English by using the name "Gail" and its homophone "gale." The name "Aura" is uncomfortably like the Roman name for Eos, used by Ovid, which is "Aurora."

[17] Ovid likes (relatively) happy endings. Procris, with her dying breath, begs Cephalus not to turn to "Aura" after her death. He is able to enlighten her and she dies "with a happier expression and content." See *Metamorphoses* 7.862. In *The Art of Love,* where the story is not told by Cephalus, but reflects Procris' view of how events unfold, there is another twist. After tormenting herself when she notices a depression in the grass where she assumes he lies with his beloved, and hearing him call to "Aura," she suddenly realises that he is talking not to a nymph but to the wind and

moves to approach him, so pleased is she that her suspicions were all a mistake. This is when Cephalus hears her and kills her. Austin Dobson (1840–1921) in his *The Death of Procris* has a particularly poignant ending. Cephalus lets loose an arrow when he sees "The brown of Procris' hair/Move in the covert." He doesn't even bother to check what the arrow hits. Procris dies where she falls, "among the white wind-flowers," and only the dog, Laelaps, witnesses her death.

[18] In Ovid, Cephalus himself describes the futile chase. He was just about to put an end to it by hurling his trusty javelin at the fox when he looked away for a mere moment. When he looked back, there were two marble statues on the ground. But eternal chases are more reasonably placed among the stars. (So Orion appears to chase the Pleiades for all time. They disappear just as he comes into view.) At *Poetica Astronomica* 2.35 Hyginus writes that Zeus (he calls him Jupiter) turned both hound and fox into stone. He does not record how the chase came to be immortalised in the heavens, though it is clear that he is identifying Laelaps with the Dog Star. Pausanias records, at 10.29.6, that after Procris' death Cephalus married Clymene, daughter of Minyas, king of the Minyan territory in northern Boeotia (and thus not far from Thebes). She bore him one son, Iphiclus. Pausanias describes a painting in which Procris and Clymene are both shown, with their backs turned to each other.

EIGHT

Althaea's Story

Althaea's story[1] is an offshoot of one of the most famous tales of antiquity, the Calydonian Boar Hunt. The group of hunters who assembled in Calydon to rid the kingdom of a dangerous animal were as dazzling a collection of heroes as Jason's companions on the first Greek sea voyage.[2] The lone female hunter, Atalanta, was the star of the show in most versions, being the first to wound the monstrous creature. Althaea, of course, was not involved in the hunt. She was, however, involved in the ironic postscript to it, the unheroic death of a major participant, her son Meleager.

The blessing that becomes a curse is the common stuff of stories. We see it often in tales of the misused-wish type, like Midas' golden touch[3] or Eos' desire that her lover live forever.[4] Althaea, in her story, seems to have been granted the greatest boon of all— power over her new-born son's fate, the ability to keep her child alive as long as she chooses. Right away, we know that this is dangerous: in Greek myth, mortals do not have control over their own fates, or anyone else's. Not even the gods have power over the destinies of any mortal children they happen to have. When those children die, they die. It is the Fates who decide when and how, and only the Fates.[5] But Althaea, for no apparent reason, and perhaps in a dream, becomes privy to the plans of the Fates regarding her son, and sees a way to alter them, apparently to her own advantage. This is an extreme example of hubris, trying to overstep one's mortal mark.

How can we expect such an ambition to succeed? For years, it seems to. Meleager grows to manhood. But as a young man, he commits an act of murder that puts his mother in the classic double bind: the duty of avenging the murder falls to her, but the person who has committed the murder is her own son.[6] *In order to fulfill her duty she must kill him, a terrible and unthinkable crime. For most mothers in myth the decision whether or not to kill an adult son would be affected by their sheer physical lack of strength in comparison to that of the son—but this mother can kill hers without laying a finger on him. All she has to do is put a certain log on a fire. As she says herself in the story below, it is not her son's life that she holds in her hands, but his death. This story is about that realisation.*

I remember the log and the flames as if it were only moments ago. My bedchamber was dark, save for the light of the fire. My son, new born, lay in my arms. Meleager, my first child. I saw him in my mind's eye, full grown, tall and powerful, his smile broad. He would be king after his father, loved by his subjects, honoured by posterity, spoken of by tellers of tales long after his death. I imagined him able to command an army, but able to weep too, for the razing of a village or even for a creature newly dead.

My husband, Oeneus, handler of mares, was king of Calydon. He was a good man, as men go. I had no complaints. He was merry and generous; I rarely saw him angry. He loved company, hated to be alone, and never, never, turned a visitor away. He was not a brave man; talk, not action, was his style, but that way he stayed alive. He joined no expeditions, saved no cities from destruction, fought no monstrous animals. After my death he married again and his wife bore him new sons, to replace the ones he loved who were gone. To enjoy life as much as Oeneus did is a great gift. Those of us who are more solitary, more contemplative, may have other gifts, but it cannot be said that we relish our lives. We are too familiar with melancholy, and too fond of it.

I remember that my son was nursing from my breast, straining to fill his belly. I heard the voices.

"Whose thread is this?" said one; it was the voice of the Spinner.

"It is Meleager's," said another, the voice of the Measurer, "newborn son of Oeneus, king of Calydon, and Althaea his bride."

"Will he live long?" said a third.

"He will live," said the second, "only as long as the log burning now on the fire still burns."

I fancied I heard a laugh. "I will be ready," said the third voice. This was the voice of the Intractable one, the one who would cut the line of my son's life.

Then the first voice spoke again: "It is a pretty thread, such a pretty thread. So sorry. So sorry."

I called out to them but they did not answer. There was only the Spinner chanting over and over. *Such a pretty thread. So sorry; so sorry; such a pretty thread.* Her voice at last grew fainter and with her sisters she left my room.[7]

Meleager, asleep now in my arms, was to die as soon as the log on the fire was burnt out. To the log and to my child, the Fates had allotted the same number of hours.

No mother wants her child to die, does she? I could think of no reason, that day, why this tiny child should cease to be when others lived. Now I know better, but he was my son, my baby, born hours before of my body, and I could not let him go.

I laid him on the couch where he and I would sleep that night. I called to my servant for water. Thinking I needed to wash she brought a bowl of warm and scented water. My baby began to cry. The log was beginning to burn. She went to pick the baby up; I screamed for her to leave, and, uncomprehending and hurt, she withdrew from the room. I pulled the log from the fire with my bare hands and placed it in the bowl. No more smoke from it, no more cries from my son. When the log was cool, I took it and placed it in a chest. I gave orders that the chest be touched by no one but me, and I told no one what I had done.

The years passed, and there were other children, my son Toxeus among them. He was more like Oeneus than like me, always mischievous as a child, and impudent as a young man.

Just as Zeus visited my sister,[8] Dionysus visited me, and I bore him a daughter, Deianeira. Oeneus cared not at all. Dionysus gave him the vine, and taught him to make wine. He was merrier than before. He loved his sons. He took them hunting and riding. They sang together in the evenings. When I think of Meleager now, I remember his face, lit by the light of the fire, as he sang with his father and brothers at our late evening meal. *A pretty thread, such a pretty thread.* Was Meleager my favourite son because he was born first of my womb, or was it that I held his life in my hands with the knowledge of no other mortal?

When my second son, Toxeus, died, at Oeneus' hands, I could almost understand. Many a king has had to choose between kingdom and kin. And Toxeus pushed him too far. You cannot watch the fortifications of a city be built, day after day, month after month, by countless labourers, and then stand aside as some young fool mocks their work by jumping effortlessly over the ditch that surrounds the wall, laughing that this will keep nobody out. Oeneus was there, he saw it. He saw the men who had sweated to dig and to build gasp in horror at Toxeus' act, for everyone knows that if the first man to cross the ditch from outside does not die, neither will any enemy who follows him.[9] Kings understand that more battles are lost through bad omens than through cowardice. Oeneus barely hesitated. He drew his sword and ran it through his son's neck, my son's neck, and the ditch ran red with blood. Toxeus, how your voice darts through my mind. You, the first of my sons to die; I hear you laughing, always laughing, your scorn for your father undiminished. If a woman has the power to keep one son alive, should she condemn herself for failing another? Perhaps not, but I do. I did not berate Oeneus for what he did, I spoke not one word of blame. But he felt guilty enough to rebuke me for words unspoken. Did I think it was a woman's business to have power of life and death over her children? Or to question a man's decisions? What could I know of the burden a father carries? Or of the pain felt when duty must come before love? How could I know how it feels to kill one's child? I let him rant. I hope it eased his heart.

The loss of one child makes the others more precious. When Artemis sent the boar, I would not allow my youngest sons, Thyreus and Clymenus, to join the hunt for it.[10] Meleager I let go with light heart, knowing he could not die as long as the log remained unburned.

I should tell you about the boar. After Toxeus' death, Oeneus was less careful, perhaps, in his dealings with the gods than he had once been. He had been known all over the Greek world as the most pious of men, meticulous in ritual, inspired in prayer, but when the gods allow it to happen that a man must butcher his own son, there is a loss of trust, a certain lessening of conviction. For Oeneus, the prayers and ceremonies were a formality now, enacted because he was king, and this is what kings must do.

On the day of the harvest offerings he climbed the sacred hill as if in iron shoes. But he conducted all the ceremonies, placed the first fruits of our land on each of the gods' altars and thanked each one for their blessings. The altar of Artemis, off to one side, he ignored. Whether he forgot or miscounted, I do not know.[11] His heart was elsewhere that day. When they told him, he returned immediately to the hill, by moonlight, now, by the light of the wild, white-armed[12] goddess herself. He offered her gifts of all sorts, fruit from orchard trees, laid on the altar and burned, wild birds, thrown alive into the flames, and a wide-eyed gazelle.[13] But she was not pleased. It was not enough.

I have wondered, many times, what really angered her; the boar and all the horror that surrounded it seemed too harsh a punishment for mere distractedness. I think she knew about the log and understood that Meleager could not die as long as it remained unburned. He loved to hunt. Did she think it unfair that for him, hunting was without danger? Did she send this boar to restore the balance, to make the risk equal for hunter and hunted? Lady Artemis, Goddess, you have allowed other young men to die; Orion, who loved you, and Actaeon for seeing you unclothed; did you also want my son to die for you?[14] But who am I to second-guess a goddess? Why she did it does not matter. *Ah, such a sweet life, such a pretty thread.*

The punishment sent by the goddess of the wild was swift and harsh. It touched more than the delinquent one. When a king nods his subjects suffer. The boar trampled the sprouting grain in the fields. It tore the grapes from the vine and the olives from their branches. Overnight, whole flocks were massacred, herds decimated. Once, when the fishermen of a seaboard village were dancing in honour of the laughter-loving goddess, the one born of the foam who gave them good catches by day and pleasures in their beds by night,[15] the boar charged their circle, killing six of them at once and goring others so badly that they were recognised by the shreds of their clothing, not by their faces.

From all of Greece great heroes came to hunt the boar. Castor and Polydeuces, my sister's children, came;[16] Jason, son of Aeson and Alcimede, came from Iolcus; Iphicles of Thebes, son of Amphitryon and Alcmena; Telamon of Salamis; Peleus of Phthia; all made their way to Calydon, and so did others. I was most excited to meet for the first time Amphiaraüs of Argos, son of my sister Hypermnestra, and already a noted seer, despite his youth. But he acknowledged our kinship hardly at all and barely looked me in the eye. At that time, I did not know why. It is perhaps a curse to know what will become of those one encounters.[17] I do not envy him.

My own brothers came, younger than me by many years. I had not seen them since I left my father's house. They had grown into elegant young men, smaller than my sons but sturdy nonetheless, more than a match for all but the strongest of champions. When I left my mother's care to become the bride of Oeneus, Aphares had been a toddler still, clutching at her skirts with grimy hands, and Iphiclus a babe in her arms. Meleager, my first-born son, was younger than Iphiclus by just a year. My brothers brought word that my mother was dead, she who had borne only daughters in her youth but had loved them as I loved Meleager, knowing that they would leave her. Middle age had brought her sons at last, but she had not lived to see them grown. My father, they said, was old and ailing. They would be gone from his kingdom just a little while, a long trip being too risky when his death was so near. I had no other brothers living.[18]

The story goes, I believe, that when Atalanta, daughter of Iasus and Clymene,[19] from Tegea, came to join the hunt, my son Meleager fell in love with her. He may have done; I do not know, I was not there. A boar hunt is no place for a woman.

Oeneus entertained his guests for nine days and nine nights. The wine had never flowed more freely. The gifts that Oeneus gave, and those he promised after the kill, were abundant and elaborate. The heroes were pleased. Many of them were old friends, come together for excitement, and honour. I watched my brothers, marvelling at the handsome young men they had become. And I watched my sons. Thyreus and Clymenus, the children of my later years, were angry that they could not join the hunt except as observers, and eager, almost frantic, to have the talking done and the adventure started. Sometimes, though, they were mesmerized, despite themselves, by the stories of the scoundrel Peleus or of Iphicles. And Meleager. Not frightened, not disturbed at all. *Such a pretty thread. Nearly time now. So sorry.*

On the tenth morning they set out. I know very little of the hunt. I was told later that Atalanta shot the arrow that lodged first in the beast's flank, and then that Amphiaraüs shot it in the eye.[20] But it was Meleager, they told me, who killed it. I remember so clearly how it was when they came home. I saw the procession of hunters returning from the chase. I was standing on the very hill where my husband had neglected to offer sacrifice to the goddess of the wild. I was placing gifts of fruit from the trees in our orchards on her altar, not, this time, to be consigned to flames, as an appeal to her good will. But she wanted more than fruit from me. She wanted my son. I saw him. I saw my son Meleager marching at the head of the procession. Behind him came men holding aloft the head of the boar, its tusks curved like Artemis' own moon, and men carrying its bristling hide. There, my lady Artemis, I said under my breath, your beast is dead, and my son killed it. We have won.

I heard the wailing before I saw the twin biers held aloft on the shoulders of the servants. Two hunters were dead. Not such a great loss, I reckoned; the boar had taken many lives already.

Hunters know they take on dangerous work. I thought no more of it, went quickly back to the palace to greet my victorious son, for whom hunting was not dangerous at all, with never a care for the mothers and kin of the dead.

My son was quick to accept the congratulations of his father and his sisters, but he avoided my eyes. It was my youngest sons who told me. Meleager had skinned the boar and presented the hide to Atalanta, since she had been the first to draw blood. My brothers were appalled that a man's honour should go to a woman, and outraged that, if he were intending to give his prize away, he would give it to a stranger, not to his closest kin, themselves. They lay in wait for Atalanta in the dense brush, knocked her to the ground, and took the hide. Meleager saw them with it, and asked them how they came by it. When they told him, he asked them, so his brothers said, to give it over to him, to undo their crime the easiest way. They refused. He drew his sword and ran it through the heart of Iphiclus. Aphares must have known the skin was not worth his death. He seemed, my sons told me, about to run. But Meleager pulled his sword from Iphiclus' corpse and ran it through Aphares' heart.

It is the duty of surviving relatives to avenge their dead. My young brothers were motherless and their father, my father, near death himself. Only their sisters remained: Leda, far away in Sparta; Hypermnestra in Argos; and I. It was my responsibility to be mother, father, and all kin to them, my own flesh and blood, my brothers young enough to be my sons. It was my task, now, to arrange for the death of their killer. Mine the shame if this were not done. Mine too the horror.

To be in control of the fate of one's own loved child. Women dream of this, see it only as a blessing, a priceless gift. Had Thetis had this power, how she would have rejoiced.[21] To decide when one's own child should die. Of course, you will say, no mother will allow her child to die. The child will live forever. When does a blessing become a curse? Not, in this case, gradually; no dawning realisation that the gift was no true gift, that it had been better ungiven. No weighing of the factors and the truths, but a sudden, sharp apocalypse.[22] It was not my son's life I held in my hands, but his death. Better by far if the log had burned and he had died in my arms all those years ago. And Artemis had known. She had known all along.

I took the log from the chest in my room, where it had lain all Meleager's life. I bade my puzzled servant light a fire. The voices of the three sisters echoed all around me, the one who spins, the one who measures, and the one who cuts. *Such a pretty thread. Such a pretty thread. It is time now. It is time. So sorry. So sorry.* I placed the log on the fire. I thought of the birds and young animals burnt alive on Artemis' altars whenever she demanded them.

They told me later how he died. In pain, of course, and terror. He was walking, with Atalanta, by the river. He fell and his limbs thrashed on the ground, and he called out his father's name and Atalanta's, and he called for me. The agony was long.

At last, the thread was cut, the flailing ceased. The breath left his body as the last of the log turned to ashes in the fireplace.

Oeneus knew grief again, and the wine of Dionysus dulled his sadness not at all. He tore his hair like a woman and wept for the life of his child so soon ended.

Meleager died not knowing that his mother had killed him. No one knew, save me. I did not wish to live and found great comfort in the noose. And Artemis was at last content.[23]

In the fields of Asphodel[24] I see my own dead sons, and they do not acknowledge me. I see my dear brothers, and they do not thank me. Knowing what I have done, they stare in horror at me, uncomprehending of my act. It seems the dead do not, after all, require tributes of vengeance from the living. If we avenge their deaths we do it not for them. In the eyes of the dead, I killed my son, no more, no less. *Such a pretty thread; such a pretty thread.*

Notes

[1] The major source for the story of the Calydonian Boar Hunt and the "murder" of Meleager by his mother, Althaea, is Ovid, *Metamorphoses* 8.268–546. Apollodorus, 1.8.2–3, in the main tells the same story, as do Hyginus, *Fabulae* 171–74, and Aeschylus, *Choe-*

phori 602–11. Homer tells a substantially different story (*Iliad* 9.543–99) in which the boar hunt of the more usual story is followed by a war, Calydonians against Curetes. Meleager kills his mother's brothers and she curses him. Angry, he withdraws from the war, and only returns when the Curetes storm the walls of Calydon. Homer's version of this story does not include Meleager's death. See also Diodorus Siculus 4.34.2 and Bacchylides, *Epinicians* 5.

2 In fact some heroes went on both adventures: Meleager himself was an Argonaut, according to Apollonius Rhodius, *Argonautica* 1.191. Also according to Apollonius (1.191–201) Meleager's father, Oeneus, presumably unaware that Meleager could not die, sent his own brother, Laocoön, to keep him safe. Meleager's uncle on his mother's side, Iphiclus, son of Thestius, whom he was later to murder, also went on the expedition to keep an eye on him. Jason himself came to help in Calydon, as did other Argo veterans, Castor and Polydeuces, Idas and Lynceus, Peleus, and Admetus among them.

3 Midas, given the gift of a wish by Dionysus, asks that everything he touch turn to gold. It does. This is fun and pleasant until he realises that he cannot eat or drink. See Ovid, *Metamorphoses* 11.90–145.

4 See Procris' story, chap. 7, n. 6.

5 There are three Fates, usually thought of as old women: Clotho, the spinner; Lachesis, the apportioner; and Atropos, who cuts each individual's thread at the moment of death. The Greeks called them Moirai, the Romans called them Fata, or Parcae. This last name, meaning "women who bring forth," suggests that they were connected with birth, as in this story, as well as with death.

6 How similar this is to the plight of Orestes, whose duty it is to avenge his father's death. But his father's murderer was Orestes' own mother. See Clytemnestra's story, chap. 2.

7 According to most ancient authors, the three Fates arrive "bodily" in Oeneus' palace and place the log on the fire themselves; they then pronounce Meleager's destiny, and leave. According to Diodorus, Althaea is visited by them in a dream.

8 One of Althaea's sisters was Leda, wife of Tyndareus of Sparta. She was "visited" by Zeus in the form of a swan, and gave birth to at least two children who were not her husband's. See Clytemnestra's story, chap. 2.

[9] In Roman pseudo-myth, after Romulus and Remus have argued over who should found a new city, Remus jeers at the foundations of the wall Romulus has begun to build, and leaps over them. Romulus kills him, in the hope that none of his enemies will cross the wall successfully, and calls the new city Rome, after himself. See Livy, 1.7.2–3.

[10] The sons of Althaea and Oeneus are variously named, and there is disagreement as to their number. Bacchylides has Ancaeus and Agelaus, not as the only sons of the pair, but as the two who are killed during the boar hunt. Thyreus and Clymenus are the names given by Apollodorus. Some authors claim that Meleager was not Oeneus' son, but Ares'. Gorge and Deianeira are the daughters of Althaea, though Oeneus is the father of Gorge alone. Apollodorus reports that Oeneus was the father of Tydeus by this daughter (1.8.5).

[11] Homer says that Oeneus may have forgotten Artemis, or he may have miscounted (*Iliad* 9.537). Nowhere is it suggested that the act of omission was deliberate.

[12] Though this is usually an epithet reserved for Hera, Bacchylides uses it of Artemis in his version of this story, at *Epinicians* 5.99. The word seems particularly appropriate for a goddess of the moon.

[13] This description of an offering to Artemis is based on Pausanias' account of a festival held in honour of Artemis by the people of Patrai in historic times. See Pausanias 7.18.7.

[14] Artemis was the goddess of the hunt, among other things. She was also the protector of animals. This means that it was considered her task to ensure that the hunt was conducted "fairly," that pregnant animals were not killed, for instance, and that no herd was ever depleted to a dangerously low level. If a hunter could not be killed, perhaps he could slaughter too many animals. Orion and Actaeon, both hunters, also met their deaths at Artemis' hands, Orion possibly because he assaulted her, possibly because he boasted that he could kill all the animals on Earth (see Hyginus, *Poetica Astronomica* 2.34). Actaeon died after he stumbled accidentally upon the goddess while she was bathing (see Ovid, *Metamorphoses* 3.138–252).

[15] This is Aphrodite, goddess of sexual love, always the rival of Artemis in the classical authors. Their personalities and the lifestyles required from their devotees are not compatible.

[16] Castor and Polydeuces were Leda's twin sons, the first Tyndareus' child, the second Zeus'.

[17] See Eriphyle's story, chap. 5. Amphiaraüs' mother, Hypermnestra, is not the Hypermnestra of chap. 10.

[18] Althaea's mother was Eurythemis, her father Thestius. Thestius was a king, probably of Pleuron in Aetolia. The daughters of the pair are consistently given as Leda, Hypermnestra, and Althaea. The names of Althaea's brothers are variously recorded: Apollodorus does not name them but clearly imagines more than two, all of them present at the boar hunt. Bacchylides calls them Aphares and Iphiclus, as I have done. Ovid, acknowledging two brothers, calls them Plexippus and Toxeus; Hyginus, preferring three, Ideus, Plexippus, and Lynceus. Nowhere in the ancient sources does it state that the boys were younger than the girls.

[19] Since Clymene was the mother of Jason's mother, Alcimede, as well as of Atalanta, there is a problem with chronology here, at least in the modern view, since both Jason and Atalanta come to Calydon for the hunt. After many years of telling these stories, I have concluded that ancient mythtellers did not allow themselves to be bound by the rules of linear time. With a few exceptions (Heracles, for instance, is consistently said to have lived in the generation before the Trojan war) heroes can consort happily with the contemporaries of their grandmothers. All the participants here noted are mentioned by Apollodorus, and most by Ovid.

[20] This is Apollodorus' story. In Diodorus Siculus' version, Meleager is the first person to score a hit. Ovid has Atalanta's arrow followed by Meleager's spear.

[21] See Thetis' story, chap. 12.

[22] This word, which has such specific Christian connotations, is Greek. It means, literally, "uncovering."

[23] Artemis has no jurisdiction over, and little sympathy for, mothers. As a girl enters puberty, and even at marriage, Artemis will protect her, but the birth of her first child puts her outside of Artemis' domain. There are limited examples of Artemis actively turning against a woman about to bear her first child, but they do occur. The story of Callisto is a case in point. See Ovid, *Metamorphoses* 2.409–531.

[24] The fields of Asphodel are the area of the Underworld frequented by most of the dead. Meleager, according to Bacchylides, encounters Heracles there when Heracles comes down to the

Underworld to kidnap its guard dog, Cerberus. The dead Meleager offers Heracles the hand of his sister Deianeira in marriage. See Bacchylides, *Epinicians* 5.165–75. This marriage will result in Heracles' death.

Myrrha's Story

Myrrha is sometimes known as Smyrna. Her story, in the ancient sources, is a story of a girl who desires her father sexually.[1] So strong is her longing for him that she sees no escape from it other than suicide. Her nurse intervenes and arranges for the girl's passion to be satisfied. When the father discovers that it is his own daughter who is being brought nightly to his room he is enraged. He determines to kill her. She escapes him, but is turned into a balsam tree. As a tree she gives birth to her son (and her father's), Adonis.

The ancient story rings with distorted or fragmented voices. Myrrha claims to desire her father, but perhaps something else lies behind her sleepless nights. Then there is Myrrha's mother, who is absent. What does this mean? Can she know what is happening to her daughter and yet be unable to rescue her? There is also the nurse. She loves Myrrha unconditionally and will do anything to make her happy, but she loses her all the same. And yet the results, for her, of the mistakes she makes are never examined.

For many years I told this story in mythology classes as an introduction to an account of the relationship between Adonis and the goddess Aphrodite, but I had never given it much thought, except to include a trite disclaimer to the effect that this was a story about incest, and I hoped it wouldn't offend anybody. In the fall of 1989 a student stopped me, remarking that the story "was the wrong way round." She later wrote a paper pointing out that Myrrha has much in common with victims of father-daughter incest, especially those who have *suppressed their memories—suicidal tendencies and inability to sleep, for instance, are symptoms experienced by girls who have been subjected to sexual violence by their fathers.[2] This story could then be seen as a story of such abuse, contorted so that the abuser's actions are rendered excusable and the victim appears deranged. I was unable entirely to shake this notion from my mind, and when I began to choose stories for this book it surfaced again.*

In the version of the story told here, the details of Ovid's account are followed closely: Myrrha can't sleep, goes over her problems in her mind endlessly, rejects her suitors, loves her father (though she does not here desire him). She attempts suicide, is saved by her nurse, and confesses to the nurse not, as in Ovid, that she lusts for her father, but that her father has sexually assaulted her regularly. The nurse goes to the father and tells him not, as in Ovid, that a nameless and beautiful young girl of Myrrha's age desires him, but that Myrrha is disturbed and has said strange things about him. The nurse, with the best of intentions in either case, delivers Myrrha to her father. The father threatens Myrrha with a sword, she runs away, she becomes a balsam tree and gives birth to Adonis. So, with minimal rearrangement, a tale of repugnant female lust can become a tale of father-initiated incest.

The version of the story told here is not intended to replace Ovid's story. His work should be read and appreciated.[3] Perhaps, though, it would be wise not to have his story read in a vacuum, lest it ever be used to "prove," or even to suggest, that the victims of sexual abuse enjoy what happens to them. It must be clear that whatever the ancients thought, we now know young girls do not initiate sexual activity with their fathers.[4] At the very least the story needs a disclaimer, at best a commentary or an alternative story to accompany it. The story that follows is one such alternative.

There is another difficulty with Myrrha's tale, not as grievous, certainly, but troubling to the storyteller all the same. What to do with the balsam tree? Every teller has encountered a problem like this: almost everything in a story moves beautifully into the present even if the story itself remains set in the past. The characters are true and life-like, their motivations logical. Then one of them, with less than adequate preparation, is turned into a tree, or a weasel, or some such thing. How can a storyteller handle what seems, to modern ears, absurd? There is no universal answer. In this case, the tree is crucial. It represents Myrrha's powerlessness, her lack of individuality and voice. It also, almost paradoxically, represents the endurance of her story. In the version told here, no character admits to having seen the transformation. The nurse relates how a messenger told her he had heard that Myrrha had become a tree. She implies that she finds the story barely credible, but suggests that those desperate for answers may be willing to believe anything. The story also hints at the possibility that the metamorphosis into a tree is a blind, and that Myrrha did not manage to escape with her life on the night that her father chased her with his sword drawn.

I

No place, even in her mind, was free of him. In the day she lived in his house, sat at table with him, greeted visitors at his side. In the night she lay awake, afraid of the darkness, afraid that he would call her to his rooms again, afraid even of sleep. The words he had spoken whirled in her mind: there was nothing wrong in what they did together; kings of old had done it,[5] animals did it, even the heavenly gods had been known to bed their own daughters. In some places, he had said, fathers married their daughters and sons their mothers, thus doubling the bonds of affection between them.[6] She tried to persuade herself that it was so.

All girls loved their fathers, and hers was a king, Cinyras, king of all Assyria, a grand and clever man. As a child she had thought him handsome, too, and had loved to sit by him and listen as he handled matters she had not understood. And now, she still did not understand. Why would the father she revered be so eager to frighten and shame her?

When Myrrha closed her eyes in the hope that Sleep would send one of his thousand sons from their Cimmerian cave[7] to sweeten her night with soothing dreams, he let her down every time. The sons of Sleep became Cinyras, looming above her as he did in life, sometimes cajoling, sometimes threatening, always terrifying. Increasingly, her thoughts turned to death. If death were one long dreamless sleep, then what had she to lose by dying?

In life there was no escape. She had told no one what he had done to her; who would have believed her had she done so? Her nurse? Her mother? Sometimes, she thought her mother knew, and then again it seemed unthinkable that she did. Escape was impossible. The daughters of kings did not run away. Marriage? Marriage would mean leaving her home, perhaps leaving her father's kingdom, and never seeing her nurse and her mother again. There was no guarantee that this would be better, and besides, though suitors had gathered from all around to win her hand in marriage, no match had been made. She had been reluctant to talk with any of them, had hung her head as if in shame, and so her father had recognised none of their suits, and, puzzled, they had gone away.[8] She had been sorry afterwards; many of them were handsome, and some of them seemed kind.

But Death was the most engaging suitor of all.

One night, when the servants in the house all slept, and when she had seen her father go off to his rooms alone, she rose from the bed that gave her so little comfort. She took the belt from her dress, held its soft fabric momentarily to her cheek, then climbed onto a stool and fastened one end around the heavy beam above her. The other end she tied around her neck. "Farewell, dear Cinyras," she whispered. "Understand the reason for my death!"[9]

Outside the door of Myrrha's bedroom, in a small chamber reserved for her use, lay Myrrha's nurse.[10] Years before, this woman had given the new-born Myrrha her breast. She had been brought to the palace when her own child had been born, dead, and she had loved Myrrha in his place. This was the child whose health she took pride in and whose laughter stirred her soul. Now, her hair was greying and her life passing in servitude, but she still loved Myrrha. She had watched the baby

*become a pretty child, sweet natured and merry. She had taken
a guilty pleasure in the fact that Myrrha preferred her nurse to
her mother. Her mind was full of memories: Myrrha running to
her arms with the first anemone[11] of springtime clutched in her
hand; Myrrha's sweet voice rising in song louder and more true
than the voice of any other girl.*

*But in the last while Myrrha had been unusually silent,
prone to tears,[12] unable to meet her nurse's eyes. How can I
help her, asked the nurse of herself. She thinks I'm a fool. But
she is so young, and she knows so little.*

*This night, like many before it, the nurse had slept poorly.
Just as when Myrrha had been a tiny child, and all night long
the nurse had remained on the edge of wakefulness ready to run
to her darling if she cried out in the dark, so now she stirred
in her sleep when Myrrha stirred in hers. She heard the girl get
up from her bed, heard her move the three-legged stool across
the floor and struggle to attach the belt to the ceiling beam. She
rose in a hurry, gathered her shawl about her, and opened the
door to Myrrha's room. The girl looked at her and stood still,
caught piteously in this act of hopelessness. The nurse, taller
still than her charge, reached easily to untie the belt from both
neck and rafter, and took the girl in her arms. "How can I help
you?" she asked. "You cannot help me," was the reply.*

The nurse's tears and questions were bothersome to Myrrha. If
she couldn't die, she wanted to be alone.[13] "Are you insane?
Are you bewitched? Has someone laid a curse on you?" The
questions were endless. "I have magic that can help you. Spells
to weave, and herbs to soothe you. I have charms and witches'
knots." Myrrha heard her as if through a veil. Absurd that she
thought she could help. "What is it, child? We are in no danger
in the royal house from brigands or marauders. The kingdom
is strong. Your mother and father are well. What can be wrong
with you?"

The girl wept and the nurse held her to her breast as she
had done when Myrrha was a tiny child. She spoke gently. "Is
there someone that you love that you cannot marry? We women
are easy prey for laughter-loving Aphrodite and her craft. I will

find a way to help you. Your father need never know." It was the desire to be rid of her that made Myrrha tell. If she told her perhaps she would stop her prattling and leave.

The nurse listened to Myrrha's story with disbelief. Myrrha told how her father had summoned her many times to his rooms and there had raped her, instructing her to tell no one, threatening to hurt her more if she did. She repeated what her father had said to her. Kings and animals and gods. The nurse could only think that Myrrha was deluded, that some fiend possessed her. She knew magic, but none strong enough for this. "Myrrha is right," she thought to herself. "I cannot help her." She resolved to tell Myrrha's mother.

But Myrrha's mother was away from the house, celebrating the feast of Demeter, goddess of Earth, with other married women. For nine nights she would not be there. Eager to pass the burden of the girl's illness onto those better equipped to deal with it, the nurse asked to see the king. She told him that Myrrha had tried to die. She told him that his daughter had strange delusions. She told him what Myrrha had told her.[14] "Send her to me," he said.

For nine more nights Myrrha endured her father's attentions. But it was worse now. She had betrayed him, he said. She had told her nurse what had happened between them. Luckily the old fool had not believed her, but it was only a matter of time. On the ninth night he took his sword down from where it hung on the wall of his room. He took it from its sheath and showed Myrrha its sharp and shining blade. He held it at her throat.

Myrrha ran. Taking nothing with her but the clothes on her back, she slipped past the guards and out into the night. Her father followed. The darkness cloaked her, and by morning she was far away.[15]

Soon afterwards, her father died by his own hand.[16]

II

I woke to find her gone. All the next day I waited for her to return. Since the second hour of her life we had not been apart

for so long. But she didn't return. I was never to see her again,
though I did not know that then. Only when she was gone did
I understand that what she had told me was the simple truth.

I had failed her as surely as if I had led her to her father's
rooms myself. I tried to find her—had scouts and messengers sent
all over the kingdom. One by one they came back, with no news
of her. There had been sightings at the beginning, but nothing
since. And then the last messenger returned, from Sabaea, with a
story so incredible that I hesitate to relate it here. But it is the only
end I have for her, the only epilogue. This is what he claimed
he had been told: she ran for many nights and days in terror
for her life. Knowing that she could never return to her father's
house, she wandered far away. She grew heavy with child, her
own father's child. (If only I could have been with her. I was
scarcely past middle age. I could have supported her, carried
her, guarded her while she slept. I would have begged food for
her. I would have brought her everything she asked for.)

As the time for giving birth drew closer, Myrrha was heard
to pray. She wanted death but was afraid to die. Living was
beyond her now. She asked the gods to change her form. Her
bones became hard wood. Sap, not blood, flowed through veins.
The trunk of the balsam tree she was becoming grew up past her
womb, her breasts, and her neck, and covered her face. She wept
and her tears became the bitter myrrh that dripped from the tree.
And from the balsam tree her son was born. The nymphs washed
him in his mother's perfumed tears and laid him on the forest
floor. "People say the child is very lovely," said the messenger.
And then he left and I was alone without her. I have heard
nothing of her in all the years since then. I am an old woman
now, but this I shall remember as long as I live.

Notes

[1] The readily available ancient sources for this story are few. Ovid tells it at greatest length, at *Metamorphoses* 10.298–518. The details of his version are repeated here, though the interpretation is different. In Ovid, Myrrha's father is the Assyrian king, Cinyras, son of

Pygmalion's daughter, Paphos. (Pygmalion was king of Cyprus.) Apollodorus (3.14.3–5) also knows of a Cinyras, who founded the city of Paphos on Cyprus. He married the daughter of the king of Cyprus, Pygmalion. Her name was Metharme. They had five children, including Adonis. Apollodorus also tells another story of Adonis' birth, wherein Adonis is born of the balsam tree as he is in Ovid's tale. His mother is Smyrna transformed, and his father is her father, Theias, king of Assyria. Clearly there was much confusion. Antoninus Liberalis (*Transformationes* 34) has Theias and Smyrna also. Smyrna gives birth prematurely from the shock of having her identity discovered by her father. She is then granted her tree shape by an indulgent Zeus. Antoninus' tale is otherwise similar to Ovid's. Hyginus (*Fabulae* 58) and Fulgentius (*Mythologiae* 3.8, though this is a late source, probably from the sixth century C.E.) also tell the tale.

2 See *Reaching for Solutions* (Report of the Special Advisor to the Minister of National Health and Welfare on Child Sexual Abuse in Canada) (Ottawa, 1990).

3 See Amy Richlin, "Reading Ovid's rapes," in Amy Richlin, ed., *Pornography and Representation in Greece and Rome* (New York, 1992), 158–79. Richlin discusses various strategies to render the text of Ovid's *Metamorphoses* manageable for women who read it today.

4 It is certainly true that a child can claim to want to marry her father when she grows up, and may therefore wish for the removal of her mother. If the mother then disappears through divorce or death, the child may feel responsible and guilty. It could be the case that Myrrha's story conceals nothing more sinister than this.

5 This may have been so, in reality. There may once have been communities in which the heir to the throne was the husband of the current king's daughter. There must have been more than one king, who, when his wife died (he would have had the right to rule only through her) sought to prolong his rule by marrying his own daughter, rather than accepting the suit of other would-be kings. In the story of Myrrha, it is Myrrha herself who rejects the suitors, but in the story of Hippodamia, for instance, it is Hippodamia's father, Oenomaus, king of Pisa, who refuses to allow her to marry, eliminating all her suitors, until Pelops happens along. Pelops causes Oenomaus to die in a chariot race, marries Hippodamia and takes over the kingdom. (See Apollodorus, *Epitome* 2.3–10.) If there ever were such communities, they existed long before Ovid lived. In his time (43 B.C.E.–17 C.E.) there were no

societal standards that would have rendered father-daughter incest acceptable.

[6] These words are essentially Ovid's, at *Metamorphoses* 10.324–34. In his story they are part of Myrrha's "justification" of her passion for her father. In Ovid, her thoughts are troubled, not because she has been frequently raped by her father, as here, but because she is overwhelmed with desire for him.

[7] This metaphor for sleep is taken from elsewhere in Ovid's *Metamorphoses* (11.592–677). The Cimmerian country, a mythical place, seems to be located near Scythia. The cave where Sleep lives is always dark and always quiet, so his slumber is rarely disturbed. His thousand sons include one who appears in dreams as humans, one who appears as animals, and one who appears as inanimate objects.

[8] In Ovid's story, when the suitors come, Cinyras does not know what to do and so asks Myrrha whom she wants to marry. When she cries and cannot answer, he asks her what kind of husband she wants, and she answers, because she is in love with him, "one just like you" (11.315–17 and 356–67).

[9] These are in fact the words that Ovid gives Myrrha to say. They fit these different circumstances equally well, since girls who are abused by their fathers do frequently feel affection for them.

[10] The nurse is unnamed in the ancient sources.

[11] The anemone, a common springtime flower in this part of the world, is associated with this story in Ovid, though in a very different way. When Myrrha's child, Adonis, dies as a young man, his blood becomes a dark red anemone.

[12] Ovid describes Myrrha as silent and tearful, though he is referring to a specific situation, namely a discussion with her father about whom she will marry. This is before her lust for him has been satisfied (11.359–60).

[13] In Ovid, Myrrha remains stubbornly silent while the nurse begs her to reveal what is wrong. She asks whether Myrrha is mad, bewitched, or targeted by angry gods. She has remedies for all three situations. Myrrha's continued silence leads the nurse to assume that she is in love, and she promises not to tell her father if Myrrha tells her all about it. Myrrha begs her to go away. Pleading turns to threats: the nurse will have to tell Cinyras about his daughter's suicide attempt. Finally, with much difficulty, Myrrha

whispers, "My mother is a lucky woman to have a husband like my father," and the nurse understands what she is trying to say (11.383–425). Ovid's writing is masterly here. He describes, exquisitely, the love of the nurse for the child she nursed as a baby, and the teenager's impatience with an annoying old woman, who nevertheless offers the only comfort she is likely to find.

[14] I have made a change here. In Ovid, the nurse goes to see the king, but tells him that a beautiful young woman, of Myrrha's age, desires him. He insists that she be brought to him. The nurse's plan, which she then carries out, is to take Myrrha to her father's bedroom in darkness, so that he will lie with her without knowing who she is.

[15] In Ovid's story Myrrha also leaves at night, but her father wants to kill her not, as here, because she has betrayed him, but because he has found out that his bed partner is his own daughter.

[16] Ovid does not record Cinyras' death, but Hyginus (*Fabulae* 242) includes him in a list of men who committed suicide. Antoninus Liberalis' Theias also kills himself.

Hypermnestra's Story

This story[1] reflects a time of terrible tension in a Greek woman's life—the time of her marriage, at which her life changed
profoundly. Never truly a person in her own right, she went
from being a member of her father's family, with an identity
taken only from him, to being a member, on sufferance, of her
husband's family, who may have been strangers to her. If we
examine what is known about the day of the gamos, the ritual
transference of a bride from her father's household to her
husband's, in fifth-century Athens, this is what we find: the
bride's hair is shorn; she undergoes a bath in water drawn
from a sacred spring; she sits veiled during a final feast with
her family; when it is dark she is taken, by her husband and his
"best man," in a carriage to the husband's home; she is introduced to her mother-in-law and is placed under the protection
of the gods of her new household; she is led to the marriage
chamber, where the marriage is consummated; a doorkeeper
guards the door. There is a lot for the bride (who is perhaps
fifteen years of age) to be anxious about here, even if the
undertones of abduction and imprisonment are lost on her: she
has no choice in whom she is marrying; she is suddenly dis-
engaged from the only family she has ever known; she must
give up her virginity to a strange man.[2] Mythical women generally travel far from home when they marry, since myth tends
to deal with kings and queens and princesses, and although
there are many kings they tend not to live next door to each
other. So severance from the family of origin is often not only
abrupt but total, as it is for Procne of Athens when she is

married to Tereus of Thrace.³ In a little-known story about Penelope the tension and trauma of the wedding day are reflected: her father Icarius has given her only reluctantly to Odysseus and begs him to settle in Laconia, where he, Icarius, lives. Odysseus refuses and drives away with his bride. Icarius follows them in his own chariot. There is a showdown and Penelope is forced to choose between her father and her husband. Penelope chooses her husband.⁴ But in the story told below, forty-nine of the fifty daughters of Danaüs, the sisters of Hypermnestra, choose their father. Hypermnestra's decision is different, and that decision forms the basis of her story. It is strangely apt that for all time Hypermnestra's sisters have been referred to as "the daughters of Danaüs" or "the Danaïds" (which has the same meaning) by storytellers, since this is precisely the identity they choose. They are nobody's wife and, with one exception,⁵ nobody's mother.

Hypermnestra chooses her husband, Lynceus, over her father, refusing to kill him as her father instructs her to do, but this decision, too, is fraught with problems. She is put on trial for her disobedience.

Despite its ancient context, the story has much to interest a modern audience. The fifty women are opinionated and dynamic. They quite reasonably resent the idea that their fifty cousins wish to marry them and are not in the least deterred by the fact that the women are unwilling. The ancient sources suggest that they do not wish to marry anyone, but that they are particularly averse to this violent and lustful group of men and are not shy about saying so. They are talented women: they apparently row themselves from Egypt to Argos; they teach the Argives how to sink wells; and in Aeschylus' Suppliant Women, the only surviving play of four that he wrote on this subject, they force the king of Argos to fight a war on their behalf by threatening to act like ordinary women in a time of trial and hang themselves! Danaüs is an enigma. Is he willing to protect his daughters from their over-enthusiastic cousins because they want him to, or is it because an oracle has told him that he will be murdered by a son-in-law? Hypermnestra is presented, in the ancient sources, as bold and thoughtful enough to reject blind *obedience to her father in favour of doing what she feels is right.*

It must be noted that elements of this story are fiercely misogynist. Its message for men about to marry is that their brides, apparently docile and externally so beautiful, conceal the ability to bring ruin on their new families. There is a suggestion that women might get together and plan destruction and thus are particularly dangerous in large numbers. Amongst the Greeks of the classical period, who have not managed to conceal their misogyny from even their greatest enthusiasts, girls were handed over to their husbands with a dowry. In other words, their fathers paid their husbands to take them away. In myth, there are very many stories of suitors being willing to undergo ordeals of strength, endure tremendous peril, or display great wealth to win a wife. This story marks the change-over of systems in myth. It is told how Danaüs, left with daughters who were difficult to marry off since they had murdered their first husbands, held footraces for suitors, who would be excused from paying the customary bride-price. There were few takers.[6] It was probably once a well-known part of the story that Danaüs then offered specially made shields as prizes to victorious runners. The snag? Each winner had to take a daughter as well. Perhaps this transition in myth represents a real-life transition from a time when women were seen as a prize rather than a burden, and men paid for the privilege of marrying, to the dowry system with which we are familiar.

The task of the daughters of Danaüs in the Underworld, carrying water in leaky pots to fill a jar with holes, has intrigued many. What are they doing? Filling bridal baths? Bringing rain to Argos? Attempting to purify themselves in vain like Lady Macbeth? Undergoing a test of virginity that they can only fail?[7] Descriptions of their eternal task, a chore that is undone again as soon as it is done, bring to mind the work that often falls to women in our own time—washing floors, clothes, and dishes that are instantly dirty again, filling the refrigerator with food that is all too soon eaten, and tidying rooms that fall back into immediate disarray. Most of us know how it feels to be a Danaïd.

By patriarchal standards, the daughters of Danaüs are the ultimate in useless women—caught in a loop of their own making, they are not virgins, but they have no husbands and no chance of producing children. Is this, perhaps, what they are being punished for, as much as the murders they have committed? Better for everyone, the message seems to have been, if women accept the life pattern determined for them.[8]

In the story as told here, Hypermnestra and her sisters are in a double bind typical of Greek myth. In order to please their father they must kill their husbands, and so ruin their chances of leading a normal life. Forty-nine of them do so. Though Hypermnestra does not take action as provocative or as contradictory to the female norms as her sisters', trouble is still forthcoming. She is rejected by her father, but never truly accepted by her husband. Nor can she accept him, since he avenges his brothers' deaths by killing her sisters. The father she once adored she begins to despise, and she is acutely aware that through the choices she made she has rendered herself choiceless. She has saved the life of a man who lives to do her great wrong, and she must be his wife. Perhaps, after all, she should have listened to her father.

"Often I tear my Sidonian veils"[9]

The beginning of my story is a quarrel. Twin brothers fought for land. And from that quarrel came flight, war, murder, betrayal. The story has not ended yet. My sisters languish in the Underworld, forever seeking to wash the blood from their hands.

I am Hypermnestra, the eldest of fifty sisters. Our father is Danaüs. His brother is Aegyptus. They are sons of Belus, who was king of Egypt. When Belus died they could not agree on the division of the land. Aegyptus did not wish to reign only in Arabia, the territory that had been assigned to him. He planned that his fifty sons would marry my sisters and me—the fifty daughters of Danaüs. He knew that if this was accomplished, all Libya and the broad plains of Egypt would be theirs when my father died. My father wanted none of it; he refused his brother's offer, but he was afraid for his own life and for ours.[10]

His refusal came as no surprise, at least to us. Since childhood we had been warned against marriage. How there comes a day when a girl must leave her mother, and her sisters, and her father. How she must sit, veiled and apart from them, through one last meal in her father's house. How she is disconnected from them, and becomes a stranger to her own kin. How she is taken to a new place, her husband's home, where she must lie on a bed in a locked room and wait for him to come to her. It is a kind of death. She is never again the same.

My sisters and I grew up in Egypt. You would have thought us Egyptian. Our hair was dark and our eyes also. We dressed in the Egyptian style. But our lineage is Greek. We are descended from Io, who was loved by Zeus. Loved so much that she was obliged to flee Greece, pestered by the gadfly that was Hera's revenge.[11] If there had been rain, to give relief, she could have stayed. But Argos was dry like a corpse turned to dust. Io came to Egypt, to Memphis on the many-mouthed Nile. Her son, Epaphus, was born to her there, and when Hera, still implacable, stole the child, Io's tears flowed so abundantly that the river flooded for the first of many times. Epaphus, returned at last to his mother, grew to manhood. His daughter was Libya and her son was Belus, my grandfather. We, like Io, were exiles from our homeland, and we came to Greece, to Argos, the place of her birth, to escape a marriage we wanted no part of.

We landed, fifty women and one man, our father, on a shore where there was sacred ground. A row of stone images greeted us. We recognised them, as Danaüs had taught us, as the gods of Greece. Poseidon we knew well. We had travelled across his seas in the first fifty-oared galley, one of us at every oar. Poseidon was my father's grandfather. He had looked after us throughout our lives, but to the Argives he was cruel—their rivers ran dry because they had chosen Hera over him.[12] Athena we knew. She had shared her skill with my father so that he could build the boat, and she will have no man as her husband. And Zeus, who is her father, and whom she loves and does not leave, we also knew. He was our saviour and our protector.

We had heard of Aphrodite, though I had not felt her power and have not still. She seems to me a mere euphemism for the lust of men and the violence with which they satisfy it.

Pelasgus[13] was king of Argos in those days when we sailed from Egypt. The Argives came to meet our ship in chariots of war. They are a violent people, these kinsfolk of ours. We had no swords. What danger did they imagine we could offer them? We were women. We carried suppliant branches in our hands.

"Dark ships they have, and strongly built."

It was our plan to ask Pelasgus for sanctuary. Behind us on the seas were sailing the fifty sons of Aegyptus, my father's brother. They were enraged and insulted because we daughters of Danaüs did not wish to become their wives. They planned to force us to their beds. Their father did not sail with them, but gave them orders to return to him with Danaüs dead or not return at all. He wished his own brother dead. I find that hard to comprehend. They say that brothers rarely love each other. If so, then they are not like sisters.

King Pelasgus was much troubled. Fifty women landed on his shores, draped themselves over the statues of his gods, and threatened to hang themselves there in the sanctuary if he did not agree to defend them against the sons of Aegyptus! There is not much about my life that makes me want to laugh out loud, but when I think of Pelasgus standing baffled on the strand, I cannot resist. Hours before he had been an admired and confident king. But nothing like this had ever happened to him. What would his people say if he risked a war for strangers, women no less, dark-skinned women with painted eyes? And only because they did not wish to marry. All Greek women marry. It is what they are for. How would his people feel about dying on our behalf when the crazed and brutal sons of Aegyptus arrived in their harbour?

But fifty women dead, dangling from the statues of his gods, their corpses rotting in the sun! This vision must have rendered him near senseless. The sanctuary forever polluted. The kingdom defiled. Miasma so heavy you could feel it in the air.[14] Taste it.

What, precisely, was the man to do?

"Yet subject to men would I never be"

We remained in Argos. The Argives took a vote on it.[15] That was their way. We were housed in the royal palace, all of us and our father. Where else could fifty women have stayed but in its vast halls? Then Pelasgus talked to us. "Marry your cousins," he said. "You will save yourselves much trouble if you do. Their claim on you is just. You say you are Greeks; then do as Greek women do and marry your kin."[16] It was more plea than advice. "We will not marry," we answered. "Our cousins are rude and violent men. We will not marry them or any others."

"Father, I am spent by fear"

There were many ships when the sons of Aegyptus came, more than the Argives had imagined. My sisters and I saw them loom, dark on the horizon, and felt terror flow deep. I heard my sisters cry: "They are mad men, Father; they will hurt us."

"Father, they are worse than dogs."

"Father, I am spent by fear."

"I would sooner die, Father, than have a man touch me."

"Father, where can I hide?" The Argives came out bravely, with their horses and curved chariots. But their fear showed. The Egyptians, to them, looked like gods of another world, with their flesh black as Erebus, their linen tunics radiant white. Pelasgus died in the fighting. Our reluctant champion; dead on our behalf.

"Let us offer for the Argives good prayers"

The Argives needed a leader. Without one they were like lost children, dumbly clutching anything that was secure. My father was used to kingship. It rested lightly on his shoulders and he wore it well. Before we knew it, the Argives were being steered by him, guided to new decisions.

The plan was to retreat to their citadel, now called Larisa after Pelasgus' virgin daughter. To hide behind their walls and leave the Egyptians on the shore. The Argives gathered what they could and brought in everyone who would come—old women who had never left their huts before, wide-eyed dirty children, full-cheeked country girls.

"Never fruitful water might I see again"

But there was one big flaw in this plan. Larisa was dry. We needed Io and her tears. There were no springs on the citadel and the Argives did not know how to sink wells.[17] In times of peace it was the task of watercarriers to bring water in from the rivers in the countryside, though even they were all too often dry. An endless stream of women carried water to the houses. At first when we all withdrew into Larisa, the women went as usual to find water. Only some came back, and they with terrible stories of the Egyptians' brutality. The elders among the Argives conferred and spoke to my father. The situation seemed hopeless. They could last only days without water. Could he could not encourage us to wed these cousins of ours? It was natural that we should one day marry and have children, beautiful dusky girls like us. Surely a marriage celebration of immense proportions would be an event long talked about in the Greek world—preferable to a quick siege or a bloody battle? They were offering him a part in Argive history.

As luck would have it, several of the sons of Aegyptus came to him too. They would desist, they claimed, from their violence against Danaüs and his new-found allies, compatriots, whatever they were, if Danaüs handed us over with no more fuss. My father could taste power. The richest kingdom in the land almost his but about to slip away. Imagine, the people named Danaäns after him.[18] "Very well," he said. "My daughters shall be the brides of my brother's sons."[19] He chose his words carefully, you note. Even then, I think he knew what he would bid us do.

I loved my father, dearly, very dearly, but I could see his weaknesses. He craved power. But he was a squeamish man who wanted others to do his dirty work for him. He wanted to rid himself of his brother's sons but keep his own hands clean. And he wanted to be king of Argos.

In many ways we were not like Greek women, my sisters and I—and I am not referring to our hairstyles or our eyes. In Egypt before we sailed for Argos, we had taken up arms ourselves against the sons of Aegyptus.[20] And what Greek women could have rowed a penteconter half across the Earth, as we had done? Later, my sisters were to go out alone into the Argive countryside and find new springs. They would show the Argives how to sink new wells. My father had played fair. He had not wanted us to marry, to submit ourselves to men, but he had taught us how to do for ourselves what husbands might have done for us.[21]

He spent some time deciding which daughter would be the bride of which cousin. A list of killers and their victims. He had his fun. Sthenele would murder Sthenelus because their names were similar. Theano would murder Phantes because their mothers were both Naiads.[22] He was not without a sense of humour.

"Before that, ravisher, would you die"

The day before the wedding our father gathered us together. He gave each of us a knife, a small, delicate, lethal thing, and instructions:

"Hide the knife in your clothing. When you retire to your bridal chamber, submit to your husband. He will give you no choice. But then, when he falls asleep, plunge the knife into his heart. When he is dead, cut off his head and place it outside the door of your chamber." Some of my sisters tittered nervously. Others began to whimper in fear.

"Do you swear that you will do this?" Our father asked this question of each one of us in turn.

"Yes, Father," each of us replied. My sister Oeme hid her dagger in her thick black hair.

Danaüs had taken over Pelasgus' palace on the citadel. It was easy enough. We had been invited there as guests but had made it our own. And after Pelasgus' death at the hands of the Egyptians, my father had begun to sit at the dead king's place at table, and later to sleep in his bed.

There was one long corridor in the building's west wing, which had once been storerooms, but which later had been set aside for guests. The rooms were high, airy, comfortable, and fifty in number. My father had a bridal bed placed in each.

On the day of the weddings, the sons of Aegyptus came to the palace with their attendants. But their armies were nowhere to be seen.

"We come in peace," said one of them to my father; Chthonius his name was. "Violence and marriage do not blend."

You think not, cousin?

"But I, how shall I act?"

Argos had never seen such revelry.[23] The celebration of fifty marriages all in one day calls for the killing of many fattened beasts and the flowing of much wine. All day the sun shone splendidly on the parched earth, and as darkness fell hundreds of lamps trimmed with Argive gold were lit in the palace courtyard. The altar fires burned well into the night. I cannot readily describe how it was. Neither day nor night, it was a new time—a time for surprises, a killing time. I felt the knife, hidden beneath my breasts by my clothing. Its point moved against my skin as if it would impale me. My sister Gorgophone, the one best loved by me, for we shared the same mother,[24] caught my eye as we were led, by the light of still more oil lamps, down the long corridor of bridal chambers. She looked very lovely; her women had braided her hair with flowers. She stood so tall and proud. She smiled at me; a sly, slow smile of collusion. I smiled back.

I was to wait in my chamber for Lynceus. That was his name, Lynceus. I tried saying it out loud, practised whispering it as I thought a harlot might. I wondered about him, this Lynceus. Was he a powerful man or a frail one? Under different circumstances should I have been proud of him, or ashamed? I would like you to believe that I had every intention of doing as my father had instructed me. I had always obeyed my father. I would kill this Lynceus as soon as he slept.

I have heard of brides waiting for hours in the bridal chamber, while their new husbands consorted with the slave girls or drunk themselves into oblivion. But not that night. I heard shouting, and some singing, the heavy footfalls of men in the corridor. Some of them argued with their servants, knocking them out of the way in their haste. I could hear them bursting into bedrooms all around me. I could hear men everywhere, but not a sound from any of my sisters. Some were bold like Gorgophone, but others were so much younger, children still. I imagined them waiting in terror for the rape of their bodies to begin.

One set of footsteps came all the way along the hall, to the rooms right at the end. It was Lynceus coming to me. He did not stumble, or shout, and I guessed he had drunk only a moderate amount of wine. I did not look him in the eye even when he lifted my veil. You do not want to know the eyes of the man you will murder.

He spoke to me. "I understand you do not wish to marry me and I understand why. I will spare you the ordeal you fear. I have neither need nor desire to force a reluctant bride." That was all he said. I can't even tell you if he looked at me to say it.

I know the rumours that have flown since that night: that I enjoyed the weight of his body on mine so much that I wanted more of him and therefore did not kill. That I felt the power of Aphrodite and fell in love with him and therefore did not kill.

The truth is simpler. He did nothing to me. I did not kill him because there was no reason to kill him.[25]

He removed the golden bracelets that he wore around his wrists and placed them by the marriage bed. He removed his own sandals. Then he lay down and fell asleep. I looked at him at last. So trusting, he. I removed the dagger from the folds of my dress. I held it in my hand, weighing its deadliness. Strangely, I thought with some amusement of Pelasgus and the dilemma with which we had presented him. What to do? To kill this man, my husband, as my father ordered, or to help him escape? Or else to turn the dagger on myself? It was an easy choice.

All around me I could hear the groans of dying men. I touched Lynceus' arm and shook him awake. "Stand up. Unless you leave, your sleep will be eternal."[26] I showed him the dagger. He seemed to understand immediately what was happening and ran from the room without glancing back. I noted then, and I stress now, that he made no attempt to save his brothers.[27]

"Darkness flutters in my heart"

I ask you to imagine the scene. A long corridor, bedchambers all down one side. Lamps extinguished. One by one the daughters of Danaüs, drenched in Egyptian blood, place the severed heads of their husbands outside their doors. Dawn breaks; at its first light Danaüs arrives. He walks along the passageway, noting and counting the heads. The edges of his cloak trail in blood and soak it up. He puts his hand out onto the wall to steady himself, so as not to slip in it. He is pleased. The heads seem all to be there. It is as if they will combine to form some hideous monster. He likes the expressions of horror in the dead men's eyes. Some of them had woken before they died. He arrives at the end of the passageway. The final two doors, Gorgophone's and mine, are further back than the others. Her husband's head is there, on the ground, its blood clotting in pools beside it. Its eyes look towards my door, the last door, and are surprised,

for there is no blood there. There is a space where Lynceus'
head should be. But then, this is a story of surprises.

Before I knew it I was in chains behind locked doors. On trial
for not murdering my husband. My father was king by then.
He could do anything he liked.

"Gladden this earth with waters brilliant and rich"

My sisters were kept busy. They hardly had time to ponder
their peculiar state—defiled but husbandless. My father sent
them out daily to find water. He had no fears for their safety.
The Egyptian soldiers had sailed back home and no Argive men
would risk approaching the husband-killers. My sister Amymone was raped by our ancestor Poseidon, they say, and as
recompense he struck a rock at Lerna with his trident and a
new stream appeared there. It is never dry, even on the hottest
days of summer.[28] My sisters also sank the wells in Argos for
which they are justly famous. So you see, my family repaid the
Argives for giving us sanctuary when we needed it. Argos is
well watered, now.

There were bodies and heads to bury too. The bodies they
buried under the walls of the citadel. The heads they took to
the newly made marshes at Lerna, threw them in, and watched
them sink.[29]

"May they grant justice"

I was freed before long from my prison. My father had me
tried: he ranted on and on about betrayal, but if truth be told he
seemed to be more indignant than angry—as if by refusing to
do as he ordered I had made my sisters, and him, look more
guilty than they were. If we had all joined in with his plan, the
question of whether or not it was an appropriate action would
never have been raised. I was grateful for the good sense of the
Argives, who would have none of his nonsense. "You cannot,"
they said, "find someone guilty of not committing a crime."[30]
He felt that they were laughing at him, and his pride was hurt.

He was king, and no one should laugh at a king. He and I were not reconciled.

"My life is dirges"

What happened next was very terrible. Lynceus, whom I had saved, hunted down my sisters and killed each one of them. It was easy enough. They had enjoyed the freedom of the countryside so much during their water-carrying days that they went off alone or in small groups often. One by one he killed them. Like my father, he was obsessed with the pairings. He knew exactly which sister had murdered which brother. As each died he would address her personally. "Adite," he would say, "I am killing you because you killed Menalces. Callidice, I am killing you because you killed Pandion." It took hours, and no one stopped him. I think the Argives were glad. The non-virgin, husbandless daughters of Danaüs had cost them lives and were now a huge embarrassment. Incredibly, my father had been trying to marry them off. It was his plan to hold footraces, offer a valuable prize to the winner each time, and throw in a daughter. He had had forty-eight elaborate shields made as the bait. Neither Amymone, whose belly was swollen with Poseidon's child, nor I were to be offered. The whole affair was laughable. Who would have taken them?[31] I am surprised at how lightly I can speak of my once-beloved sisters—Gorgophone, Automate, Scaea, my youngest sister Hyperippe, and the rest. Lynceus tells me sometimes, in his chilling way, that Hyperippe died the hardest.[32]

My dead sisters do not rest. In Tartarus[33] their ceaseless task is to carry water, as if to the Argives in their citadel, but every vessel leaks when it is filled. Perhaps by sprinkling water on the floor of Tartarus they will send rain to Argos, to keep her rivers flowing, by some magic that I do not understand. Though there are times when I think my tears alone can do just that. All the water in the world cannot cleanse my sisters' hands of blood. All the rivers in the world cannot wash the earth of Argos clean. There is simply too much blood.

The worst, the very worst, I have saved until last to tell you. It is this: Danaüs my father whom I loved, who became the foolish, haughty king of Argos, gave me back to Lynceus, as his wife. This was his punishment for me. The Argives could not stop him, for all their voting, since it was by their wish that we had been married to the sons of Aegyptus in the first place.[34] And so I am the wife of the man whom I could have killed but chose to save, the man who slaughtered all my sisters. I lie with him every night. He does not spare me now.

The final surprise in this sordid, bloody tale will be my father's. The last laugh will be on him. He fancies himself reconciled to Lynceus, despite my dead sisters (now there's betrayal for you), and has named him his successor to the throne of Argos. But Lynceus plans to kill him, as he promised his father Aegyptus long ago that he would. He will indeed become king of Argos, and our son, Abas, born of lust (Lynceus') and loathing (mine), will rule after him. It has been prophesied that Abas will be the father of twin boys, who will detest one another in their mother's womb and after, and the cycle—of flight, war, murder, and betrayal—will begin again.[35]

Father, let me follow you to the dark, to the black dead.[36]

But give me a lamp to light my way.

Notes

[1] Aeschylus wrote a trilogy of plays, plus a satyr play, about Hypermnestra, her sisters, and their father. Only one play from the trilogy, *Suppliant Women,* almost certainly the first, survives. It tells of the arrival of Danaüs and his daughters on Argive shores, the predicament of the Argive king, Pelasgus, and the subsequent arrival of the sons of Aegyptus, although none of the sons appears in the play. Various attempts have been made to reconstruct the other plays, based on little evidence. Surely Aeschylus told of the daughters of Danaüs being somehow coerced into marrying their cousins and Hypermnestra's refusal to kill her husband. It is thought that he went still further in the story, because there exists

a fragment of a speech by Aphrodite from one of the missing plays (quoted and so ascribed by Athenaeus at 13.600b), in which some of the properties of Eros (Love) are listed. A common view has been that Hypermnestra was put on trial for disobeying her father and not killing her husband, and that Aphrodite appeared at the trial and secured her acquittal on the grounds that love for a husband was such a powerful force. I have assumed that the trilogy dealt with the displacement of Pelasgus as king of Argos in favour of Danaüs. Perhaps he was discovered to be treacherous towards the Danaïds, only pretending to give sanctuary to them but in reality planning to hand them over to the sons of Aegyptus. Perhaps he died fighting on their behalf.

There are numerous other sources for sections or details of Hypermnestra's story. Several are ancient commentaries on other works, and thus difficult to find in English translation, but yet more problematic is the fact that no two sources seem to agree on any one aspect of the story. The only consistent features are that two brothers, Danaüs and Aegyptus, who are not friends, have, respectively, fifty daughters and fifty sons; that when the daughters marry the sons, they are ordered by Danaüs to kill their husbands on their wedding night; they do this with one exception—Hypermnestra spares the life of her husband, Lynceus.

Apollodorus, at 2.1.4–2.1, tells the story from start to finish, but though he lists all fifty daughters and their fifty husbands by name there is little detail otherwise. For the most part I have followed his outline, but his story includes the following elements: the king of Argos when the Danaïds arrive is Gelanor, who "handed over the kingdom" to Danaüs; the murderous daughters are purified of their crimes by Hermes and Athena; they are then married off, again, to the winners of athletic contests. There is no trial for Hypermnestra, and Apollodorus does not seem to know about the punishment of the Danaïds in the Underworld. Hyginus, at *Fabulae* 168, 169, 169A, and 170, shows that he knows the story of the quarrel between the brothers, the flight from Egypt, the seduction of Amymone, the remarriage of the Danaïds (to Argive men, and though races and shields enter the story, they do not do so in the context of these marriages), and their punishment after death.

Other sources for the story, some of which give details that contradict those used in the version told here, are Ovid, *Heroides* 14, which takes the form of a letter from Hypermnestra to Lynceus after she has spared his life; Pausanias 2.15.5–16.1 (Pausanias here tells us that "everyone knows" how Danaüs died and how Lynceus became king of Argos, but in fact those stories have survived only in barest outline), 2.19.3–6, 2.20.6, 2.21.1, 2.24.3, 2.25.4, and 3.12.2; Pindar, *Pythian Odes* 9.111–14; Aeschylus again, *Prometheus Bound* 851–73; and Horace, *Odes* 3.11.23–52.

The story of Amymone's encounter with Poseidon appears to have been the subject of Aeschylus' missing satyr play. It is also told by Propertius, at 2.45–50; Lucian, in *Dialogues of the Sea-Gods* 8; and Philostratus in *Imagines* 1.8.

² See Robert Garland, *The Greek Way of Life* (New York, 1990), 217–25.

³ See Philomela's story, chap. 1.

⁴ See Pausanias 3.20.10–11.

⁵ The exception is Amymone, an enigma in this tale because she can only sometimes be classified with the other sisters. The story goes that while she is out in the countryside searching for water for the Argives at her father's bidding, Poseidon discovers her, finds her lovely, and rapes her. In payment, Poseidon sticks his trident in the rock of Lerna, asks her to draw it out again, and when she does, causes three streams of water to flow from the holes left by its prongs. The new water supply is called the fountain of Amymone, after her. She later gives birth to Nauplius, who becomes a famous mythical navigator. Ancient writers tended to find stories like this amusing, and this one was a particular favourite for depiction in vase paintings. See n. 1, above, for the extant sources. Some writers include Amymone with the daughters of Danaüs who are married to second husbands and later punished in the underworld. Pindar, however, specifically states that Danaüs finds replacement husbands for forty-eight daughters.

⁶ See Pausanias 3.12.2. To be fair, Pindar suggests that the race idea worked so well that the daughters of Danaüs were all married off by noon!

⁷ Jane Ellen Harrison's views on the original significance of the Danaïds and the meaning of their actions in the Underworld are still worth reading. See *Prolegomena to the Study of Greek Religion* (Cambridge, 1908), 613–22, and *Themis* (Cambridge, 1912), 231–33, 529–30.

⁸ Amymone has a child, as we have seen; see n. 5, above. Hypermnestra bears one son, Abas, to Lynceus. The assumption that women are driven by the desire to bear children has led at least one commentator in modern times to assume that this is what caused Hypermnestra to spare Lynceus' life. The ancient sources

do not support this, unless the speech of Aphrodite mentioned in n. 1, which describes the fruitfulness of Earth, can be said to do so. None of the other daughters comes close to living the sort of life of which a classical Greek man would have approved. It is as if they belong to some earlier time, when women could choose to live free of men, but have blundered into a world in which what was once acceptable is now criminal.

[9] Unlike many female characters in Greek myth, the daughters of Danaüs have a voice in ancient literature. In Aeschylus' *Suppliant Women* they are, collectively, the main character. The headings above each section of this story are taken from their speeches in that play, though the context in which they are spoken in the play is not necessarily the context in which they are used here. I have used S.G. Bernadete's translation in *Aeschylus II,* ed. David Grene and Richmond Lattimore (New York, 1967).

[10] Some ancient versions of the story (all found only in scholiasts' notes) have Danaüs receive an oracle that tells him he will be in personal danger from or will even be killed by one or all of his daughters' husbands. This would be reason enough for him to be reluctant to let them marry. Told this way, the story resembles the story of the oracle given to Acrisius, the father of Danaë (and actually a descendant of Hypermnestra; see the family tree in n. 11, below), who, afraid that his grandson will kill him, refuses to allow his daughter to consort with men. See Danaë's story, chap. 11.

[11] Hera, Zeus' wife, is presented in myth as perpetually jealous of her husband's affairs with other goddesses and women. Apollodorus' story is that Zeus fell in love with Hera's priestess, Io. Io was disguised as a cow, but Hera, knowing full well who she was, asked to be given the cow as a gift. Though she kept Io carefully guarded, Zeus was able to continue his association with Io. Enraged, Hera sent a gadfly to sting the cow. Io wandered to the ends of the Earth in her attempts to escape the gadfly. She gave birth to Zeus' child, Epaphus, in Egypt. Hera arranged for the child to be stolen, and Io's wandering continued as she searched for her son. Eventually, she "became" Isis, a goddess worshipped in Egypt and elsewhere (2.1.3).

This is the Danaïds' family tree:

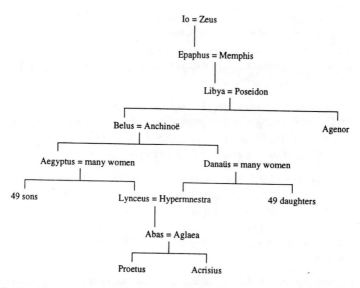

Io = Zeus

Epaphus = Memphis

Libya = Poseidon

Belus = Anchinoë   Agenor

Aegyptus = many women   Danaüs = many women

49 sons   Lynceus = Hypermnestra   49 daughters

Abas = Aglaea

Proetus   Acrisius

[12] Poseidon had a tendency to quarrel with other deities over guardianship of prized Greek lands. In the case of Argos, three river gods were appointed to decide whether Hera or Poseidon should be the patron. When they chose Hera, Poseidon retaliated by drying up the lands. In fact, though Argos was afflicted periodically by drought, it was one of Greece's most fertile regions.

[13] There is some confusion amongst ancient authors about who was king of Argos at the time of the Danaïds' arrival there. Although a Pelasgus is known as a king of Argos from other stories, Aeschylus may have invented his part in this legend. Other names given are Gelanor and Hellanor. Pausanias tells a story entirely different from Aeschylus': when Danaüs arrived in Argos, he and the reigning king, Gelanor, quarrelled over the throne. The people of Argos were to decide between them. Both candidates gave eloquent speeches and the people, unable to make up their minds, delayed making a decision until the following day. During the night, a wolf attacked a herd of cattle and killed its leading bull. The people decided that the wolf represented Danaüs and the bull Gelanor, who was therefore stripped of his kingship. See Pausanias 2.19.3.

[14] Miasma is the "fallout" of death undeserved, unexpiated, and unavenged. It can take the form of plague or barrenness of women or land. For instance, in Thebes when King Laius is killed and his murderer never found, miasma settles on the city and shows itself years later in the sickness and starvation that drive Oedipus to

consult Apollo to see what past action was their cause. See Jocasta's story, chap. 3. The possible consequences of fifty deaths in a sanctuary (traditionally, in a Greek sacred precinct no one was allowed to be born or die or engage in any other polluting act) are too terrible to contemplate.

[15] Aeschylus stresses that the Argive people (or at least the men), guided by the king, are accustomed to making decisions. They vote by show of hands. In this case, Danaüs tells us at *Suppliant Women* 608 that the air bristled with hands when the vote was taken.

[16] In fifth-century Athens marriage between cousins was quite normal, and in fact for a girl with no brothers it was unavoidable. Her family's wealth or property could only be kept in the family in this way. If Egyptian law conformed to Athenian law, then the sons of Aegyptus would have a legal claim on the daughters of Danaüs.

[17] See Strabo 8.6.8 and Hesiod's *Catalogue of Women,* fragment 128. The Danaïds may have originally been well-nymphs, as Jane Ellen Harrison suggested (see above, n. 7). A well is a very magical thing, resembling the vagina (much of the imagery in literary versions of this story is sexual), but also a giver of life and a passageway to the otherwise unreachable centre of the Earth.

[18] See Strabo 8.6.9. Originally the people called the Danaäns inhabited Argos, but the word is used by Homer as one of the names for the collected Greek forces in the Trojan war.

[19] The ancient sources are not forthcoming as to why Danaüs gave in and agreed to the marriage. Apollodorus writes only that the sons of Aegyptus begged him to set aside hostilities and let them marry their cousins. Only Hyginus and two scholiasts mention a siege. The idea that the Argives were worried that they would have insufficient water is from Robert Graves, *The Greek Myths,* vol. 1 (Harmondsworth, UK, 1960), 201–2. It is possible that in Aeschylus' version the king of Argos proved treacherous and that Danaüs was forced to change his position. I am assuming this plan is only made under great pressure, since it requires Danaüs' daughters to sacrifice their virginity and commit murder.

[20] Two lines of an epic poem called *Danais* survive that suggest the daughters of Danaüs themselves fought in Egypt against the sons of Aegyptus. The fragment is preserved by Clement of Alexandria, at *Stromateis* 4.9.989.

²¹ Lucian has Triton tell Poseidon that Danaüs brings his daughters up to be hardy and teaches them to fend for themselves. The once-common image of the Danaïds as frail, meek maidens is not supported by the sources.

²² Naiads are nymphs of springs and lakes and small rivers.

²³ Hyginus, in *Fabulae* 273, states that Danaüs staged games and singing contests to celebrate the weddings of his daughters. (This may refer to a second set of weddings, to come later.)

²⁴ This was Elephantis.

²⁵ What might Hypermnestra's reason have been for sparing Lynceus? A favourite motive among ancient writers and modern commentators alike is that she fell in love with him. But this is surely a tale more likely to be told by men than by women! According to Ovid, she acted out of "*timor et pietas*," fear and dutiful affection. Apollodorus states that she does not kill him because he respects her virginity, which is a logical position for her to take.

²⁶ Hypermnestra's words here are taken from Horace's version of the story.

²⁷ I have omitted here a portion of the story that is told by several authors—Lynceus and Hypermnestra signal to one another by light-ing beacons—he from Lyrceia to indicate that he has arrived there safely and she from Larisa, presumably to show she is alive. This would fit a version of the story in which the two are mutually enamoured, rather than the one told here.

²⁸ The stream, called Amymone, was real. If anything the land was over-watered, since Lerna was a swamp.

²⁹ A many-headed monster, the Hydra, usually said to be the offspring of Typhon and Echidna, was to emerge from the marshes at Lerna at a later mythological time. Heracles, a descendant of Hypermnestra, would kill it and use its gall to poison his arrows.

³⁰ Roberto Calasso, in *The Marriage of Cadmus and Harmony* (Toronto, 1994), 67–68, explains the (still paradoxical) significance of being charged with not committing the murder of one's hus-band.

³¹ As we have seen (n. 6, above), according to Pindar it worked very well. Hyginus puts the footraces in another context, but states

that the daughters of Danaüs married Argive men, and even had sons by them.

[32] Although various obscure sources mention the death of Danaüs, only the scholiast on Euripides' *Hecuba,* at 886, states that Lynceus kills both Danaüs and Hypermnestra's sisters. It is clear from Ovid that the sisters are dead, though nothing is said about how they died.

[33] Tartarus is a section of the Underworld reserved for those who are to be punished after death.

[34] Apollodorus states that Hypermnestra and Lynceus are reunited. To the best of my knowledge it has always been assumed that this reunion was welcomed on both sides.

[35] Abas will be the only son of Hypermnestra and Lynceus. His wife, Aglaea, will give birth to Proetus and Acrisius. The new cycle of disaster will include the events told in Danaë's story, chap. 11.

[36] I know of no story of Hypermnestra's death. Pausanias states at 2.21.2 that she shares a grave with Lynceus.

ELEVEN

Danaë's
Story

The plight of Danaë[1] has long been overshadowed by the adventures of her son, Perseus. His most famous quest was his divinely aided search for the home of the Gorgons, and the murder there of Medusa, whose glance, even after her death, could turn anyone who looked on her to stone.[2] Perseus' special talent is that he can kill her, and subsequently use her head successfully as a weapon, without ever looking at her himself. With the aid of the head he saves Andromeda from a dread sea monster and marries her. His story is a riot of fairy- tale motifs: the hero's rash promise, the wicked king with whom there is a score to be settled, the death of an ugly monster, the clever use of divine apparatus (he is given a cap that makes him invisible, sandals that enable him to fly, and a special pouch to keep the head in), and the rescue of the princess. These are glued together with some interesting characters, such as the fisherman Dictys and the feuding brothers, Acrisius (Perseus' grandfather) and Proetus. The women in the story are less prominent: there is Andromeda, waiting to be rescued, and her mother Cassiopeia, who hangs forever upside down in the sky as punishment for boasting of her daughter's beauty. There is the Gorgon, Medusa, whose role here is only to be killed, and her sisters. And there is Danaë.[3]

The Danaë of the story told below is not a conniving wo- man. She does not need to be. Like the circles of stones that haunt this tale, her story must come back to where it began. If her father is doomed to die at the hand of her son, then die he will, however outrageous the crimes he commits in the hope of avoiding his fate. That fate is inescapable. There is little for Danaë to do.

I have added here a recognition scene, not found in any ancient source. The story, once told from Danaë's point of view, demands it. If a child is "exposed," as both Danaë and her son are when Acrisius puts them in a box and lets it drift out to sea, she or he must come home again, and must be recognised by the parent who contrived the exposure. This recognition provides Danaë's satisfaction.[4]

Some doubt is expressed in this version of the story about the identity of Perseus' father. The candidates are the Sky God, Zeus, and Danaë's father's brother, Proetus. Proetus' affair with Danaë is well attested in the sources, but favoured among the ancients was the explanation that she gives her father for her pregnancy, namely that Zeus came to her in a golden shower, since of course Perseus is thus provided with a divine father. Many a young woman might have explained a surprise pregnancy by announcing that she had been divinely fertilised, either in true ignorance or to try to avoid some of the consequences of her predicament. In myth, as an excuse it rarely works. Semele (the mother of Dionysus)[5] wasn't believed either, though Leda seems to have been.[6] Acrisius certainly believes the child Perseus to have been fathered by his brother Proetus. It may be that, before the conception process and the male's role in it were fully understood, women were thought to be fertilised by moonbeams, or the rays of the sun or drops of rain. It is quite clear that at some level the mating of Zeus and Danaë represents the Sky fertilising the Earth. Whether the golden rain would be the Sky God's urine or his semen is less clear.

I

I have waited for this day for most of my life. On this day a man will die. It is my prayer that he does not die without seeing my face.

I am Danaë, daughter of Acrisius, king of Argos. My mother was Eurydice. My son is Perseus, of whom you have doubtless heard. Today, though he does not know it, my son will kill my father. This was foretold before ever he was born.

II

We are in Larissa, in Thessaly, as guests of King Teutamides. He is holding games in honour of his dead father. I am awkward at court after all these years of living with the island people. I feel ignorant, and tongue-tied. My face is weather lined, I know, and my hands are not smooth as they once were. I have mended too many nets for that. The girls of the court are sneering at me behind their cloaks. I hardly look like the daughter of a king. My son is not uncomfortable at all. He has charmed everyone here, and in a while, when the accident happens, they will be kindness herself. What is decreed by Fate, they will say, no man or woman, however resolved, can avoid.

I am seated in the royal enclosure with my son's wife, Andromeda, daughter of Cepheus and Cassiopeia, who were once king and queen of Joppa. We are alike, she and I. Her father played her false as mine did me.[7] She speaks little of our language and does not know what will happen today, though she senses my excitement.

Perseus, my son, is competing in a new contest today—the discus-throw. At running and jumping he will never be a champion, but he can throw a disc as far as any man alive.[8]

III

The foot race is over. So too the long jump. My son has done well enough. Not that it matters. It is the discus that counts. He will be the last to throw. The discus is made of stone and is heavy enough to kill a man. If you kill a man with a stone, there is no blood, so they say.[9] My son knows about stones: his first toys were the stones on the floor of our underground prison; as he grew older and stronger in the fisherman's hut by the sea he learned to send beach pebbles skimming over the waves, further and further out from the land. He has just one more stone to throw.[10]

My son stands ready. His hair is golden. His dark naked body glistens with oil. He is alert and unsmiling, his whole being concentrated on the throw. He holds the disc in his right hand behind him, twists his body sideways and down, turns on his right foot, and lets the disc fly upward and away. So powerful is his throw that it soars over the markers of the other contestants, still high in the air. The stadium falls silent as the wind picks it up, and it sails far off course. An old man is standing in the crowd. He is here, so he thinks, to escape his fate. To avoid the death at the hand of his only grandson that has been prophesied to him. He knows his grandson lives and has come to the mainland, but he believes him to be in Argos, many miles from Larissa. That man is my father.

IV

I was a child when this all began. Acrisius' only child. He was king of all the Argolid when I was born. In those days it was all one kingdom, ruled from Argos. He shared the throne with his brother Proetus, each ruling for a year at a time, as their father, Abas, had decreed, with no thought past one generation. Not an arrangement, this, to cause brothers to love each other.

There is one thing that kings need above all others. And that is sons. My father had none. He consulted oracle upon oracle, asking of each the same question: How can I ensure the birth of a son? He drank potions of eggs in honey and rubbed himself with oils and ointments. His bed chamber was a shrine to fertility, filled with amulets and goddess-charms.

As I grew older, I became accustomed to his loathing of me. My mother he merely despised. She grew old with sadness long before her time. But me, he hated. I sat at table with him where a son should have been, and he never forgot it for a moment. If he talked to me, it was only to be cruel. His brother Proetus, his twin, but younger by nearly a day, was a kind man, or so he seemed to me. He showed me fondness where my father showed me none. They had quarrelled all their lives, everyone said. They had fought even in the womb, both wishing to be the first born. They were alike to look at but not otherwise. My uncle was tender with me. As a child I sat on his knee and kissed his cheeks above his red beard. He laughed his soft laugh and called me his darling. As I grew older I still loved him. And I did not protest at what he did to me when we were alone. It seemed, because I loved him so much, a grand thing that he should take pleasure in me. Even now, I cannot be angry with him for it. It was all I had. Sometimes he wept for love of me. And if his eyes were troubled, as they often were, I thought it was because of some sadness connected to my father. "Your father and I are kin but not friends," he told me once. "Anything that brings me joy he will make an end to." Then I was afraid.

One day, the world changed. My father's year as king ended and he refused to relinquish the throne. My uncle left Argos. When next I heard of him, he had married a Lycian woman and with her father's troops[11] he had come to claim the kingdom he considered his. Many died though there was no clear victor, and at last, after many months of fear, it was agreed that the kingdom should be divided. My father would continue to rule at Argos. My uncle would build a great palace at Tiryns and rule his portion of the realm from there. The stone walls encircling Tiryns now, which were built during his reign, are the work of the one-eyed giants.[12] They say the walls will never fall. They are unscalable by armies and by gods alike.

V

My father's chagrin at his lack of a son increased now a thousandfold. More oracles consulted, as many answers. But one gave him news that he had not heard before. He would have no son, for all his goose grease and his potions. But one child, a boy, would be born to me, and that child would kill him.

Some men might have made a show of caring, of claiming that they loved their daughter too much to condemn her easily to a life of solitude so that she would bear no child. Even that was beyond him. He had a dungeon carved out of the earth, only an arm's length of it above the ground. And he locked me in there, with just one woman to look after me. Oh, I had the finest of clothing, but no one to see me in it, and salves for my face, but no chance of a man ever kissing my lips.[13] At one end of the chamber, an opening above the ground, too small for escape, let in the sunlight and the air and, sometimes, the rain.[14]

When my body changed I did not know what was happening to me, and had the woman not told me, I would have been altogether surprised by the birth of my child. He was golden haired when he was born and his eyes were bluer than the sky. I nursed him myself, and named him Perseus, a good name, I think.[15]

From one winter through till the end of the next we kept him hidden. The guards who brought us our food could not have cared less. If they knew they said nothing; my father never ventured near. One day as Perseus was playing, and chattering to himself as children do, a new guard heard him laughing, and soon word reached my father. He came himself to the dungeon underground.[16]

"How was this child conceived?" he asked, his face white with anger.

The woman prompted me. "Tell him the Sky God himself came in a shower of gold and fathered him on you," she whispered. And I told him that. It made as much sense as anything. His anger grew even greater. I have learnt since that people say that only the most shameless of women blames a god when she conceives a child.

We were not much longer in the dungeon. I realised now that he needed to get rid of us without bloodshed. He had to stop short of murder. One cannot kill one's kin without the powers of darkness knowing.[17]

A child, alone, can be exposed in a mountain cave,[18] and will die before the next morning, like as not. But a young woman in the hillside can survive. He could not get rid of me so easily. This is not a problem one can pose to one's advisers. Even he could not bring himself to say, "Tell me, my friends, how to rid myself of my daughter, so that I need never die?" No, the solution he came up with was all his own. I wondered then and wonder now what his thoughts were: Did he hope not to die at all, ever? Did he think that if his grandson did not kill him, nothing would? Are there really some mortals who strive to live forever, not understanding that the essence of being born mortal is that we must die? That this is the only certainty of our lives? Perhaps he needed to live forever since he had no heir, only the brother whom he loathed. Or was it the shedding of kindred blood he dreaded? Did he fear that if he died at the hand of his own grandson, his house would lie in ruins and his kingdom never recover? Never mind, father. I assure you that your death will be bloodless. To little avail, perhaps, for it is prophecied, so they tell me, that the royal families of the Argolid will shed enough for all of us in not so many years.[19]

The method he chose to dispose of us was this: a box was made of wood, with a lid, not large enough for me to lie full length in. It would float a little and be dashed to pieces in a day.[20]

I watched it being built. Perseus was too young to know, of course, what was being made. He wanted to play with the carpenter's tools as all boys do. He spoke his first words while he watched, pointing at the drill and laughing with the work-men.[21] When the box was ready my child and I were taken down to the water's edge. I remember that morning: sky and sea dark as wine; a chilling breeze; the water's edge like a woman's skirt brushing the sand; the crash of the breakers, noise endless and unearthly; my father, his men, and the wo-man, hair wind-blown, holding the child, weeping. I remember being lifted into the box; I remember cold, fear, no food, no drink, no warm clothing, only a blanket, a small purple blanket woven by the woman. I asked my father if I could keep this. I thought its colour fitting. Perseus was descended from kings, after all. But my father's heart was harder than stone. He refused. He took the purple blanket from around the child, held it in his hand for just a moment, and then threw it on the sand. But the woman ran past him and covered the child just as the lid of the box was being closed, and he did not stop her. I doubt she lived. The men took us out to sea a little way, and lowered the box into the water. Then they were gone. No noise now save the lapping of the waves, a gentle sound, and the woman, screaming.

I prayed to Zeus the Sky God and my prayers were answered. He sent no storms, and his brother Poseidon no rough waters. Perseus slept in his blanket, hardly felt the motion of the box, scarcely knew how cold and dark it was.[22] A child is not afraid if his mother is with him. I crouched with my son in my arms, singing to him sometimes, shielding him from cold, but knowing, as he did not, that I could not keep him from Death, when Death came for us.

VI

Day and night and day again we drifted. Near death, we slept, both of us, and I awoke to the sun in my eyes, and the voices of men in my ears. They spoke my language and from them I learned that this was the island of Seriphos, a rugged place where strangers seldom ventured. They were fishermen and the box was caught in their net.[23] They seemed excited—as if an adventure was beginning. It was, in a way. Because of my presence, brothers would renew their hatred of each other and men whom those fishermen knew and feared would become stone statues in the palace banquet room. But that was far in the future.

Now, for the first time, I wanted to die. Death, I thought, could be no crueller than these men with rough hands and vulgar jokes. But I was wrong. Dictys took me home with him. He was an old man, childless, with a wife whose smile was sweeter than the rising sun.[24] I have never known such gentle people. When I was strong they set me to work, cleaning fish and mending nets. But I was no slave. We were well fed and my son grew tall and strong. By the time he had lived eleven summers he was taller than I. The lives of the fisherman and his wife were hard and I like to think we brightened them.

Gradually I learned that Dictys lived in fear. His brother was the island's king, Polydectes. Years before, when they were young men, they had come from Thessaly,[25] where their grandfather, Aeolus, was king, and, searching for a place to settle, had discovered this deserted, rocky island. They and their followers had settled there. But Polydectes had proved the stronger of the two, had made himself king and, fearful that Dictys would want his throne, allowed him only the most meagre existence. But Dictys was an easy man. He was happy enough with his wife and his nets if no one bothered him. While his wife still lived, I learned to amuse them with stories from my father's court. They called me daughter and we laughed together at Perseus' boyish ways, but after her death he smiled less and was uneasy.

The announcement that I would be Polydectes' bride seemed to come out of the blue, at least to me, though Dictys, I think now, had expected it. Was it designed only to remove me from Dictys' home? Would this king, like my father, destroy anything that made his brother happy? Polydectes had no love for me, though I was a handsome woman still. When I refused to marry him and he saw my son was strong enough to resist on my behalf he changed his tactics. He feigned interest in Hippodamia of Elis, and pretended that since I would not marry him he would court her instead and needed gifts from the men of his island kingdom to strengthen his suit. My son had lived sixteen summers, enough to be considered a man. Polydectes feared this handsome boy, born of the Sky God in a golden shower, and determined to be rid of him. He sent Perseus to bring to Seriphos the head of the Gorgon, Medusa, whose glance turns any living soul to stone.[26] Perseus cut her head from her shoulders and brought it in a sack to Seriphos. On his return journey he found his wife and rescued her from the very jaws of death. He is considered a hero in the eyes of men. But it must be said that Medusa died by her own stare, not by any skill of his. In the mirror of his shield she saw herself and died. His true work is not yet done.

Months after Medusa's death, Perseus came home. He was just in time. Dictys had given his brother no gift for the winning of Hippodamia, thus calling his bluff and showing that he knew the suit was feigned. Polydectes was angry. We were forced to leave our home to escape violence from him and had gone to sacred ground and taken refuge at the altar of Zeus there. Polydectes laid no hand on me; there was no need. He knew that without food and water Dictys could not last for long, and that I would relent to save him. I cradled the old man's head in my lap, and I remembered other days and other prisons. Polydectes kept us there under guard, without food and water in the end. He did indeed intend to marry me, it seems, though he knew how I hated him. I agreed, so that Dictys would live.

When my son returned, with the head of Medusa in a bag slung over his shoulder, the wedding feast was under way. Polydectes and his friends were seated around a table, drinking and eating.

"You!" said Polydectes, surprised enough to stand. "You! I told you not to return until you brought with you the Gorgon's head."

"I have it," said my son, and took it from the bag, holding it high, at arms' length. They turned to stone right at the table, the friends of Polydectes. The king as well. A circle of stones.

Dictys is king on the island now, but he was happier with his nets, I think, and with my child when he was young.

VII

There is little left for me. My son will be embarrassed at the accident of Acrisius' death. The throne of Argos, his for the taking, he will not have. He will say that he cannot kill a king and then expect to rule in his place. In Tiryns Proetus is dead now,[27] but his son Megapenthes rules. He and Perseus will exchange thrones. Then Perseus will rule in Proetus' kingdom with the wall of the one-eyed giants around him. Perhaps this is more fitting, after all. It is said, by those who know these things, that he will found the richest city Greece will ever see.[28]

I have not seen my father's face for more than twenty years, but I would know him anywhere. His hair is long and absolutely white, his beard still full. He does not wear the cloak of a king, but rather is dressed in a plain blue tunic, the colour of his eyes. He thinks there is safety in anonymity. But the Fates know who he is. They have spun the thread, and they hold the shears.[29]

My eyes are on him as the discus nears. It falters at last in its flight. It hits him across the temples, and he falls.[30] He is just a man in a crowd. No one but me knows that he is a king.

I want him to know who has killed him before he dies. I want him to know that I am here. It is fitting, after all, that a daughter be beside her father when he dies.

The stadium is still hushed. Perseus runs from the field into the stands. He kneels and cradles the dying man's head in his lap. There is indeed no blood.

"Who are you, sir?" he asks. "Give me your name that I may tell your kin what I have done and beg their pardon."

He speaks the words that are to be his last: "I am Acrisius, king of Argos."

My son is horrified. "Then I am your daughter's son, sir. My name is Perseus. I think you knew that I still lived."

I am behind my son now. I bend down, and put my face within inches of the white beard. The blue eyes are clouding, but they can see well enough. "And I am your daughter," I say, "Danaë, for whom you arranged a certain death. I too still live." The dying eyes meet mine. I have enough of my beauty left, despite the years, that he knows me. I have in my hand a token, the blanket, the purple blanket in which my baby was wrapped when he was placed in the box; if he had not known me, he would have known the blanket. I have heard that other women keep mementos of their children's babyhood, but not for this; not for this. In his eyes I see the old hatred, and, as they grow dim, defeat. They close and he dies. I let the purple blanket drop. Its work is done.

Notes

[1] A little-known author called Pherecydes included this story, probably in the fifth century B.C.E., in a prose work on Greek myth. The work is lost, but another writer, a scholiast, or ancient commentator, on Apollonius Rhodius' *Argonautica* quoted Pherecydes' story of Danaë, Acrisius, and Perseus at length. The discursions of scholiasts are seldom translated into English; in this case, though, the relevant passages are given by Jocelyn Woodward, in

Perseus: A Study in Greek Art and Legend (Cambridge, 1937), 4–7. No other ancient version of this tale gives the whole story. Details of major episodes are lacking. Apollodorus' version (2.2.1–4.5) is the most complete. See also Simonides, fragment 543; Aeschylus, *Dictyulci* (this is a fragment, not a complete play); Pindar, *Pythian Odes* 12; Pausanias 2.16.2–3; Horace, *Odes* 3.16; Ovid, *Metamorphoses* 4.607–5.249; and Hyginus, *Fabulae* 63. Hyginus' version is unique in that here King Polydectes is not an evil king, but a good one, to whom Perseus' mother Danaë is happily married.

James Frazer relates a parallel story from another tradition in *The Golden Bough* (New York, 1981), 237.

[2] Medusa's story is told in chap. 4.

[3] It has been pointed out that Danaë's story follows a known fairytale pattern for women's stories: she is forbidden to have intercourse with men and is secluded; she is violated none the less; she comes within an inch of death; she is rescued. See Barry Powell, *Classical Myth* (Englewood Cliffs, NJ, 1995), 429.

[4] According to Pherecydes (Woodward, *Perseus* [op. cit., n. 1 above], 7), Perseus and Acrisius recognise one another in Larissa shortly before Perseus accidentally kills Acrisius. The recognition scene is central to Greek myth. An exposed child always comes home. Some recognitions are happy: Orestes' of his sister Iphigeneia, for example (see Clytemnestra's story, chap. 2). Most are terrible: Agauë's of her son Pentheus, whom she has herself killed (see Euripides' *Bacchae* and Ino's story, chap. 6), and Oedipus' of himself (see Jocasta's story, ch. 3, foreword and n. 4).

[5] See Euripides' *Bacchae*. Semele claimed that her lover was Zeus. While she was pregnant with the child Dionysus she died, either burned by Zeus' brightness as he approached her or by his thunderbolt if she was telling lies. See also Ino's story, chap. 6.

[6] Zeus came to Leda in the guise of a swan. See Clytemnestra's story, chap. 2.

[7] Cassiopeia boasted that she and Andromeda were lovelier than the Nereids, the nymphs of the sea. The result was a sea monster, sent as punishment by Poseidon to destroy all the coastal communities of Cepheus' kingdom. The king consulted an oracle, and learned that only if Andromeda were chained to a rock by the sea and left for the monster to devour would the kingdom be safe. Andromeda was duly chained. Perseus promised to rescue her on

condition that he could also marry her, and was able to do so by killing the monster. Cepheus and Cassiopeia tried to wriggle out of the bargain, championing the suit of one Agenor for Andromeda's hand. Perseus turned them all to stone with the Gorgon's head. Poseidon placed their images in the sky among the stars. Hyginus tells this story at *Fabulae* 64.

[8] Apollodorus (2.4.4) writes that Perseus was a contestant in the pentathlon, which in historical times consisted of running, jumping, throwing the javelin, wrestling, and the discus-throw. Pausanias (2.16.1) states that the discus was Perseus' own invention, and that he was giving a display of the new sport at Larissa. Since an ancient discus was made (at least until the sixth century B.C.E.) of stone, and Perseus is connected with stones because of his link with Medusa's head, through association of ideas rather than strict logic he becomes the inventor of the sport of discus-throwing.

[9] There is blood, of course, in reality, but technically there is none. In ancient thought, if it is decided that a man must be put to death by his own side in a war, in the absence of suitable cliffs or underground tombs he will be stoned to death. If his throat is slit or he is stabbed, blood-guilt for killing a friend will be incurred, but death by stoning is death from the Earth herself. Thus Palamedes is let down into a well and buried with stones at the hands of his fellow soldiers in the Greek army at Troy after Odysseus, on false evidence, has him convicted of treachery. See Dictys Cretensis, *Bellum Troianum* 2.15.

[10] I have invented the stones-as-toys and the tossing of pebbles into the sea, but Perseus was jokingly associated with stones by the Greeks. Strabo (10.5.10) writes that Seriphos, the island where Perseus spent his youth, was very rocky and notes that comic actors attributed this to the fact that Perseus took Medusa's head there. It is an old joke amongst students of the classics that Perseus must have been responsible for the fact that Greece has so many stone statues.

[11] She was either Stheneboea or Antaea and her father was Iobates.

[12] Seven Cyclopes, the Gasterocheires, built them, using blocks of stone too large for humans and mule teams to shift.

[13] A famous vase-painting, in the Hermitage Museum in St. Petersburg, shows Danaë in an elaborate garment tying, or untying, the scarf in her hair. A mirror hangs on the wall. The couch on which Danaë sits is unusually ornate also.

14 Pausanias saw the underground building; see 2.23.7. Horace makes it a tower.

15 Perseus means "the destroyer."

16 The only ancient author to relate this part of the story is Pherecydes. According to him, the woman who has been imprisoned with Danaë is killed at this point.

17 The Erinyes or Furies, daughters of Earth, will avenge the murder of a blood relative (usually, but not always a parent at the hands of a child) by driving the murderer mad. See Clytemnestra's story, chap. 2.

18 Numerous instances of classic exposure, the placing of a newborn child outside to die from cold or be eaten by animals, are known both from stories and from life. Acrisius' plan, which is to let a child and his mother drift out to sea in a box, is merely a variation on the theme. In neither case is blood-guilt incurred, since no actual killing takes place and since the victim's fate is let in the hands of the gods. Oedipus, of course, is exposed. See Jocasta's story, chap. 3.

19 Perseus will found a new city, Mycenae, close to Argos. This city will later be ruled by the family of Atreus, which is destroyed by kin-murder. See Clytemnestra's story, chap 2.

20 The symbolism is interesting in this part of the story, for those who like to look at myths this way. The box, especially if we imagine the lid closed, surely represents a secret, something undiscoverable, like the abandonment and virtual murder of daughter and grandchild. A boat, or sea-borne box, is the route by which one travels from life to death or back again according to the beliefs of many cultures. It is both womb and coffin.

21 A red-figure vase in the Boston Museum of Fine Arts shows Acrisius, a craftsman, Danaë, and Perseus in another woman's arms. Perseus is watching the craftsman, who is working on the box using the bow-drill, and is pointing.

22 Simonides, fragment 543, is a prayer to Zeus from Danaë, while she is in the chest. The purple blanket, necessary for the recognition scene at the end of the story, appears here.

23 *The Dictyulci,* a satyr play by Aeschylus, dealt with the arrival of Danaë on Seriphos. A surviving fragment has her discovered by a fisherman, Dictys, and at least one other person, whose identity is not clear. Danaë is clearly frightened.

[24] No wife of Dictys appears in the ancient sources, but the relationship between Danaë and Dictys is not a sexual one, even there. Pherecydes states that Dictys takes Danaë and her son into his home because he and she are of the same kin (both being descended from an early king of Argos, Danaüs).

[25] See Apollodorus 1.7.3 (Magnes is the father of Dictys and Polydectes) and 1.9.6.

[26] See Medusa's story, chap. 4 and Appendix.

[27] According to Ovid, Proetus is dead because Perseus has killed him, using Medusa's head. Proetus had invaded Acrisius' section of the Argolid and usurped his throne. Ovid remarks that Acrisius does not deserve his grandson's aid. There is no suggestion here that Proetus might have been Perseus' father.

[28] The richest city was Mycenae. Its name is derived by Pausanias from "mykes," the Greek word for scabbard-cap. Apparently Perseus dropped his, and, thinking this an omen, built a city on the spot. Pausanias also gives another story—that Perseus pulled a mushroom (also "mykes") from the ground, drank the water that rushed out, and built the city where the mushroom had grown. See Pausanias 2.16.3.

[29] For the role of the Fates in death see especially Althaea's story, ch. 8.

[30] According to Pherecydes and those authors who followed his account, Acrisius is killed by a blow to the heel, not the head, as if he is vulnerable there.

Thetis' Story

In its simplest form Thetis' story is an expression of a mother's love for her child. But this is easily missed in traditional renditions.[1] When I first encountered the story I saw the teen-aged Achilles as its main character, with Thetis just appearing every now and then, and annoying him. She interfered in his life and she babied him, running to his side whenever he had a problem. In addition, she had tried either to drown him[2] or to roast him as a baby. What kind of mother would do that?

But traditional renditions amount to an examination of the life of Achilles against the backdrop of the war in which he fights and dies, with the built-in assumption that this war is a necessary and even a desirable thing, offering young men the chance to perform deeds of incredible valour and even allowing them the ultimate but over-rated honour—death on the battlefield. It is only when the story is told from Thetis' angle that the awful agony of an immortal woman who has given birth to a mortal child emerges. The women of Homer's time,[3] or those of the classical period in Greece, or even the women of Rome, where this story was still beloved, might possibly have believed it was a glorious thing for their sons to die in war. Even into our own century, women have accepted medals from appreciative governments for being the mothers of sons slaughtered in action. But perhaps there were some, like Thetis, who said, or wanted to say, "Stop. Enough. I did not bear this child so that he might die in someone else's war while still a boy."

Another important facet of Thetis' story is this: it concerns a collision between the immortal and mortal worlds. Gods and

*mortals meet on a mountain top to celebrate the wedding of
Peleus and Thetis. But Thetis is divine and Peleus is not and
they can never be truly united. The story is about Thetis'
attempts to adapt the human world to hers, and her failure to
do so.*[4]

If you were an immortal goddess with an immortal god for a
mate, your experience of motherhood would be different in one
crucial aspect from your experience of it in this life: you would
not need to fear the death of your child. That cold dread that
takes hold of you and makes you shudder in the night would be
unknown.[5]

When Thetis was young, she had no cause to shudder. It
seemed likely that she, a Nereid,[6] a deathless sea goddess,
would become the bride of the immortal Poseidon, ruler of the
oceans, and Poseidon certainly looked at her with desire in his
eyes. But Olympian Zeus desired her too, and this was the start
of her trials. A prophecy reached his ears: a goddess, unnamed,
would bear a son mightier than his father. This was unnerving
news for Zeus. He had himself proved stronger than his own
father, Cronus, had replaced him as ruler of the universe,[7] and
the one thing he feared was the birth of a powerful son. But as
bad as that, for Zeus, was the fact that until he knew which
goddess was the subject of this prophecy, he dared consort with
none.

Prometheus[8] alone knew which goddess was meant, and
Prometheus enjoyed Zeus' discomfiture and would not talk. But
Zeus tortured him, staked him to a crag at the end of the Earth
where the heat of the day and the chill of the night drove him
to cry out Thetis' name in his agony. Thetis heard that she was
the goddess who would bear so powerful a son, and was
pleased, though the implications of such a destiny were not lost
on her. She had some powers of prophecy, though they were
not well honed, and knew enough to realise that she would be
seen, now, as dangerous. She could not have predicted, however, the speed with which Zeus would act. Sadly, because his
fondness for Thetis was genuine, he arranged for her to be

married to a mortal man, Peleus, king of Phthia, a coward and a fratricide[9] and no worthy match for an immortal goddess.

Preparations began for the union immediately. Had Thetis guessed that her fate would be so swiftly sealed, she could have hidden deep in the ocean, and Zeus could not have found her, but she was off her guard and asleep on the soft sand of her favourite cave when Peleus approached her. She woke to the breath of a mortal man on her face and the weight of his body on hers. She countered with the age-old powers of her ancestors: she changed her shape.[10] She became a snake and crushed him and yet he held on to her; she became a tigress and tore at his flesh and yet he held on to her; she became fire and burnt him and still he held on to her. Heaven was on Peleus' side. The gods laughed and gave him new strength. He subdued her[11] and a child was engendered within her, along with the knowledge that the child would one day die. Thetis shuddered for the first time.

The wedding was a grand affair. The nine Muses sang for Thetis, a song lost to us now, perhaps a song of foreboding, perhaps one of love. And her sisters came from the sea to dance for her.[12] The Olympian gods were so relieved that their comfortable lives would not be threatened by Thetis' child that they came, every one of them, to the celebrations. Dionysus came and presented a golden urn, a funeral urn, to Thetis, a preposterous gift to give a goddess. And Apollo came; Apollo had not been in love with Thetis, had no cause to harm her, no excuse for what he did. He promised, with all the powers of prophecy behind him, that Thetis' child would live long and free of pain and that Thetis' own destiny would be blessed by Heaven. Thetis heard and was comforted, for Apollo, she thought, could not tell a lie and his powers of prophecy were great.[13] The lesser gods came too, save one, Eris. Eris was forgotten.[14] Her revenge was so far-reaching that it is absurd that we think of her still as a lesser god. It was cruel, too, and touched those who never wished to hurt her: three proud goddesses; an apple for the fairest; a squabble; a bribe: "If you award the apple to me, you shall have the most beautiful woman in the mortal world as your wife"; the judgement; the kidnapping of Helen; the war; thousands of young men dead, among them the son ... but I am moving too far ahead.[15]

Thetis' child, by Peleus, was born in the spring—a boy, lusty and loud. Peleus was well pleased and swaggered more than usual, but nothing stirred in his soul. Thetis, though, was changed, abruptly and completely. It was as if there was no one in the universe now save her son and herself. Nothing was to her more thrilling than his smile, nothing more compelling than his cry. But think: she was the immortal mother of a mortal child, a fate so harsh that we can scarcely comprehend its cruelty.[16] She remembered Apollo's promise, though, and believed him to be a fair and faithful prophet, a more powerful one than she. Could his prophecy mean there was a chance that she could prolong her son's life? Could she edge him perhaps towards immortality? Could she take into her own hands this responsibility with the blessing of Heaven?[17] She rubbed his little limbs with ambrosia daily to make him more like the immortals,[18] and she tried to think. Somewhere, at the back of her mind, was a memory of a rite as old as time itself, but a rite so horrible that she fought against remembering it. Yet what else was there to do? One night she retired to her bedroom, laid a fire in a brazier there, kindled it, and watched its flames become regular and then low. She took the child and, removing his swaddling bands, whispered the name she had chosen for him over and over, Achilles—the very name is pain and a cry of sorrow.[19] She kissed him, laid him naked in the fire, listened to his screams,[20] and felt the searing of the flames along with him. Peleus, not hearing the noise, not sensing Thetis' anguish, but looking, in his wine-stupor, to find his wife or some servant girl to lie with him, stumbled suddenly against the door of the bedroom, and it gave way. He was immediately alert; he ran forward and, to his credit, snatched the child from the flames with his bare hands. Thetis endured his ranting in silence. She did not care that he cursed her, that he spat at her, that he tore her garments and struck her in his rage. Her women said later that she had the look of a madwoman, a tormented soul. I am not surprised. Her son had suffered to such little avail, for the rite had not been completed.

The mortal parts of his tiny body had not been entirely burnt away and he would still die,[21] though it might be harder to kill him. Thetis never spoke to Peleus again.[22]

As Achilles grew it became apparent that only in his heel could he be wounded.[23] Thetis' sisters comforted her. It was enough, they said. No weapon could lodge there, save perhaps an arrow, and what mortal archer could aim an arrow at the heel and find his mark? The child grew strong and sound. He wrestled his playmates, modelled weapons out of wood, and Thetis shuddered. But still she was not ready to accept their destiny, her son's and hers, if it was to be that they be parted for ever at his death. If she could keep him from fighting, he could not die. She took him to Cheiron, the healer, half horse and half man, a gentle creature of the wild who played the lyre and sculpted flowing figures. "Teach him to love the arts of peace and to despise the horrors of war. But teach him, please, to run—swifter than the wind, swifter than the fastest arrow ..." Cheiron solemnly embarked upon his task. He fed the child honeycomb to make him fleet of foot, taught him to ride, to sing, to play the lyre, to heal a wound, and, because they lived in the forest, to hunt. So fast did he run that he could overtake a stag himself and had no need of hounds to bring it down. But he enjoyed killing the stag and Cheiron stood by and shook his old head, for he recognised a warrior born.

Achilles grew stronger, sturdier, swifter, and his mother feared for him. She knew the Trojan War would come—Paris had kidnapped Helen by now—knew too that if he fought in it he would die in it, and knew that her only hope was to keep him away. Anger at Helen's abduction had mounted in Greece. Agamemnon, wealthiest of the Greek kings, had gathered a vast army at Aulis and was preparing to sail to Troy. He wanted Achilles. It had been prophesied that Troy would fall and Helen be recovered only if Achilles, son of Peleus, went to war. Thetis took him, protesting, dressed him as a girl, and hid him at the court of King Lycomedes on the island of Scyros. Lycomedes had seven daughters, and Achilles, with his golden curls and his down-free cheeks, passed easily as one of them. Agamemnon suspected that Achilles was hidden there and sent

Odysseus to find him. Odysseus, seeing no obvious boy among the girls, laid a trap. He placed piles of gifts on the couches—bracelets, brooches, embroidered dresses, cloaks, one breastplate, and one spear. The daughters of Lycomedes fell upon them greedily as Odysseus watched. He had ordered a trumpet blast to be sounded outside the palace. Seven daughters ignored it when it came, but the eighth, Achilles, was stripped to the waist, ready for the armour, and brandishing the spear in an instant. Odysseus chuckled, and Achilles himself was not displeased. He followed Odysseus to war and certain death. He was fifteen years old.

Thetis laid woolen rugs and warm cloaks in a wooden chest and brought them to her son at Aulis. He was impatient with her embrace, eager to be free of her, and he laughed with all the arrogance of the young when she told him it seemed to her, with her imperfect powers of prophecy, that Destiny was giving him a choice in his route to the grave. If he went to Troy, he would be famous forever but he would never come home; if he went back to Phthia he would live a long life, but a life without glory.[24] He wanted glory. Thetis returned to the sea, in sorrow, to wait.

However much we disapprove of war, it is hard not to be filled with admiration for Achilles' fighting skills. He was, simply, the best. His spear flew straight and did not stop until it pierced human flesh. He chased his victims with the fury of a madman and the speed of a panther, and the earth grew dark with blood wherever he fought.[25] His grief when his best friend Patroclus was killed, by Hector of the flashing helmet, prince of Troy, all but overwhelmed him.[26]

His mother came from the sea to comfort him, but there was no comfort for her. She had tended him, she said, as one tends a tiny plant in a garden bed, and watched him grow, and seen him go to war. And she would never again welcome him home.[27] She knew now, without a doubt, with foresight unusually acute, that Achilles would die soon after he had killed Hector. That he would succeed in killing Hector she was certain; not that much skill in prophecy was needed, for she found him driven only by one desire—to avenge the death of Patroclus.

Beyond that he had no interest in living. He also had no armour, for Patroclus had borrowed his and died in it and now Hector was wearing it himself, to taunt his enemy. Thetis went to the forge of Hephaestos, on Mount Olympus, and asked him to make a shield and a helmet, a pair of fine greaves fitted with ankle clasps, and a breastplate too,[28] and, carrying the glittering armour, she hurried down from snowy Olympus to the battlefield at Troy.

She found Achilles weeping still, his arms around his dead friend, his face stained with tears. But once again the sight of armour inspired a warrior born. He shook off his grief and put on the new armour. And Thetis, to please her son, used her magic arts again and rubbed the body of Patroclus with ambrosia to preserve it from decay. And she let red nectar drip into its nostrils.

Once more, only, did she speak to her son. He had killed Hector and had taken the body back to his tent, refusing to return it to Hector's father. He had treated the corpse with contempt, inserted leather straps into the ankles of it, attached the straps to his chariot and driven, with the head dragging in the dirt, round and round the walls of Troy. Hector's mother, Hecuba, saw and tore her hair and wailed, and Thetis heard and asked her son to return the body to the Trojans.[29]

Thetis did come once more to Troy, with a golden urn this time, in which to place the ashes of Achilles. It had been the wedding gift of Dionysus, a gift she should never have needed. The news of her son's death had reached her in her home under the sea. Achilles had been killed at the Scaean gates of Troy, chasing the enemy as usual as they fled, dozens of them, back inside the gates, his own fleetness of foot an insurance, one would have thought, against attack. "Where was Apollo, then," scoffed Thetis, for she had all eternity to grieve, "Apollo, who prophesied that my son would live long and free of pain and that my own destiny would be blessed by Heaven? Where was he?" And they told her. He was at the Scaean gates of Troy, a bow and arrow in his hand, guiding the arm of the Trojan Paris as together they shot a poisoned arrow into Achilles' heel.[30] It took a cheating god to kill Achilles.

Around the body of Achilles on the Trojan shore by the tents of the Greeks his comrades assembled, grief shaken. Thetis' many sisters rose, arms linked, from the sea and stood in their immortal robes beside the soldiers. The voices of the nine Muses, raised in song, filled Trojan skies with death chants for Achilles. For seventeen days and seventeen nights mortals and gods together wept for him. On the eighteenth day they burned his body. Kings and princes gathered his white bones at dawn and placed them in the golden urn. And Thetis? She grieves still, for all eternity; a mother with no child.

Notes

[1] Thetis' story is not told in its entirety by any one author. The story of Thetis' marriage to Peleus is told in Apollodorus at 3.13.5, and in Apollonius Rhodius' *Argonautica* at 4.790–813, where Hera chooses Peleus to be Thetis' husband, fully intending her to be a happy bride. Pindar also tells the story at *Isthmian Odes* 8.27–47, as does Ovid at *Metamorphoses* 11.217–65. Hyginus, at *Fabulae* 54 and *Poetica Astronomica* 2.15, tells of the prophecy that so threatened Zeus, and Prometheus' knowledge of it. The actual wedding is described by Pindar (*Pythian Odes* 3.86–95), Euripides (*Iphigenia in Aulis* 1036–79) and Catullus (64).

Apollonius Rhodius describes the attempts of Thetis to immortalise her son (*Argonautica* 4.869–79), as does Apollodorus (3.13.6). According to Apollodorus (3.13.6–8), Thetis deserts Achilles when she cannot fully immortalise him, and Peleus sends him off to live with the centaur Cheiron, so that the boy will be toughened up. When it is prophesied that Troy will fall only if Achilles fights on the Greek side, Thetis hides him. See also Hyginus, *Fabulae* 96; Statius, *Achilleid* 1.20–2.167; and Ovid, *Metamorphoses* 13.162–71. The desertion of a mortal husband and child by the immortal Thetis is consistent with the "fairy bride" story type. See below, n. 22. Homer's *Iliad* is the major source for the story once Achilles is at Troy, though Achilles is the central character and Thetis merely his interfering mother. The *Iliad* concludes, however, before Achilles' death. On Homer, see n. 3 below. For the death and funeral of Achilles see Homer, *Odyssey* 24.43–92; Apollodorus, *Epitome* 5.3–5; and Quintus Smyrnaeus, *Posthomerica* 3. This list of sources is by no means exhaustive.

The story of the Trojan war was the most popular of all Greek myths; many authors told segments of it and many others alluded to it. Some details of Achilles' life and many variant stories are necessarily omitted from these notes.

2 The better-known story of Thetis' attempts to immortalise Achilles, but not the one told here, is that Thetis took the baby Achilles, held him by the heel, and dipped his body into the river Styx, a river of the Underworld, or place of the dead. The idea would be that anyone who has been down to the Underworld and has returned alive has survived death and is therefore not subject to it again. But a spot on Achilles heel was not touched by the water and thus he was vulnerable in that spot. Statius mentions this tale at *Achilleid* 1.133-34 and 269-70.

3 I assume Homer to be the person who, about 800 B.C.E., collected, collated, and wrote down the *Iliad* and the *Odyssey,* poems that had been performed orally for hundreds of years. The poems, each as long as a modern paperback book, were immensely popular in the ancient world. The *Iliad* in particular promotes the warrior ideal to which Thetis' story is a response.

4 The site, the mountain top, in this case Mount Pelion, is crucial. The ancient Greeks had no flair for mountaineering and it was thus safe to locate the homes of the gods, in their imaginations, on the top of a mountain, Olympus, since no one was likely to climb it and discover that they were not there. As long as no one checks up, the belief can continue. (For the same reason, you would never look behind you when conducting a ceremony in honour of the dead or gods of the dead—not because you might see them, but because you might not.) In myth, significant meetings between a mortal and an immortal frequently take place on mountain tops. See Richard Buxton, *Imaginary Greece* (Cambridge, 1994), 91-92.

5 In this century, in the industrialised West, the chances are that your child will outlive you, barring vehicle accidents and rare disease, but of course this was not always the case. Children died from infections or malnutrition; they could be kidnapped or murdered and they could die in war. Boy children fought in wars, but girl children died in them too, when cities were taken or villages raided. Girls died in childbirth, also, bearing children while still children themselves. There is a practical problem with having your child die before you if you do not live in a welfare state. Who will look after you when you are too old to earn an income? Premature loss of children was one of the harshest fates the Greeks could imagine.

[6] The word means "daughter of Nereus." Nereus was the Old Man of the Sea. His mate was Doris. Their daughters numbered fifty. Most had the status of nymph rather than goddess, and their activities were confined to the sea. Thetis may once have been a fully fledged and worshipped goddess, becoming associated with the Nereids later as her importance diminished. In existing literature she frequents Mount Olympus, the home of the major gods, which other Nereids do not. Euripides calls her the eldest of the Nereids.

[7] This is Hesiod's story, *Theogony* 617-735.

[8] Prometheus, the son of a Titan, had fought on Zeus' side in the battle between Zeus and Cronus, unlike the other Titans and their offspring. He had some prophetic power and knew who would win. Afterwards, however, Zeus and Prometheus were perpetually at loggerheads, and Zeus inflicted various tortures on him, including sending an eagle that perpetually tore at Prometheus' liver. According to Catullus, Prometheus, still bearing the scars of his torture, came to the wedding of Thetis and Peleus (294-97).

[9] He had killed his half-brother and been banished from Aegina, the place of his birth. He had acquired land in Phthia by marrying Antigone, daughter of the king, Eurytion, whom he inadvertently killed with a javelin. He later became king in his stead. Antigone later conveniently committed suicide. Few of Peleus' recorded deeds were truly 'heroic'—he once won a competition for killing game—though he sailed with Jason on the *Argo* and joined the Calydonian Boar Hunt. He was no great prize, and his son, even if "mightier than his father," could have been quite insignificant. See Apollodorus 3.12.6—3.13.8.

[10] Most sea deities could change shape. Proteus, another Old-Man-of-the-Sea character like Nereus, is best known for this ability.

[11] Traditional accounts, translations, and commentaries tend to understate the severity of Peleus' attack on Thetis. His conquest of her has traditionally been seen as a heroic exploit. Thetis is said to be trying to escape from the arms of her lover, or he is said to be courting her. But this is rape.

[12] The wedding of Thetis and Peleus is almost a story in itself. Only the wedding of Harmonia to Cadmus (see Eriphyle's story, chap. 5) attracted such interest. In both cases, the immortals joined mortals in celebration. At Thetis' wedding, according to Euripides, her sisters, the remaining Nereids, all forty-nine of them (he writes fifty), linked arms and danced on the silver sands. The nine Muses

danced up the mountainside in their golden sandals, filling the forests of Pelion with their song. According to Catullus, the Three Fates, quite a contrast in that they are ugly, palsied, and old, are present. They spin (they have brought the necessary equipment) and they prophecy—delineating the life of the as-yet unborn Achilles. They tell more of death than of life: they describe the deaths of the Trojans whom Achilles will kill (a particularly poignant note, and one relevant to Thetis, is the description of the mothers of the dead Trojans who will acknowledge Achilles' warcraft while they tear their hair and beat their breasts in mourning for their own sons). The Fates also mention the death of Achilles himself and the death of Polyxena at his tomb. (The usual story is that the ghost of the dead Achilles demands that Polyxena, a daughter of the king and queen of Troy, be sacrificed to him. Such is the honour in which the dead hero is held among the other Greek leaders that the Greeks are willing to do this. See Catullus 64.362–70, and Euripides' play *Hecuba*.) Strangely, these predictions are seen as happy ones by the wedding guests. Among the divine guests given particular mention is Cheiron, who will later be Achilles' guardian and teacher, bringing flowers according to Catullus, but a spear made from an ash tree that he felled himself, polished by Athena and fitted with a blade made by Hephaestus, according to Apollodorus, Homer (*Iliad* 16.140–44), and the scholiast (ancient commentator) on those lines. Prometheus comes to the wedding (see above, n. 8); Poseidon comes and brings with him a pair of immortal horses as a gift. They are called Xanthus and Balius. Xanthus was given the power of speech (by Hera) and uses it to warn Achilles that his death is near. Achilles tells him not to waste his breath, since he already knows this. When Patroclus, Achilles' greatest friend among the Greeks, dies, the horses weep for him, and Zeus wonders out loud why the gods allowed the immortal pair to become involved in the troubles of mortals. Two touching passages in Homer's *Iliad* concerning the horses are 17.426–58 and 19.392–424.

[13] Apollo was the god of prophecy supreme, omniscient and able to speak to humans through the machinery of his oracle at Delphi. Thetis, like many sea deities, had prophetic powers, but they seem to have been less reliable, though it is clear from the ancient sources (Apollodorus 3.13.8) that she knew that if Achilles fought at Troy he would die there. The story of Apollo's promise to Thetis was told in a lost play by Aeschylus. Plato knew it, and disapproved of Apollo's lie. See Plato, *Republic* 2.383b. According

to Catullus, Apollo despised Peleus and refused to attend the wedding celebrations (298–302).

¹⁴ Eris' name means "Discord." Perhaps she was not so much forgotten as deliberately excluded. It is hard to imagine "Discord" being welcome at any large gathering.

¹⁵ Eris tossed an apple inscribed "for the most beautiful" into the crowd at the wedding. It landed at the feet of the goddesses Hera, Athena, and Aphrodite, each of whom claimed it. Zeus arranged the outcome to his own advantage. He wanted to watch a war. Paris of Troy was the judge. All three goddesses bribed him, but Aphrodite's bribe, marriage to the most beautiful woman in the mortal world, pleased him most, and he awarded her the prize. The most beautiful woman in the mortal world was Helen, of Greek birth and married to a Greek king. (See Clytemnestra's story, chap. 2.) Aphrodite helped Paris to take Helen back to Troy. The Greeks arrived in force (Thetis' son was to be among them) to get her back, and thus the Trojan War began.

¹⁶ An immortal mother and her immortal child can be together for eternity. A mortal mother and her mortal child will also spend eternity together, in the Underworld, after their deaths. An immortal mother and her mortal child will spend a painfully short stretch of time together.

¹⁷ A similar story of a mother attempting to save her child from death exists in Norse mythology. Balder, son of Frigga, feels that he is soon to die. His mother goes to great lengths to stop this happening, extracting a promise from every living thing that it will not harm Balder. But she neglects to include the mistletoe, and because of this omission Balder dies. A modern source of this story is Roger Lancelyn Green's *Myths of the Norsemen* (London, 1970).

¹⁸ Ambrosia, the food of the gods, seems to have been what kept them immortal—certainly most of them don't like mortals to get hold of it. Tantalus acquires a supply of the smooth and pudding-like substance, tries to distribute it amongst his fellow mortals, and is punished in the Underworld for eternity. See Apollodorus, *Epitome* 2.1. When it is required that Psyche, new bride of Cupid (as Eros was called by the Romans) become immortal, she partakes of ambrosia. See Apuleius, *Metamorphoses* 6.23. According to Greek authors, the gods rub ambrosia into their hair and onto their skin. This presumably accounts for the fact that they do not age. Nectar, the drink of the gods, may have had some of the same properties.

[19] *Achos* is Greek for "pain" or "distress." *Acha* is a cry of anguish. Another explanation for Achilles' name, given by Apollodorus at 3.13.6, is that it means "lipless." Achilles, he claims, was never nursed at the breast by Thetis.

[20] Here, of course, is where Thetis' reputation for being a difficult sort of mother begins—this seems, if not an act of downright cruelty, at the very least a barely excusable interference. But mothers whose children have undergone painful medical procedures, for the perceived greater good of the children, will understand Thetis' position, and her discomfort as her son suffers. One obscure story, not readily available in translation, has Thetis as the mother of seven sons of which Achilles is the youngest. The first six are each tossed onto the fire at birth, the premise being that any child that is wholly mortal will die, any child that is wholly immortal will survive, and any child that is half and half will have his mortal parts burned away. None of the six lived. The story is alluded to by Lycophron, at *Alexandra* 178–79.

[21] Through her interference, Thetis creates a new category of being: not a mortal who will live as long as an immortal, but a near-immortal so close to the defined edge of mortality that he will live less long than most mortals. In *The Marriage of Cadmus and Harmony* (Toronto, 1993), 105, Roberto Calasso points out that Achilles should have been a god greater than all gods (the son who would be mightier than his father)—a god to outlive Zeus—but because of the substitution of Peleus for Zeus as his father, he became the opposite—a mortal with a brief life span.

[22] According to Apollodorus and Apollonius Rhodius, Thetis departs angrily for the sea at this point and never lives with Peleus again. In fact, Apollodorus writes that it was Peleus who saw to Achilles' subsequent education. A marriage between a mortal man and his "fairy bride" generally follows this pattern in folktale—a short period of harmony followed by the bride's return to her people. She may retain affection for her husband and arrange for him to see her occasionally. There is a modern Greek folktale on this theme with great similarities to Thetis' story. It is pleasing to think, though impossible to prove since this type of story is common, that it arrived in our times through direct oral transmission. In this story, a shepherd entrances the Nereids with the music he makes on his pipes. They encourage him to play for them while they cavort in the water, night after night. He falls in love with one of them and enquires of a wise woman how he may win her. He is told that he must take hold of the scarf in her hand (compare

the veil that saves Odysseus, in Ino's story, chap. 6) at the magic moment when dawn breaks and not let go, whatever happens. When he does this she changes into a variety of frightening shapes, yet he manages to hold on. She becomes his wife, lives with him in his hut, and bears him a son. He hides the scarf, her one link with her original home, always fearful that she will leave him. Sometimes the story continues. The marriage is not unhappy, but the Nereid never speaks to the shepherd. He returns to the wise woman and asks how he can encourage her to talk. "I will tell you," she replies, "but you will not like what you hear. Place your son on the fire, and she will talk to you." He does as he is told: while she sleeps, he takes the baby and places him on the fire. The Nereid wakes, misses her child, finds him on the fire, snatches him away, and shouts at the shepherd that she is leaving him. She wraps the child in her scarf, which she has retrieved from its hiding place, and takes him back to the sea. One night a year, the shepherd goes down to the place where he first set eyes on her, and she appears to him and shows him his son. See John Cuthbert Lawson, *Modern Greek Folklore and Ancient Greek Religion* (New York, 1964), 136–37; and Roger Lancelyn Green, *Once Long Ago: Folk and Fairy Tales of the World* (London, 1962), 50–51.

[23] Whatever the manner of Thetis' attempts to immortalise Achilles, it is always part of his foot that is left vulnerable. Hence, our "Achilles' heel" is our weak spot. The story related above, n. 20, has Peleus snatch Achilles from the fire when only his heel has been burned. To repair his son's body, Peleus digs up the bones of a dead giant, finds the ankle bone, and slots it into his son's foot. See Robert Graves, *The Greek Myths*, vol. 2 (Harmondsworth, UK, 1960), 280.

[24] Homer, *Iliad* 9.410–16.

[25] This is a paraphrase of Homer, *Iliad* 20.494. Not mentioned in Thetis' story as told here, but a major ingredient in the *Iliad*, is Achilles' quarrel with Agamemnon, during which the young woman whom he was awarded as a prize after the sack of the town of Lyrnessus is taken from him by Agamemnon. This results in Achilles' refusal to fight. For much of the *Iliad*, though Achilles is considered the Greeks' strongest fighter, he stays in his tent, sulking. Thetis does play a part in this episode. Angry on her son's behalf at the ill treatment he has received, she petitions Zeus for temporary victory for the Trojans, so that the Greeks will be forced to beg Achilles to return to the fray. Zeus, who still has tender feelings towards Thetis, consents.

²⁶ The friendship between Patroclus and Achilles is of great significance in Homer's *Iliad*. When Achilles refuses to fight, and the Greeks are consequently failing on the battlefield, Patroclus is able to convince Achilles to let him, Patroclus, put on Achilles' armour and lead their troops, the Myrmidons, into battle. Achilles warns him, however, only to drive the Trojans back from the Greek ships, and then to come back. But Patroclus, spurred on, perhaps, by the novelty of being a lead player for once, and certainly guilty of having delusions of grandeur above his station, makes his way right up to the walls of Troy, killing Trojans on all sides as he goes. Hector, the bravest of the Trojan warriors, and their most skilled fighter, kills him and has the body stripped of Achilles' armour, armour that once belonged to Peleus, his father.

²⁷ Homer, *Iliad* 18.438–41.

²⁸ Hephaestos, the divine smith, was indebted to Thetis since she had raised him when his own mother would not. This story is told by Homer at *Iliad* 18.394–405. The exquisitely decorated armour is described at *Iliad* 18.478–608.

²⁹ According to Homer, the return of Hector's body to his parents requires more divine interference than I have suggested. Apollo and Zeus in particular are uncomfortable with Achilles' treatment of the body. Zeus sends for Thetis and instructs her to have a talk with her recalcitrant son, and Iris, his messenger, goes down to Earth and informs Priam, Hector's father, that he must cross the enemy line and come himself to Achilles' tent with a ransom for his son's body. He does so and Achilles receives him with uncharacteristic grace. See Homer, *Iliad* 24.31–691.

³⁰ The poem "Infidelity" by Constantine P. Cavafy, in *The Complete Poems of Cavafy,* trans. Rae Dalven (New York, 1948), was the inspiration for this version of Thetis' story. Apollo's promise to Thetis, and his betrayal of her, is the subject of this poem.

THIRTEEN

Medea's
Story

This story[1] is really three: Medea in Colchis, Medea in Iolcus, and Medea in Corinth.

Medea in Colchis is the story of the stranger, Jason, who arrives on Medea's father's shores in his ship the Argo, *demanding to be allowed to take a certain "golden fleece" back to Greece. He would be unable to accomplish this without the ingenuity and magic of Medea, who, in helping him, betrays her family and her people. It is likely that Medea, like Ariadne in the well-known story of the Minotaur in the labyrinth,[2] is a diminished goddess, helping a mere mortal much as Athena helps Perseus to acquire the Gorgon's head.[3] Medea's story suggests that she is a relic of once-held beliefs that a Great Goddess possessed the birth-giving and regeneration magic. That the Greek writers of the fifth century B.C.E. and after portrayed her as a fearsome and dangerous foreigner is understandable, given how completely such beliefs contradicted their own.*

The first episode of Medea's story contains traditional motifs that make it a very simple story for a storyteller to tell. The wizard or king, Aeëtes, sets impossible tasks for the hero, Jason. The king's daughter falls in love with the hero and helps him to perform the tasks with magic that can undo her father's. The hero and the daughter must then flee for their lives. A chase ensues in which they put obstacles between themselves and their pursuer. In other such stories, from elsewhere in Europe, the obstacles are such things as a comb that becomes a forest when thrown over the shoulder of an escapee, or a mirror that becomes a lake. Here, they are much more gruesome—

the chopped-up pieces of Medea's young brother, Apsyrtus, thrown into the sea for her father to harvest.

The early adventures of Medea and Jason are told, partly from Medea's point of view, by Apollonius Rhodius. In his Argonautica *he describes Medea's agony as she imagines Jason, with whom she has fallen deeply in love, dying a horrible death as he attempts to yoke fire-breathing bulls to the plough. She ponders suicide before deciding to help her beloved and abandon her home. But Medea, for Apollonius, is a strange combination of love-sick girl and powerful witch, a character that would not be easy to sustain through the second and third episodes of Medea's story, which Apollonius does not tell.*[4]

The second of the Medea episodes, Medea in Iolcus, is the least well known, and yet it is a wonderful story to tell. Children in particular squirm with horrified delight when it begins to dawn on them that Medea has no intention of rejuvenating Pelias; she wants him dead, no more, no less. The simplicity of her plan, and its daring, is the stuff of the best stories. So what if Pelias' daughters suffer—they are foolish, are they not? Ovid, in his Metamorphoses, *so loves this part of the story that he goes into exquisite detail in his description of Medea searching hills and valleys for just the right herbs to go into her potions. She travels in a dragon-pulled chariot for nine days and nights. Not only does Ovid's Medea make standard boastful statements about her powers as a witch (she can draw the moon down from the sky; she can uproot oak trees and make rivers run backwards), but she also leaps around Maenad-style, with streaming hair and flaming torches. Her powers, according to Ovid, come from Hecate, goddess of magic arts. She adds various time-honoured witch-staples to her cauldron in addition to the herbs: a werewolf's entrails, a crow's head and beak, a snake's scaly skin.*

The rejuvenation of a ram, or in Ovid's version, a ram and Jason's father, Aeson, is a crucial element of the story. Not only does it establish Medea as the most powerful of mythological enchantresses (the ability of Circe, who is featured in this story, to turn people into swine and back again is a mere party trick by comparison), but it leaves any murder that Medea commits open to the interpretation, by reader or listener, that she fully intends to bring her "victim" back to life.

The third episode is the most gruelling, a difficult story for an oral storyteller because of the amount of explanation it requires. Euripides' Medea tells how Medea, angry and jealous because her husband has married the daughter of the Corinthian king and she, Medea, is to be deported, murders her two sons by Jason in order to spite him. Euripides' portrait of Medea is not unsympathetic. It is worth noting that the lot assigned her is no easy one. In classical Greece and after (not, of course, the time at which the story is set, but the time at which existing versions were told or written) a woman without a male guardian (father, husband, brother, uncle) had little chance of being able to survive. Both identity and economic support came only through such a man. Prostitution would have been a temporary "solution" for some women. Medea cannot even be looked after by friends in Corinth, since she is told she must leave, and she certainly could not return to the family she has betrayed in Colchis, even if she had the physical means to get there.

There are still traditional elements in this episode, the poisoned robe, for instance, and the parting of wife and husband, as if Medea is some "fairy bride" like Thetis.[5] One such element, the murder of the rival, and incidentally of her father, is often overlooked in our hurry to move on to what really fascinates, Medea's murder of her own children. The death of the princess, Glauce, as described by Euripides sounds like a case of spontaneous human combustion. Perhaps its very weirdness is what distances us from it.

The murder of the children is a different matter. As a society it seems we are fascinated by the notion that a mother, who is supposed to be tender to her babies, to soothe their pains and calm their fears, can in an instant deny all motherly feelings and slit their tiny throats. The "true crime" section of a bookstore, if you choose to look at it, will yield at any one time several books about the arrest and trial of mothers who are ultimately convicted of killing their own child or children. It is noteworthy that in some cases there seems to be no reason *for the mother of the children to be charged rather than some other adult.[6] Such a woman is often tried and convicted by the media and the public before ever a verdict is pronounced.*

The fascination with a mother killing her child is certainly as old as the Greeks of the classical period. (The stories themselves do not begin here. They are far older, and may date back to a time when a community's most precious resource, namely a young child, was given as a sacrifice to the powers of regeneration, whoever they were, when the community was in crisis.) If we analyse the appeal of stories like these it is clear that it comes from a paradox that the Greeks created for themselves: a Greek man of the classical period divided the world as he knew it into three groups of people: those whom he knew and who knew him and with whom a set of mutual obligations and responsibilities were operative, namely his "friends";[7] those with whom he had some argument, or who had conflicting interests, his "enemies";[8] and those whom he did not know, who lived in the next village, or country, and with whom he had no obvious relationship, who were neutral. His task was to help his friends and to harm his enemies; not just to ignore them, but to harm them. Sometimes the boundary between neutrality and friendship was crossed, for instance when a traveller was invited to stay in the home of a family he had never previously met. Women when they married crossed the boundary. Through the marriage the families of bride and groom became friends, whatever their previous status with each other, but a particular friendship was formed between wife and husband, enhanced by their sexual relationship, and by the fact that any children of the union created an indirect blood-tie for them. When a marriage soured and the relationship was severed, usually by sending the woman back to her father, the friendship ended. It was virtually impossible for friendship to become neutrality, much more likely that it would become enmity. Since children were considered to be of their father's family, and to have little connection with their mother's family of origin, a woman would be considered an enemy of her own children, and enemies were expected to harm one another. The paradox was tantalising—a woman could be a participant in the most sacred of all relationships, that between a mother and her child, in which it was her duty to nourish, educate and protect, and also she could be an enemy to the very child in question. Normally, murder of an enemy was neither sin nor crime, and required neither expiation nor penalty. But if a woman killed her enemy-children, this was murder of kin. And murder of kin was the greatest crime of all.

It becomes clear, upon investigation of women over the centuries and over the world who have supposedly murdered their own children, that there are many ways of "murdering one's children." For instance, women who have killed their children in order to protect them from terrible suffering could be said to have murdered their children.[9] So too could women who have accidentally killed a child while trying to save that same child from danger, or women who have been ordered to kill their children as part of some devastating campaign against a certain race.[10] Women occasionally kill their children because they (the women) are incurably mad, because they are in a clearly pathological relationship with another adult who demands it of them, or because of some factor not germane to the mother-child relationship that compromises it—a physical or mental handicap, for instance, or the fact that the child is born of a rape into a community that ostracises rape victims. There is also the possibility that a woman might be accused of the murder of her own child, when it has been committed by someone else, purely to discredit her. In fact, in the written tradition of Medea's story, a version like this last already exists. According to Pausanias it was the Corinthians who killed Medea's children in retaliation for the deaths of their princess and king, and then, presumably, they blamed Medea.[11]

Any of these ways of "murdering one's children" could be inserted into Medea's story, as versions that would have made more sense to women than the cold-blooded killing of children by their mother. And yet, when they are examined from the mythteller's angle, all seem to ignore the magical essence of the rest of the story. Here we have a woman with a dragon-chariot at her command who can alter the course of the moon. I have

tried to find, for this troubling story, an ending that is consis-
tent with the use of witchcraft. [12]

The major character in each of the three tales that follow
is Medea. This is true even in the ancient sources. In development and interest generated, no other character comes close.
Jason, Medea's husband, emerges from the words of the Greek
writers as a man who has other people fight his battles for him.
He is not even a lovable scoundrel—more a pompous fool.
Medea is certainly cleverer, very much more dangerous, and
altogether more absorbing.

Prologue

I see in the crystal a woman, tall, superb, beautiful. She is
dressed in a robe of purple and red, the colour of royalty, the
colour of blood. Her eyes are the colour of death. Two children, small boys, are on their knees before her. One touches
the fabric of her robe, the other flinches as she raises her arm.
She strikes him, but not as a mother slaps an errant child. In
her hand is a knife. The child whispers "Mother" as she slits
his throat. The other dies harder. He screams. He tries to run.
He is older than the first, stronger, perhaps able to escape. She
holds him by the hair, jerks his head back, runs the knife blade
across his neck. He dies at last. His blood soaks into her robe.
"My children," she says.

I

On the far eastern edge of the Black Sea there is a land called
Colchis.[13] King Aeëtes, the sorcerer, ruled there. Place and
king were much alike: cruel and comfortless. The mountains
towered above us like nightmares and we were cold as moon-
stones.

I will tell you of Medea, daughter of Aeëtes. Of her youth,
of her powers, of her love for Jason. There is a story that she
killed her own children, and another that she rose to the skies
in a chariot of gold. There is no story of her death.

Once, when Medea was still a girl, a stranger came to Colchis. His name was Phrixus. He was a Greek from Boeotia. His body was bronzed and gleaming; his hair white-blond, and curly, like a cloud.[14] He told a strange tale, of his stepmother's attempts to kill him, of his escape with his sister, of her sad death.[15]

The king and court listened with interest. They asked how he had made his way to Colchis. Though the journey was possible by land, very few had attempted it. Phrixus spoke of flying, gliding above the spray of the ocean like a shearwater. He had come to the right place to talk about flying. We believed him: Aeëtes was the son of Helius, the Sun god,[16] whose chariot ran daily across the sky. Phrixus asked Aeëtes for sanctuary, and it was granted.

The child Medea listened to his stories, and longed to visit Greece, to meet the queens and kings of whom Phrixus spoke. To live, to bear her children, to die without ever leaving Colchis—this was not for her. And Phrixus taught her magic, the first she learned: the incantations that would protect the young from harm, as he had protected himself. But his magic was imperfect. Student outstripped teacher in ability, and she grew impatient with him. Phrixus became complacent, convinced he would be the king of Colchis when Aeëtes died. He had found favour with Aeëtes by finding new wealth for him. We knew of flying, but not, till now, of gold. Phrixus showed us how to shear a ram, take its fleece, and sink it in a mountain stream. He laid a fleece in shallow water, held it still with stones, lifted it later, and found it heavy with gold.[17] Aeëtes approved of magic like this. He gave his elder daughter, Chalciope, to Phrixus as his wife and did indeed promise him the kingdom. Years later, when Chalciope's sons by Phrixus were grown, Aeëtes had him murdered.

The young Medea filled her mind with magic. She learned to read the strange words etched into stone by the priestesses of the Earth-Mother long ago. These told Earth's story and her secrets of rebirth, secrets I cannot tell you. Medea knew Sun-magic too. Her father, you remember, was the child of the Sun, who renews himself daily. Children of the Sun, and their children, can burn themselves with fire and never flinch. Enchantment was in her bones. Aeëtes himself was grudging with his secrets, as he was in all things, but he had sisters who loved the child Medea and met her at night in her dreams—Circe of Aeaea and Pasiphaë of Crete.[18] Perhaps this blend of sorcery is dangerous, if mortals are to be mortal. The magic of Earth is wholesome and good. The magic of the Sun is the magic of deceit.

Medea, for whom the night was a time of learning, not of sleep, sought out the old women of the mountain, women of a time before Aeëtes, who told her how to use flowers and the bark of trees, crushed into dusts of many colours, to heal and to enchant. She sat with the shepherds on the hillsides and learned to read the sky. She learned to pet and wear the sacred snakes like jewellery around her arms. She learned to stare into the crystal and see this world from outside as the gods see it. What she saw made her light-headed with horror. To know one's destiny is to be afraid.

This witch-child had no mother living. Eidyia the wise had died at the birth of her third child, a son, Apsyrtus.[19] Medea was mother to her brother, and yet she was to kill him for love of Jason.

She was still young when Jason came; not innocent, but young. She loved him on sight. The poets were right about that.[20] In a ship powered by oars, the first the Greeks ever built, Jason entered the mouth of the River Phasis by night. He hid his ship, the *Argo,* in the river's reeds and walked, with his comrades, to the palace. He had come from Greece, from Iolcus this time, for a fleece heavy with gold to take back to the land of his birth. He was no mere adventurer. With the fleece he hoped to regain his kingdom. He told the court that Pelias, the brother-slayer, the usurper, would retire from the throne of Iolcus, a throne that was rightly Jason's, only for Colchian gold.[21] Aeëtes laughed. He would give him gold in plenty, he said, if he could perform just one task. His voice cracked with the joke of it. Aeëtes, son of the Sun and heir to his fire-magic, led Jason to a field beyond the palace buildings, past the willows and the reeds where the ship lay hidden, brought two oxen with hooves of bronze and flaming breath beneath the yoke strap, and ploughed a furrow, straight and true.

"Do that," he said to Jason. "Do what I have done. Plough this field in a single day, and you shall have your gold." And then he handed Jason the teeth of a serpent, teeth filled with old Earth-magic, which he could use, but did not understand. "Armed men will grow when you sow these," he said. And the air echoed with his laughter.

Medea knew magic more powerful than her father's. She made a lotion from the juices of a flower that grew in the Caucasus, a flower that had sprung from the blood of Prometheus when he was chained there by Zeus.[22] She met Jason by night and offered it to him, telling him to melt it and use it like oil. Smeared on his body it would protect him from fire and bronze. Rubbed onto his shield and his spear it would render them invincible. Such was Medea's power that the next day, the day of Jason's trial, when surely he would have died without her help, the bulls were yoked and the field ploughed long before sundown. When the Earth-born warriors grew from the soil Jason killed them all—with ease.[23] Aeëtes watched in horror and recognised a magic more powerful than his. He thought Jason was some wizard, that Greece, perhaps, was full of them, and he was afraid. Better that he had given Jason a fleece of gold when he first arrived. Now he would steal one, or many. But that mattered little. What counted was the boy, Apsyrtus, Aeëtes' only son. Those who weaken a father take the chance to kill a son. Aeëtes made his way back to the palace, shouting to his slaves to find the boy.

But Medea was faster. She left the field where the warriors were dying. She raced through the palace; doors flew open for her. She sought her salves and ointments, her polished crystal, and her beloved brother. Apsyrtus was a child still, who did as Medea told him. He took only the small bundle of loved objects that a motherless child will have, and he followed her, uncomplaining. She met Jason at his ship. In darkness his crew pulled the ship from the reeds and rowed downstream, the moonlight their only friend. Though the river threatened to trap them in its shallows, by some good fortune they did not run aground.

They came to the grove of oaks by the river where the golden fleeces were hung when they were brought down from the mountain. The guard was lulled to sleep, through Medea's magic again, and Jason stole the heaviest fleece, as you would snatch a rattle from an infant. In the hours before morning the *Argo* carried on downriver and emerged into the Black Sea just as dawn was breaking. It would be a long time before Medea saw her home again. She and the child found a place to crouch, in the stern of the ship, his small hand in hers.

At the palace all was chaos. Aeëtes, caring little for the fleeces—there was more gold in the mountain rivers than we could ever use—ran to his son's room and found him gone. Medea had gone too, and willingly, her women said. They knew they would die for it. The palace, its courtyards, and its balconies were filled now with the king's screaming. Not orders so much as a plea, to gods and to servants alike: "Bring the boy home."

In Colchis we had no ships as sturdy as Jason's *Argo,* but our people had been trading along the edge of the Black Sea since the time of the Earth-Mother, and Aeëtes' best crews headed out now to follow the *Argo,* the king himself at the helm of the first ship. The ships were faster than the *Argo,* the rowers more vigorous, the steersmen more accustomed to the coast. Jason saw them in the distance, closing in like hounds for the kill.

"Your magic, Medea," he said. "Use it for us again."

But Medea's magic was of the Earth and the Sun, not of the wind and the sea. She knew no charms to change the paths of the waves. Instead she took a knife and drew it across the tender throat of her brother, thinking that she killed him only for a while, believing that her father still possessed the renewal magic of the Sun.[24] The boy looked into her eyes without fear. This was not murder, you understand. It was not death he consented to.

She cut her brother's body into pieces and threw them, like one crazed the crew said later, into the water behind the *Argo.* The swell ran red behind the ship. The crew were men who had seen slaughter enough to haunt their dreams forever. They were killers themselves. They had taken girls no older than this boy and raped and maimed them before they died. Cut off their breasts for sport. Yet by this woman's act they were horrified. "Is she not human," they asked of each other, "that she can butcher children? What kind of witch is this?"

And Medea was wrong: Aeëtes gave up the chase and stopped his ship and picked up each piece of his son's small body as she had known he would, and he placed the pieces in a cauldron as she had known he would. But she did not know, and nor did he until the incantations failed and the child was not reborn, that his magic had left him when Jason yoked the fiery bulls and ploughed the furrows, straight and true.[25]

II

The journey to Greece seemed unending. The *Argo* at last reached Iolcus, the place that would be Medea's first home in her new land. Here her magic would help women conceive, ease pains of birthgiving, and heal. The Greeks, she had heard, did not know how to set bones that were broken or to suture wounds. She would teach them.

Jason was a naive man. He believed, all the way home, that he need only give Pelias the Colchian gold and the usurper would resign the throne. He thought the hardest tasks were done. He was wrong: Pelias laughed in his face, and sent him away like a dog disgraced. What else could Jason do but turn to his witch-wife and ask, once again, for her help?

Oh, she was clever, was Medea. When people talk of her now this is what they should remember—that she found a way to rid the world of a vile man. Kings are well guarded against sword and poison. They are not easily killed.

She became a companion of Pelias' daughters. He had several. No one remembers the name of any, save for Alcestis.[26] They were senseless beyond belief. She sat with them on their couches, talked of ridding their skins of blemishes, of rouging their lips. She gazed into her crystal and told them of their husbands-to-be. They thought her a friend. The fools. Always a surprise when women are fools. They told Medea that their father feared death—not because he would be punished as a wicked man, though he surely would be, but because he had no male heir to rule in Iolcus after him. He had one son, Acastus, who had sailed with Jason on the *Argo,* and was no longer considered kin. "What can we do, Medea?" the sisters asked. "Our father does not want to die." They spoke as though he were the only mortal who had ever felt this way.

"Then he shall be young again," said Medea, with a comforting smile. "It will be my pleasure to aid my friends." When they looked unbelieving, she reminded them that witches can alter the very path of the moon in the sky. To change the course of one man's life was a trifle.

She went out into the hills, at night when all of Iolcus slept. She gathered herbs, pulling them out of the earth by their roots, and plucked grasses from the riverside.[27] In the courtyard of the palace, absurd though this was, for witches in Greece have their caves like all other witches, she put a large pot over a fire by the altar of Artemis. "The Goddess will help me," proclaimed Medea. "She is a guardian of new life." But it was not Artemis who helped Medea that night.

Medea loosened her clothing, removed the pins from her hair. She called on the powers of the Earth and the powers of the Sun. And then, "My lady Artemis," she intoned, "be with me." She danced a strange, wild dance, tossing her head so that her long black hair flowed free in the air. She boiled her potion on the fire. She took a ram, an old one, with knotted horns, white bearded like an ancient man. She cut its throat. She carved it into pieces, remembering her brother with a smile, for she did not yet know that he had died forever. She stirred, she chanted. She gazed wild-eyed at the skies. When the sisters were impressed enough, and at the magic hour when the Sun returns, she took from the pot a new young lamb, bleating, she explained, with the joy of life renewed. The silly women babbled their delight.

"This," she said, "is what we must do for your father. Tonight I will fly to the hills and gather my herbs again and you will go to his chamber and do what must be done." She did not say, "and slit his throat."

The sisters whimpered. They were frightened, squeamish. But Medea saw that she had won.

And so it was that Medea gathered herbs a second time, but wove a different spell, as you know but the sisters did not. They stole into their father's bedchamber while he slept and surrounded him. The youngest took the knife. There was much blood. The walls dripped with it. The enchantress waited as they carried the corpse from the room, for it was, and would be, nothing but a corpse. The liquid was boiling already by the altar in the courtyard. It boiled noisily, like a stomach singing for its supper. The sisters tumbled the body onto the ground. In turn each cut off a limb, solemnly, with reverence. Their efforts covered them in blood. They placed each piece lovingly, with tenderness, into the cauldron. The witch crooned her incantations like so many lullabies. The sisters waited, quiet.

Imagine the dawning realisation, the growing conviction that you have been tricked. That an atrocity beyond words has been committed.[28] They stood there, those women, stupidly staring at the cauldron, a riot of blood on their clothing. Oh but he deserved it, did Pelias. A true death for a false king.

No blood on Medea's hands. No guilt for Jason. But Acastus, the usurper's son, was angry, though he had shown little love for his father until now and had sailed for adventure with Jason in defiance of him.

"Jason," he said, "I risked my life for you. Suffered hunger and hardship for your glory. It was I who laid down the fleece as the marriage bed for you and Medea.[29] I saw her kill her brother, a gentle child, and I made no move to stop her or denounce her. Had I done so, my father would now be alive and my sisters in their right minds. Take your witch and get away from here, or you will be sorrier than you know." A noble speech from a villain's son. Jason was surprised, but slunk away, Medea with him. He was never to return to the land of his birth. Did he foresee that fame and fortune awaited him in Corinth? I think not. There was never any sign that Jason had the gift.

III

Corinth was a wealthy city, poised on the neck of land that joined mainland Greece to the southern peninsula. The white buildings of Corinth were as alluring as jewels to Medea. She imagined herself flying above them, admiring the patterns they made on the earth.

Two sons were born here to Medea and Jason: Mermerus, a slender, solemn child, with hair dark as a crow's wing, and Pheres, still baby-plump after six summers, with a smile that would melt the ice of the north. Jason was devoted to his sons, people said, was ambitious for them. He paraded them at the court of Creon, who was king in those days.[30] Medea was feared in Corinth; the people felt her power. She was known to have killed—Pelias at least, and maybe others. And here they had heard rumours from Colchis about the boy, Apsyrtus.

"Why is the great hero Jason," people wondered, "the one who by his valour won the Golden Fleece from the king of Colchis, bound in marriage to this witch? Why would any Greek man born and bred keep as a wife this foreigner, this child-killer?" Never mind that women came to Medea unable to bear children and later bore several; never mind that old men walked with the stride of younger men, their sticks discarded, after Medea had touched them; never mind that when sickness fell on Corinth, brought by traders from the west, not one person in that city died. They called her sorceress, butcher, whore. They called her witch.

Oh Jason, how readily you were convinced to abandon your wife. For the first time, she seemed to you loud, flamboyant of dress, an embarrassment. You already knew that she was dangerous. This had not troubled you before.

Jason, if truth be told, wanted a kingdom. All his life he had been denied one, first by Pelias, then by Pelias' son. But Corinth, richer, grander, was within his grasp. King Creon was an old man, childless save for one adored daughter, Glauce.[31] He liked Jason, knew the stories of his valour in yoking the fire-breathing bulls and his cunning in stealing the Golden Fleece before the very eyes of the monster who guarded it;

knew how he had dedicated his life to avenging the wrongs done his father. Strange how mere men, cowards even, became heroes in the telling of their tales. Creon saw in Jason a fine husband for his daughter and a future king for Corinth. And Jason had one quality unusual in one so accomplished—he did as he was told.

Jason married Glauce with hardly a thought for Medea, his eyes on his girl-bride as if he would eat her, not marry her. The people of Corinth rejoiced: a new king for an old; the promise of a rich future; they hoped the princess would bear sons as tall as Jason and daughters as pretty as their mother.

And Medea? What was she to do? Stay husbandless in Corinth? Already in Greek cities women could live only with the protection of a man, be he father, husband, or pimp. Some said they would drive her from the city; others would have her slink away and live in the hills with the witches. "Let her go back home," said others, "back where she came from." "Kill her," said the most frightened, "she is dangerous. Look. You can see how angry she is. And she can weave spells to kill and maim, she can bring the moon down from the sky. She is dangerous." Medea smiled. They were right. She could do all those things ...

It is the day after Jason's wedding. The king is a nervous man. He has learned to trust few in his life. This barbarian, this witch-woman, must go, he thinks, and take her children with her. He says as much to Jason. "Must the children leave?" asks Jason, but he is careful not to offend, and his mind is not on the conversation. There will be other sons, he is confident of that. What need has he of these? He consents, turns to his bride to murmur into her hair. She is the most lovely woman he has ever seen. And he has travelled the world.

The king, himself, comes to Medea. She must leave and take her children with her. He seems pompous, absurd. She hardly hears his words. It is as if her wits are encased in wet sand. This is the effect of indecision on a quick mind. What to do? How to escape this place? But more than this. How to cause Jason sorrow? Make him drink it in for the rest of his days? Somewhere, as if in the distance, she hears the king's voice bleating on. "Gone ... you and your sons ... waste no time ... no safety till you're gone."

A sudden sharp vision ... wits clear again ... head lighter. The witch speaks, in tones of wonderful sweetness. Creon is shaken. Doubts his own judgement. Who could fear a woman like this, her voice soft as morning? What is she asking? He is not sure. Perhaps that she be permitted to stay. Yes ... yes ... anything. No voice emerges from his lips. It is as if all sound is forbidden when she is speaking. The words reach him at last. "May we stay, my sons and I, for just one day?" Why, he thinks, why does she ask this? And though this question is unspoken he hears her answer somewhere in his mind. "I must prepare. Send messengers ahead. Make my children ready for their ordeal. They are so young. Pity them." This time he speaks the words. "Yes, yes. Stay this one day. But before the Sun's chariot runs across tomorrow's morning sky, be gone."

The witch smiles. The king turns and stumbles from her sight.

She does indeed make preparations. A dress and crown that belonged once to Circe, daughter of the Sun, are brought from a chest in the cellar. The dress is golden, shimmering, decades old already, its sheen brighter with the years. Circe wore it once when she travelled in her father's chariot from Colchis to Aeaea.

The crown she never wore. It is a death-crown. Even witches fear to wear it.

The lotion is mixed. Smeared on dress and crown, invisible. Medea places them in a casket, also gold. She places it in Pheres' arms. "These gifts are for the Princess Glauce." She runs her hand across his curls and touches, oh lightly, his cheek. Mermerus asks why, why the gifts? She had not reckoned on this. The lies come hard to her own children. "Gold may buy you life," she says. "Perhaps she will allow you to stay."

The children are on their way. The witch weeps. It is finer, she knows, to be a healer than a murderer. That she should feel remorse surprises her. Who is Glauce but the girl who seduced her husband? Who is Creon but the king who wished her gone?

And what of Jason? Is there some penalty for him that is worse than dying? Some greater grief than loss of bride and kingdom?

There is. She knows it, and a decision is made.

Later, there is pandemonium at the palace. Jason's pale-cheeked bride is dead. So is her father. Corinth is without a king.

This is how it was:[32] The princess thought the presents beautiful. She thanked the children, but seemed eager to be rid of them, and Jason, so that she could try the gown. She had seen nothing, ever, as beautiful as this. She pulled it on, impatient with her women. She placed the death-crown on her hair. The women gave her a mirror and she smiled at her reflection. Then came Death. The poisons on the dress ate into her flesh like fire. No one dared to touch her save her father, who took her in his arms and was himself consumed. They lay together, caught in that fatal embrace, their white bones bared, disfigured in their deaths.

It is time. Before Jason arrives, the children must die. He will come to the house to accuse Medea of causing the deaths of his charming bride and his friend the king. He will imagine that nothing worse could happen.

Medea walks to the children's chambers. In her hand she holds a knife, but it is concealed in the folds of the dress she wears—no Sun goddess dress, this one, but a gown of duller stuff, blood coloured. She calls to her sons, who are playing. They fight, together, some imaginary foe. She smiles at them. They come close to her, the younger hugs her knees. The elder looks into her eyes and sees a new sorrow there. "Mother, I will help you. Mother, we will go together from this place. Mother, do not fear."

"My fear," she replies, "is that you will not understand what I do." She lifts the knife. He sees it and drops to his knees. The small boy, the baby, kneels also. Instinctively, he knows he must plead with this woman who seems not, after all, to be his mother. But still he calls her by that name, "Mother." He looks up at her and in so doing offers her his throat. She cuts it and he falls. The other clings to her skirt, not clear what has happened. Can a brother die? Medea holds him fast as he struggles to escape her. She is the stronger, though the blood on them both makes him eel-slippery and he is almost away. But his effort is for nothing. She slices his throat and he slides, lifeless, to the ground. "My children," she says.

Jason arrives. He is enraged. Medea has never seen him angry like this. She thought him incapable of such fury. He has come, he claims, to collect his sons, lest the dead king's family slaughter them in revenge. He will leave the city with them, get as far away as possible before the hunt is called. Medea's women, once his own servants, tell him what they feel he must know, that Medea has murdered twice more today, that his precious children are dead.

"My precious children are dead." He repeats the words like some parrot-bird. "The witch has killed them? Where are they? Where is she?" The women are pointing upwards, upwards to the sky. She had told him once of flying, once long ago when they lay together on the Golden Fleece. She had told him that the closeness of him aroused her as did just one other thing— being airborne on the wind. And he had laughed. Now she is above him in the sky, in a chariot of gold, the chariot of her grandfather.

"Your sons are dead, Jason. Did they tell you it was I who killed them?" She laughs exultantly, pulls on the reins of this fantastic carriage, and is gone, leaving Jason shouting after her all the insults he can find, the greatest of these still "witch."

Epilogue

The children were not dead. When Medea reached her new home—I will not tell you where that is—she cut their bodies into pieces and whispered the secrets of Sun-magic. She placed the pieces in a cauldron so that the brew of roots and water in it splashed onto the ground. The grass grew green with new life, and soon the children were with her, more handsome even than before. They embraced their mother. "Now you will live long," she said to them, "and flourish as the tall trees of the forest." And the children have lived long and they have flourished as the tall trees. There are no stories of their deaths.[33]

My name is Medea. I am healer and enchantress. This is my own story I have told you.

And now you have heard it, they will say to you "But can you believe the words of a witch?"

And you ... you will make up your mind.[34]

Notes

[1] Apollonius Rhodius' *Argonautica* is the major source for Medea's exploits in Colchis. Ovid, *Metamorphoses* 7.1–424, has the most complete account of the planned rejuvenation of Pelias and his murder. Euripides' *Medea* is the source for the last days of Medea's stay in Corinth. Apollodorus (1.9.24) has the story of the butchering of Apsyrtus. See also Pindar, *Pythian Odes* 4 (wherein Medea is no murderer; she is an immortal enchantress); Hyginus, *Fabulae* 12 and 21–26; and Diodorus Siculus 4.45–56. Pausanias, at 2.3.6–8 in particular, adds interesting and sometimes contradictory details.

[2] Ariadne's story is not told in this book because a reclaimed version already exists. See June Rachuy Brindel, *Ariadne* (New York, 1980). It is generally supposed that Ariadne was a name of the Great Goddess, worshipped in Crete (where the story takes place) for hundreds of years. The versions of the story told on the mainland, where worship of the Great Goddess did not last as long, if indeed it existed at all, give the starring role to the male king of Athens, Theseus. The story is that when Theseus is conveyed to Crete to be fed to the Minotaur, a half-bull, half-human creature who is kept in an unfathomable maze, Ariadne, daughter of Minos, king of Crete, falls in love with him. She helps him to find his way out of the maze. (He manages to kill the Minotaur all by himself, sometimes even with his bare hands.) Having betrayed her father, she cannot stay in Crete and sails away with Theseus. See Plutarch, *Parallel Lives*, "Theseus," 17–22.

[3] See Medusa's story, chap. 4.

[4] In fact, Apollonius' Medea does not murder her baby brother Apsyrtus in the way I have described. His tale is as follows: Apsyrtus, who is here a full-grown man, leads the hunt for his sister and her lover, and cuts off the *Argo*'s escape route. Medea lures him, alone and unarmed, to a lonely place, where he is murdered by Jason.

[5] See Thetis' story, chap. 12.

[6] In at least two much-publicised cases in the English-speaking world, the father was present when the child-victim disappeared or died, but the mother was charged, convicted, and jailed and the father was given custody of the remaining children. Perhaps the best known of these stories is the so-called Dingo Murder. An Australian family, the Chamberlains, had their baby stalked and stolen by a dingo when they were on a camping holiday, but their account of the tragedy wasn't believed. The mother was charged with and convicted of her daughter's murder, though no body was ever found and no motive was established. The father, charged with aiding her, was convicted but given a suspended sentence. After years in jail, Lindy Chamberlain was freed, and they were both subsequently exonerated. Before and during Lindy Chamberlain's trial, the media made much of the fact that the dead child had possessed a black dress, and that the family belonged to an uncommon religious group, the Seventh Day Adventists. Their mother, in some people's view, was a witch, and had used her baby in weird and unnatural rites. She had sacrificed her to the demons of the desert. See John Bryson, *Evil Angels* (Ringwood, Australia, 1985). This book became the motion picture *A Cry in the Dark*. See also Don W. Weber and Charles Bosworth Jr., *Precious Victims* (New York, 1991), for the story of the ordeal of Paula Sims.

[7] The Greek word is "philoi."

[8] The Greek word is "echthroi."

[9] In the Nazi death camps of the Second World War, for example.

[10] As happened in the pogroms of the early twentieth century in Russia and Poland.

[11] It was claimed in antiquity that the Corinthians bribed Euripides with fifteen talents of silver to blame Medea for the murder of her children and thus absolve them of inherited guilt for the crime.

[12] I have used the words "witch" and "witchcraft" as little as possible in this book because of the pictures they tend to conjure up, nowadays, of hags on broomsticks with pointed black hats. The

Greek word *pharmakis* means "user of drugs and enchantments" and has no such connotations.

13 This land is now Georgia. The inhospitable Caucasus Mountains, thought of by the Greeks as the edge of the Earth, are to the northeast.

14 Phrixus was the son of Nephele, first wife of Athamas; her name means "cloud." She returned to the sky to live while her children were still small.

15 The usual tale is as follows: Phrixus' father, Athamas, had two children by Nephele, Phrixus and his sister Helle. When Nephele departed, he married Ino. Ino was determined to be rid of her stepchildren. She caused a famine in the land, made sure an envoy was sent to Delphi to enquire how to end it, and saw to it that he gave a false message to King Athamas, namely that the famine would end only if Phrixus and Helle were put to death. The king was prepared to carry out what he thought were the instructions of the god Apollo, but Nephele intervened in the nick of time. She sent a golden-fleeced ram from the sky, the children hopped onto its back, and it flew off in an easterly direction. Helle fell off on the way to Colchis, and the water in which she drowned was named the Hellespont (Helle's sea) in her honour. This tale must have been invented in an effort to explain the name Hellespont and perhaps also to account for the presence in Colchis of a golden fleece. It can be found in *Apollodorus* 1.9.1. Parts of this myth are told in Ino's story, chap. 6.

16 So the Greeks said, because they considered Colchis to be at the eastern edge of the world, the supposed home of the Sun.

17 Tim Severin, who built a replica of Jason's *Argo* and sailed from Iolcus to Colchis in it, relates that the Svans, who live in the Caucasus mountains, know how to retrieve gold from the rivers there. Severin describes how they nailed sheepskins, fur side uppermost, onto wooden pallets that were placed on the river bed and weighted down. As the water ran over them, particles of gold became caught in the wool. See Severin, *The Jason Voyage* (London, 1985), 220–23. The geographer Strabo, who lived in the third century B.C.E., wrote, "It is said that amongst these people [the Colchians] gold is carried down by the mountain torrents and that the barbarians obtain it by using perforated troughs and woolly hides, and that from this comes the myth of the Golden Fleece." See Strabo, *Geography* 11.2.19.

[18] Circe is best known for her ability to turn men into swine. She does this to Odysseus' companions when he visits her island home of Aeaea. When she turns them back into people, they are younger, handsomer, and taller than before. See Homer, *Odyssey* 10.393–96. Pasiphaë's skills have already been mentioned; see Procris' story, chap. 7, where she puts a spell on Minos, and possibly also on Procris.

[19] Not according to all authors. Sometimes a nymph is the mother of Apsyrtus. In Apollonius Rhodius, Eidyia is not dead.

[20] Apollonius Rhodius is much concerned with describing the love of Medea for Jason in his version of the story. See, especially, bk. 3.

[21] Pelias was the half-brother of Aeson, who was king of Iolcus and Jason's father. Pelias stole Aeson's throne. When Jason grew up and demanded that Pelias step down, Pelias sent him off in search of the Golden Fleece. See Diodorus Siculus 4.40.1–5. Pelias forced Aeson and his wife to commit suicide and killed a son of theirs who was much younger than Jason, though not until Jason had left on his quest. See Diodorus Siculus 4.50.1. In Ovid's story, Pelias did not cause Aeson's death. Aeson lived long enough to be rejuvenated by Medea. See below, n. 27.

[22] This story is told by Aeschylus in his *Prometheus Bound.*

[23] Medea suggests that he throw a stone at one of the men, who will think another has hit him and begin a brawl in which all the men will engage and most will die. The throwing of the stone represents the Earth's way of killing her own. See Danaë's story, chap. 11, n. 9.

[24] More than once in myth, a dead character is restored to life by being boiled in a cauldron. The story of Pelops, told by Pindar in *Olympian Odes* 1.26–27, is one example.

[25] No extant ancient source, as far as I know, states that Aeëtes planned to bring Apsyrtus back to life. According to Apollodorus, Aeëtes merely gathered the pieces and buried them at Tomi, on the western edge of the Black Sea.

[26] Apollodorus gives the names as Pisidice, Pelopia, Hippothoë, and Alcestis. Hyginus adds Medusa. Pausanias suggests Asteropeia and Antinoe only. Diodorus, at 4.53.2, gives Alcestis, Evadne, and Amphinome. Alcestis has her own story. She is married to Admetus, king of Pherae. He is granted an unusual boon by the god Apollo: if he can find someone to die in his place, he need not die at his

appointed hour. Alcestis agrees to die for him. He grieves for her, though he also complains that she is leaving their children motherless. It may be that this story was intended to be amusing. See Euripides' *Alcestis*.

[27] For a detailed account of Medea's actions in preparation for casting her spell, see Ovid, *Metamorphoses* 7.179–237. Ovid has her praying to the goddess Hecate for help with her magic and being rewarded by the appearance of a dragon-pulled chariot, in which she flies to various mountains and valleys where the herbs she requires for her spell can be found. The trip takes nine days and nine nights. Medea performs sacrifices to the gods below the Earth and boils a liquid in her cauldron that contains not only the herbs she has gathered, but also such ingredients as the wings of a screech-owl and the liver of a stag. Jason's father, Aeson, is here still alive. He is rejuvenated by having this mixture poured into his veins to replace his blood. An elderly ram, its throat slit, is plunged into the cauldron and emerges as a frisky lamb. Pelias' daughters witness this second marvel and plead with Medea to attend to Pelias likewise.

[28] This is more than murder. Medea has contrived that the sisters commit kin-murder, in this case the murder of a parent. Both literally and figuratively, their father's blood is on their hands.

[29] According to Apollonius Rhodius, 4.1128–64, the marriage of Jason and Medea takes place hurriedly enroute to Iolcus. A force of Colchians pursues the *Argo* and demands the return of Medea. The issue is to be decided by Alcinous, king of the Phaeacians, in whose territory the Argonauts are currently visitors. Alcinous confides to his wife, Arete, that he has determined that if Medea is still a virgin she must be returned to her father, though this may mean terrible punishment for her. If she is a married woman, she is to stay with her husband. Arete sees to it that Jason and Medea know of this so that they can marry. A marriage bed, complete with flowers gathered by nymphs and the Fleece as bedding, is prepared in a sacred cave. It should be noted that this marriage is very easily dissolved by Jason later in the story.

[30] This is not the Creon who appears in Jocasta's story.

[31] Some sources call her Creusa.

[32] In Euripides' *Medea*, the account of the deaths of Glauce and Creon is given to Medea by a servant. The servant is torn between

two loyalties—to Medea, just recently his mistress, and to the naive young bride.

[33] No ancient version of the story states that her children were revived, though the version of the story told here is in keeping with ancient accounts of Medea's magical abilities. She has already proved that she can kill, cut up, and boil a living creature and then bring it back to life. Perhaps if she is immortal herself, she also has the power to render her children immortal. This too would be accomplished by cutting and boiling, much like Thetis' attempts to immortalise Achilles (see chap. 12). An ordeal that would kill an ordinary child will, if all goes well, result in a chosen child surviving death and thus never afterwards being susceptible to it. The idea of immortality for Medea's children does exist in the ancient sources—Pausanias seems to suggest that Medea took each of her children, directly after birth, to the sanctuary of Hera in Corinth and buried them there under the impression that they would thus become immortal. The plan apparently failed, and Jason, like Thetis' husband Peleus, was righteously angry.

[34] You could be forgiven for doubting Medea's account, because although it is true that women in myth do sometimes burn or boil children in the hopes of making them immortal, the practice does not have a high success rate. We know, for instance, that Thetis' attempt fails. There is a similar story about the goddess Demeter: while she is grieving for her daughter Persephone, who has been kidnapped, she disguises herself as a mortal woman and goes to work as a nursemaid. She tries to make her charge, a boy called Demophon, immortal by putting him nightly onto the fire. Of course the boy's mother discovers her doing this and tries to intervene. Demeter is angry and refuses to continue the treatment. The story is told in the *Homeric Hymn to Demeter*, 231–74. (Some versions of this story have Demeter so enraged at the interruption that she tosses the boy on the fire and allows him to burn.) Ino (see chap. 6) could be said to have some success, since her son Melicertes, boiled in some versions of her story, becomes a sea god after his ordeal. None of these women, it should be noted, kills the child before his ordeal.

Adapting Stories
for Oral Telling:
Medusa Revisited

What follows is a text of Medusa's story transcribed from memory after several oral tellings, two months after the version in chapter 4 was written.[1]

Once there was a woman who was very beautiful. She had two sisters who loved her dearly. The god, Poseidon, also loved her, or said he did, and he came to the Earth one day and called her name, softly, in the twilight, and she came to him. He convinced her that she loved him. He took her far into the forest, to where the oak trees stood tall against the sky, and there on the shining grass he lay with her. What he knew, but she did not, was that this grove of oak trees was sacred to Athena, the goddess in armour, who had never known the love of a man. Her anger was profound; her revenge was terrible. She could not punish Poseidon, since he was as powerful as she, but she could and did punish the woman. The two stood facing each other beneath the oak trees, and Athena cursed her:

From this moment on, no mortal, man or woman, will look on your face and live.

The woman's sisters were deeply troubled. They themselves were immortal, not subject to death, and could look on her face whenever they chose, but the woman herself was mortal. They knew that they must take her to a place where she would never see her own image, or she would die.

They took her beyond the land of the Hyperboreans, to the western edge of the Earth, where no one lives any more, where the rivers ran dry long ago and where the sun shines for just one hour a day. They made their home in a cave there, and saw no living person, not a soul, except each other.

For years, no one knew where they were. But people still talked of them. They said that the woman was now so ugly that snakes instead of hair grew from her head; that her eyes were round and bulging, that on her face grew tusks like a boar's, and that her tongue drooped and lolled from her mouth. But no one really knew, because no one had ever seen her. She didn't know herself how she looked. They said, too, that if you glanced at her face, even for an instant, you were turned to stone for all time. Some even joked and said that was why there were so many stone statues in Greece. I should add, too, that many adventurers came looking for the woman. They wanted to kill her, to cut off her head and take it away with them to use as a weapon against their enemies, but none of them was able to find her. Until Perseus came along. Perseus. A man with a mission. He was brave, and clever enough. When Athena heard about Perseus she decided to help him. She gave him two things: a curved sword and her own shield, made of a metal unknown to humans and highly polished, like a mirror. She told him that only two creatures in the whole of the world knew where the woman and her sisters lived. They were the Grey Ones, who sat on their thrones at the foot of a sheer cliff, waiting to answer the questions of travellers. They were women so old that they had just one eye and one tooth between them.

As Perseus approached them, one of them spoke.

"Give me the eye, sister, so I may see who is here." And her sister gave her the eye.

"Tell me," said Perseus, "where I can find the woman whose face brings death."

They hissed at him. "We will never tell you."

"Sister," said the second old woman, "give me the eye so that I also may see this man." But this time, as one sister held out the eye to the other, it was Perseus who took it, and held on to it.

"Where is the eye? Where is the eye?"

"I have it," said Perseus. "And I will not return it until you tell me what I need to know."

"We have no choice," said the sisters to each other, and so they told him. "Go beyond the land of the Hyperboreans, to the western edge of the Earth, where no one lives any more, where the rivers ran dry long ago and where the sun shines for just one hour a day."

And so he gave them back their eye and he travelled many days, beyond the land of the Hyperboreans to the western edge of the Earth where no one lives any more, where the rivers ran dry long ago and where the sun shines for just one hour a day.

When he came to the cave where the woman and her sisters lived, the daylight was fading fast and he knew he must act quickly. He stood at the entrance of the cave and he called the woman's name: Medusa. Medusa.

The woman was asleep, but she woke when he called her name.

I don't know why she came to him. Perhaps she was tired of living in the dark in that barren land, tired even of the sisters who had tried so hard to help her. Whatever the reason, she stood up and walked toward the entrance of the cave. When Perseus heard her coming he lifted Athena's shield, highly polished like a mirror, and held it between Medusa's face and his own. And for just one moment before she died, she saw her own image reflected in the shield, and she knew how she looked.

She lay dead on the ground, and cautiously, very cautiously, taking care not to look on the face that brings death, Perseus took the curved sword in his hand and cut off her head.

Several things have happened to this story, some through deliberate choice, others through a more subliminal and gradual process less easy to document.

To begin with, the first-person teller has been replaced by a narrator. Though it would seem to be a simple thing to tell a story in the first person, it rarely is, partly because the line between storytelling and acting is crossed, and there are new attendant responsibilities. Also, the truth is that becoming the major character of a story, however much immediacy and life this might seem to lend to it, is not the oral storyteller's task.

It is her task to be a reporter (like the messenger of Greek tragedy), to connect, as much as necessary, the people of the story, which may have happened long ago or in some foreign place, with the audience, which is very much in the here and now. How could Medusa make herself understood to an audience of today? She is locked in the past, in a time without mirrors when the Earth had an edge. The storyteller must once have been the interpreter of mysteries, the softener of hard news, the rouser to action. None of this is the duty of the main character.

There is another very practical reason why telling a story in the first person doesn't necessarily work: in Greek myth in particular, main characters die with alarming regularity. Particularly among women the suicide rate is high—Althaea and Jocasta spring immediately to mind. Eriphyle and Clytemnestra are murdered. Procris is killed by accident. It is hard enough to write "Now I am dead" and maintain your credibility; absurd to speak it. (Worse still, it should be noted, characters such as Myrrha turn into trees.) There is a technique that can be used to maintain a first-person narrative when a major character dies or is otherwise absent: two or more tellers can each take a different part; then, for example, Clytemnestra can relate what happens to Agamemnon, and Agamemnon can describe what happens to Clytemnestra. But this may mean that a crucial element of a story is told in the voice of a character who, if she or he were real, would have a vested interest in misrepresenting it. A storyteller using the third person can be unbiased. We can hardly expect such altruism of Agamemnon!

It is also worth noting that an oral story sometimes needs an injection of humour. (A written story may need some light relief too, but a reader can find it outside of the story, can simply stop reading if the going gets too tough. An audience is captive, stuck with what the storyteller offers.) Medusa can't tell jokes about her predicament, but a third-person teller can come out of the story for a moment and throw in the quip about Medusa's head being responsible for a country full of statues. The same is true of explanation. I have discovered that, when telling Greek myths to audiences who are not particularly *familiar with them, it is sometimes a good idea to step out of the story and explain what the Underworld signified, for instance, or where Crete was. Again, this is not the work of the main character.*

So, the voice has changed. What else? Clearly, repetitions have crept in, comfortable choruses which give the teller a chance to collect herself—the repeated words trip readily from the tongue while she searches her mind for the details of the next episode. Repeated sections are the inevitable mark of oral epic poetry. Homer's Iliad *contains, for example, a passage that describes a warrior arming for battle, echoed several times. But repeated passages serve a purpose for an audience too, particularly a modern one. They offer the satisfaction of recognising the teller's words. In the ancient world, the repertoire of myths was large, but limited. Audiences often listened to stories they had heard before. An ancient audience would have been composed of people from one locality with similar life experiences or of people whom some common adventure had brought together, such as soldiers crossing the sea to lay siege to a city. Part of the rapport between audience members and mythteller must have come from the security of the familiar.*[2] *Today's audience is rather different—not usually steeped in fairy tale or myth, and likely to be drawn from many different backgrounds and thus to have little internal connectedness.*[3] *The story itself needs to generate feelings of familiarity because there may be nothing else that links the listeners to the place where they are gathered, to the teller or to each other. Thus in the oral version of Medusa's story the cave where she lives is always "beyond the land of the Hyperboreans, [at] the western edge of the Earth, where no one lives any more, where the rivers ran dry long ago and where the sun shines for just one hour a day."*[4] *A story writer searches for variety in words: woodland/woods/forest/grove/thicket. A storyteller picks a phrase that has a certain resonance—like "deep dark forest"—and sticks with it.*

Much of the detail has been left out of the oral version of Medusa. Many storytellers do not give precise details. They describe a woman, for instance as being "strangely beautiful" but do not reveal the colour of her eyes, or a monster as being "the most dreaded creature in the world" without saying how many heads it has.[5] My own inclination is to say, for example, "and the branches of the tree grew heavy with the birds that settled on them" and leave it at that rather than to fill in the type of tree and the number and varieties of birds, even though I may have a very clear picture in my mind while I am speaking.[6] If the teller identifies the birds, she runs the risk of penetrating too far into the listeners' minds. It is their job, not hers, to hear the word "tree" and picture one, hear the word "bird" and imagine its song.

This notion that an audience has responsibilities beyond mere passive listening bears some looking into. There is a gap between teller and audience that is never quite filled. Both teller and audience make forays into it and retreat again. That gap is where the art is.[7] It is a dangerous magical area. Where are the words when they have left the teller's lips but before they have reached the listeners' ears? They are in a place where anything can happen, because they are in no one's custody.[8] By contrast, the writer of a story tends to see to it that the story and audience meet, because her words are not read at the moment that they are written, and she does not wish to risk misunderstandings when there is no chance that she can venture into the gap to correct them or to reassure or to explain. Once a story is written, our convention is that the writer has no further opportunity to alter it. It must be right the first time. The reader reads, but performs no action that can change the story. The teller of a story, by contrast, can use what happens when an audience ventures into the gap to reshape the story if she wishes. So here the audience acts directly on the story.

Notice that words like "happily," "immediately," "sadly" are often left out in a told story. A teller's voice, demeanour, body language, and facial expression can tell how a character performs an action. Symbols and images that belong more to a subtext than to the plot may be left out too. So may references to other stories.[9] Listeners have more to absorb than a reader does, what with gestures and expressions as well as words, and less time to absorb it. It is important not to set them a task that *they may fail at, namely the deciphering of obscure allusions. If there are allusions in a piece of writing that prove to be hard to understand, the words can be read again, and if they are still not understood, well, at least the book has already been bought, and the writer doesn't go without her supper.*

The Greek myths contain elements that provide audiences with feelings of satisfaction, or perhaps of superiority. There are puzzles in the form of riddles (like Oedipus'); there are reunions with long-lost relatives wherein the characters are remarkably slow to figure out the true identities of apparent strangers. Audiences are quick to notice that a character is making a foolish wish, or is about to perform an act that will bring about punishment from the gods. Characters don't heed warnings, although audiences smugly know that they should. Neither the oral nor the written version of Medusa's story is told here as Perseus' quest for a monster, and so they are not immediately recognisable as a well-known tale. In the oral version, the story is further disguised by the fact that Medusa's name is not mentioned until the very end. But most individuals in an audience understand much earlier whose story they are hearing and seemed to be pleased with their detective work. This ruse would work less well in a written story. It is hard to keep secrets from readers who can skip ahead in the text.

The told story is shorter than the written one. In the case of Medusa's story, it is not entirely necessary to make cuts, since the written story is itself short. Adult audiences can enjoy a story of fifteen or twenty minutes told in one voice, a longer one if told in more. A reader can read for more time at one sitting than a listener can listen, perhaps because there are no behaviour requirements for readers: a modern audience must be silent and sit relatively still on a not necessarily comfortable chair. (It may be that ancient audience members were free to come and go; it may also be that they joined in sometimes and told the story with the teller.) But there is more to it than this. The truth is that listening skills are not well honed today. Rarely are we required to hear something once, without benefit of written cues, and to understand it well enough to tell it again. We don't value the spoken word highly enough to give it our full attention (who sits down and listens *to the radio any more?), and anyway almost everything that is spoken, other than casual conversation, is recorded in some way—students take notes from lectures; we look up facts in a book, or find them using a computer. We tape songs and television shows so that we can hear and watch them again. The ancients, in a world where most people did not read or write, were much more practised at listening and remembering what they had heard. How else could crucial information have been learned and passed on? (Imagine not being able to write down a recipe, or directions to someone's house!) My guess is that the ancients could listen for hours before reaching a point beyond which no more information could be processed. Homer's* Iliad, *in its written form, takes about eighteen hours to recite, though there is nothing to suggest that its delivery was accomplished at just one sitting. But the drama festivals of Athens in the fifth century B.C.E. involved audiences sitting from morning till dark for three or more days in a row, listening to actors declaim.* [10]

All the stories in this book can be told. The fact that they are written here need not make them ineligible for a new oral tradition. Although the literary tradition may once have been responsible for the demise of the oral, in this century the oral is being revived, using the literary to enable tellers who rarely or never meet to tell the same tales. I may have set these stories on a page, but they are not like butterflies dead forever through the lepidopterist's pin. They and others like them can rise from the page and fly again—like the winged words that Homer knew— on their charmed journey from teller's lips to listener's ear.

Notes

[1] This was transcribed after a performance that I gave alone, in April 1994. In May 1994 the same story was twice performed as part of a "set" of stories by Earthstory. On these occasions we were wearing the cloaks that we sometimes wear when our stories involve the three Fates from Greek myth, the three Norns from Scandinavian myth, or similar characters. They are made of an iridescent fabric in unearthly tones of deep pink and blue. They

reach to the ground and have hoods that can cover our faces. As I told the story, Mary Louise and Kay sat behind me, suitably shrouded. They spoke the words of the Grey Ones. They also mimed the handing over of the eyeball. None of the description of Perseus taking the eye was then necessary. While they were both crying "Where is the eye?" from deep in their hoods, I called out "'I have it,' said Perseus," and the story continued much as in this transcript.

[2] Once a story had been told for the first time and had become part of a "tradition," the oral storyteller of old was essentially telling a community its own story. See Sean Kane, *Wisdom of the Mythtellers* (Peterborough, 1994), 189.

[3] The three of us who comprise Earthstory have found ourselves on occasion telling a story to an audience with common life experience and realising that we are telling these people their own story. We have, for example, told both Philomela's story and Myrrha's story in workshops for adult survivors of childhood incest and their supporters. The experience of watching listeners recognise themselves in a story is a moving one; and in these cases, because of the nature of the stories, disturbing.

[4] Watch your audience nod and smile when the repeated passages are spoken. In folk tale a similar effect is achieved when repeated actions are reported. A heroine is given three magic walnuts to open, for instance, in times of trial. Another heroine arrives three times at an uncrossable river, and magically forms a bridge for herself every time.

[5] The conventions and needs of writing a story are simply different. When you write, detail is what makes a text your own; you are individualising, writing what *you* see and what *you* think is important. It has to be different from what everyone else has written; if it isn't we call it plagiarism. But a storyteller does not own a story. She is a reporter, a medium, the person temporarily responsible for handing the story on in such a way that others can tell it later.

[6] Because Earthstory is comprised of three tellers who sometimes tell interwoven tales or three parts of the same story, we need to rehearse—not the actual words, they are rarely learned, but the cues and crossovers and any movement we want to include. Sometimes it becomes clear during rehearsals that the visions generating the words we speak are different for each of us. On one occasion each of us in turn needed to used the words "she looked up at the window and saw the red ribbon hanging there." We discovered

that we were imagining three very different windows. Kay's was a hole in a lumpy, moss-encrusted wall. Mary Louise's was in a tall tower, and a lot of craning of the neck was required to look up at it. Mine was a slit more than a window, the kind you see in old castles, wide enough, but only just, for a defender's arrow to glide through. This would not matter at all if one of us were the teller and the others the listeners who could use their different visions to retell the story at a later date. But it seems essential that three tellers of the same story at the same time have the same pictures in their minds!

[7] See "The Creative Act" in *Salt Seller: The Writings of Marcel Duchamp,* ed. M. Sanouillet and E. Peterson (New York, 1973), 138–40. Duchamp is writing about the visual arts, but his words are well worth the storyteller's attention.

[8] The Greeks originally used the written word for lists, accounts, and other mundane things. The spoken word was where the magic was. Homer refers to speech as "winged words." In my own mind, I liken the gap in which the words fly to the danger zone that a bride occupies while she is travelling from the house of her father to the house of her husband on her wedding day, protected by the guardian spirits of neither family. See Hypermnestra's story, chap. 10.

[9] This is a real difficulty in the telling of Greek myths. Very few myths are complete in themselves. They are entangled with other stories and don't willingly let go. It is often tempting to veer into related stories, but it is far easier for a reader to cope with two or more plot lines at once than it is for a listener to do so.

[10] There was no realistic scenery, and no real costumes. (Actors were dressed as actors.) Most "action" took place off-stage, and the characters described it and talked about it rather than acting it out. There were no written programs to help an audience figure out who was who and what was happening.